This collection of essays is the first to examine the impact of the French Revolution on a global scale. The legacy of the French Revolution extends far beyond the borders of France or even Europe—the ramifications of the Revolution of 1789 are truly global and continue to have an impact today. Although the French Revolution was a response to purely domestic concerns, it was immediately noted at the time by observers and many participants that its ideals were universal in scope and that its message traveled well. As a model for both discourse and action, the Revolution helped usher in a new age, one we still live in today, of nationalism, constitutional government, mass politics, citizen armies, and popular sovereignty.

Twelve authorities analyze the historical and present-day impact of the French Revolution on American political culture, nationalism and freedom in Eastern Europe, Russian intellectual life, colonial bondage, Middle East politics, the Mexican Revolution, and Chinese socialism.

*WOODROW WILSON CENTER SERIES*

The global ramifications of the French Revolution

Other books in the series

Michael J. Lacey, editor, *Religion and Twentieth-Century American Intellectual Life*

Michael J. Lacey, editor, *The Truman Presidency*

Joseph Kruzel and Michael H. Haltzel, editors, *Between the Blocs: Problems and Prospects for Europe's Neutral and Nonaligned States*

William C. Brumfield, editor, *Reshaping Russian Architecture: Western Technology, Utopian Dreams*

Mark N. Katz, editor, *The USSR and Marxist Revolutions in the Third World*

Walter Reich, editor, *Origins of Terrorism: Psychologies, Ideologies, Theologies, States of Mind*

Mary O. Furner and Barry Supple, editors, *The State and Economic Knowledge: The American and British Experiences*

Michael J. Lacey and Knud Haakonssen, editors, *A Culture of Rights: The Bill of Rights in Philosophy, Politics, and Law—1791 and 1991*

Robert J. Donovan and Ray Scherer, *Unsilent Revolution: Television News and American Public Life, 1948–1991*

William Craft Brumfield and Blair A. Ruble, editors, *Russian Housing in the Modern Age: Design and Social History*

Nelson Lichtenstein and Howell John Harris, editors, *Industrial Democracy in America: The Ambiguous Promise*

Michael J. Lacey and Mary O. Furner, editors, *The State and Social Investigation in Britain and the United States*

Hugh Ragsdale, editor, *Imperial Russian Foreign Policy*

Dermot Keogh and Michael H. Haltzel, editors, *Northern Ireland and the Politics of Reconciliation*

# The global ramifications of the French Revolution

Edited by
JOSEPH KLAITS
and
MICHAEL H. HALTZEL

WOODROW WILSON CENTER PRESS

AND

PUBLISHED BY THE PRESS SYNDICATE OF THE UNIVERSITY OF CAMBRIDGE
The Pitt Building, Trumpington Street, Cambridge, United Kingdom

CAMBRIDGE UNIVERSITY PRESS
The Edinburgh Building, Cambridge CB2 2RU, UK
40 West 20th Street, New York NY 10011-4211, USA
477 Williamstown Road, Port Melbourne, VIC 3207, Australia
Ruiz de Alarcón 13, 28014 Madrid, Spain
Dock House, The Waterfront, Cape Town 8001, South Africa

http://www.cambridge.org

First published 1994
First paperback edition 2002

*A catalogue record for this book is available from the British Library*

*Library of Congress Cataloguing in Publication data*
Klaits, Joseph.
The global ramifications of the French Revolution / Joseph Klaits
and Michael H. Haltzel.
p.    cm. – (Woodrow Wilson Center series)
Includes index.
ISBN 0 521 45175 2
1. France – History – Revolution, 1789–1799 – Influence – Congresses.
2. World politics – Congresses.   3. Civilization, Modern – French
influences – Congresses.   4. Political science – Philosophy –
Congresses.   I. Haltzel, Michael H.   II. Title.   III. Series.
DC158.8.K63   1994
944.04–dc20   93-32346   CIP

ISBN 0 521 45175 2  hardback
ISBN 0 521 52447 4  paperback

# Contents

# Foreword

This book is based on a conference held at the Woodrow Wilson International Center for Scholars in Washington, D.C., in November 1989, during the bicentennial year of the French Revolution. The conference was organized and directed by the Center's West European Studies program. Thanks are due to the Ford Foundation for a generous grant that made the conference possible.

The editors wish to thank the following participants for their comments on the papers presented at the conference: Hugh Agnew, Shaul Bakhash, Allison Blakely, Mbye Cham, Prasenjit Duara, Eric Foner, R. Emmet Kennedy, Colin Palmer, John Ruedy, Monica Schuler, and Donald Sutherland. In addition to these people and the contributors to this volume, Elizabeth L. Eisenstein and Timothy Tackett helped develop the conference theme at an early stage. We are grateful for the expert advice of Lawrence D. Orton and the assistance of Paula Bailey Smith.

Neither the conference nor this book would have been possible without the contributions of Susan Nugent and Charlotte Thompson, staff members in the West European program of the Woodrow Wilson Center. We thank them for their superb work in the organization of the conference and for their assistance in the preparation of this book for publication.

# Introduction

JOSEPH KLAITS and MICHAEL H. HALTZEL

The Age of Revolution of the late eighteenth century has occasioned an age of anniversary commemoration in recent years, of which the greatest example in magnitude and extent was the French Revolution bicentennial. Around the world there were conferences, exhibits, scholarly and public events in celebration—or at least appreciation—of the worldwide impact of the Revolution. These commemorations, planned years in advance, unfolded in remarkably harmonious coincidence with the momentous events of our current age of revolution. The replacement of Communist domination in Eastern Europe with democratically elected governments and market economies evoked for many the continuity between the eighteenth-century struggles for liberty and present-day analogues.

Such reflections were in the minds of many participants in the conference at which the essays in this book were first presented. The conference was convened by the West European Studies program of the Woodrow Wilson International Center for Scholars in Washington, D.C., early in November 1989, just as the Berlin Wall was crumbling. The initial inspiration for this volume was the sense that in all the activities spurred by the French Revolution bicentennial, the Revolution's worldwide impact and continuing significance had been insufficiently elucidated and needed direct examination.

To be sure, it is a textbook cliché that the French Revolution ushered in the "modern world," with its stirrings of popular sovereignty, patriotic warfare, nationalist impulses and imperialist ambitions, capitalist economics, and egalitarian ideals. All too often, however, the impact of the French Revolution has been cast as limited in focus primarily to France or at most to Western Europe, with any influence farther afield little more than a faint and fleeting echo of the reverberations emanating from Paris. This book proceeds from the premises that the Revolution's influence beyond Western Europe has been greatly underestimated and that its

1

impact has been truly a phenomenon of the *longue durée*, continuing to the present on a worldwide stage. Hence the chapters that follow examine the impact of the Revolution's ideals and practices in Poland, Russia, Mexico, Haiti, the United States, North and sub-Saharan Africa, the Middle East, and China. The chronological focus of the book ranges from the Age of Revolution itself down to the 1980s.

Such an encompassing approach to the Revolution's impact has been encouraged by recent shifts in the ways historians of the French Revolution have interpreted the origins and significance of the events of 1789 in France. Until the 1980s, as Jack Censer explains in Chapter 1, the leading conceptual model of the Revolution was derived from a Marxian analysis of social change. The Revolution was generally viewed from a perspective first sketched in the late nineteenth century by historians who saw class struggle as the hidden dynamic of the political changes of 1789 and after. The debate—very much alive in France until recent years—between supporters and opponents of republican institutions and egalitarian ideals made the Revolution a continuing issue in French political life. For the largely class-based parties of the Third and Fourth republics, the Revolution variously represented a great treasure to be protected, a disaster to be undone, or an as yet unrealized ideal. But quite suddenly and to the surprise of nearly everyone, this well-worn political mold was broken in the postwar world, so that François Furet could plausibly proclaim in the late 1970s, "The French Revolution is over."

The fading of the class-struggle model in political action and historical imagination has encouraged the reemergence of an even older tradition of interpreting the Revolution. Instead of emphasizing the clash of social forces, many recent historical writings about the Revolution have stressed the clash of ideas. The vision of the Revolution as an ideological force, first perceived during revolutionary years and greatly clarified by Alexis de Tocqueville and Augustin Cochin in the first half of the nineteenth century, has once again found the spotlight in works by today's historians. Censer analyzes the contributions of several of these historians, all of whose interpretations differ but who share a common framework in a rejection of the social interpretation of the French Revolution and an acceptance of ideological issues—variously defined—as central to the elucidation of the Revolution's meaning.

This recasting of the terms of discussion serves also to bring into focus the wider and more permanent influence of the Revolution. While historians conceived of the Revolution's turmoil in terms of class conflicts, it was difficult to transfer their model of the French Revolution to the very different social terrains of countries beyond the borders of France or Western Europe. Thus, until recent years—and prominently in many works occasioned by the bicentennial of the American Revolution—the Revolutionary War was typically distinguished from the French Revolution on the grounds that, whereas events in France constituted a true social revolution, in America there was mere rebellion and a relatively superficial change in political forms. This distinction has come under increasing criticism as the social interpretation of the French Revolution has faded (and as that of the American Revolution has received new attention).

In Chapter 2, Lloyd Kramer describes both the affinities that drew Americans of the 1780s and 1790s to the French Revolution and the ideological divisions in American political life that prompted a split in the way the astonishing events across the Atlantic were seen by contemporaries in the new United States. Kramer's thesis is that the French Revolution was central in forming enduring American attitudes toward foreign involvement, democratic culture, and secularism. Stances first developed in the 1790s, he shows, became permanent features of the American scene and are still recognizable in the late twentieth century. Much of the content of American political debate and ideological division seems to have been first articulated in reaction to news of the French Revolution.

The fissures that opened in American public life after 1789 also appeared in Eastern Europe. In Poland and Russia, according to Jerzy Borejsza and Dmitry Shlapentokh in Chapters 3 and 4, authoritarian rule—and in the case of Poland, dismemberment and foreign domination—made the French case, in Borejsza's words, "an example of political and military struggle, . . . a pattern for social revolution and . . . an ideological model." Borejsza shows how the early links between Poland's leaders and the revolutionary governments in France, built primarily around common political interests on the international scene, were replaced after Poland lost its independence by an ideological commitment to the Revolution on the part of nineteenth-century Polish dissidents and nationalist revolutionaries. Shlapentokh's account of the attraction of the French model to Westernizers, who saw it as a beacon for political reform and cultural reorientation, demonstrates that much of the history of Russia in the nineteenth century can be written around the crucial question of how the French Revolution was perceived. The divergent paths of the revolutionary tradition in Eastern Europe made nationalists in Poland sympathetic to the ideals of 1789, while nationalists in Russia usually rejected the French model as contrary to true Russian values. These chapters show the ongoing influence of the ideals of 1789 in countries where such doctrine was deemed subversive by the rulers.

Equally striking are the instances of rejection of the Revolution's ideals by the French revolutionaries themselves, as in Saint-Domingue (Haiti) in the 1790s, and, more broadly, in the French colonial world throughout the next two centuries. Robert Forster's contribution, Chapter 5, analyzes the French Revolution's debates on slavery and the actions of people of color in the Caribbean during the revolutionary years. Principles of *liberté* and *fraternité*, though deeply felt by some revolutionary leaders, were quickly overridden by the economic and nationalistic considerations of protecting French sugar interests in an immensely rich colony. On the island, the response to the stirring message of liberation was immediate and clear-cut—compatible as it was, Forster shows, with African traditions still vivid in the minds of many slaves. But the ambivalence in France over the question of the applicability of the Revolution's ideals to a colonial setting revealed at the outset the limitations and inherent contradictions of a revolution that espoused both the universalist ideals of brotherhood and equality and the particularisms of nationalistic and imperial domination. As Forster observes, a consequence of this ambivalence was revolutionary France's "forfeiture of its claim to be the Motherland of Liberty for *all* humankind."

Such a clash of values could not easily be resolved, and in practice through most of the last two centuries, the ideals of the Revolution have regularly been harnessed to rationalizations for colonial expansion and cultural hegemony. As Christopher Miller elucidates in Chapter 6, on the French Revolution in sub-Saharan Africa, colonial domination was justified as the "exportation of the ideals of 1789." In the writings of Lamartine and Tocqueville, as well as in the works of more recent African authors writing in French, the conflict between revolutionary ideals and colonial rule is either ignored entirely or resolved by formulating some version of the doctrine that colonial government is somehow liberating. In Miller's view, the contradiction remains fundamental: "What has happened to the values of the Revolution within the discourse of colonialism [is that] the heart has been cut out."

The French Revolution's influence in the Muslim lands of the Middle East and North Africa was also mixed, although the proportions of ingredients differed considerably. Chapters 7 and 8, by Elbaki Hermassi and

Nikki Keddie, describe the political and military impact of French influence in the Napoleonic era and throughout the nineteenth century. Here, the primary stress was on reform in the name of rational, and sometimes also constitutional, government. The statist and militaristic legacies of the Revolution were the first to find an echo among the reforms of leaders in Egypt and the Ottoman Empire. Later, when the Revolution's values of popular sovereignty, secularism, and nationalism began to be felt in the Arab world and Iran, some leaders embraced all these values; fissures emerged separating them from others who to varying degrees invoked traditional ideals indigenous to the Muslim world and, Keddie shows, from spokesmen for a dissident intellectual Islamic revolutionary tradition in Iran that proved receptive to some aspects of Enlightenment thought and the principles of the French Revolution. Though often identified in practice with France's imposition of imperialistic controls, the Revolution's idealistic message of constitutionalism and democracy and its encouragement of nationalistic feeling, Keddie and Hermassi demonstrate, continue to exert an influence on Middle Eastern thought and practice.

The constitutionalism of the French Revolution is the element Charles A. Hale discusses in Chapter 9. He considers three "moments" in the history of nineteenth-century Mexico when the writings of French liberal theorists shaped political discourse. Within the context of attempts—ultimately unsuccessful—to establish a constitutional balance, French liberal thought strongly influenced Mexican political culture. Although other elements of French revolutionary ideology had an impact on the Mexican scene, Hale emphasizes the liberal constitutional legacy of the Revolution, as mediated through such nineteenth-century liberal theorists as Tocqueville, Benjamin Constant, and Edouard Laboulaye.

In contrast, Maurice Meisner's discussion of the Revolution's influence in China (Chapter 10) isolates another side of the revolutionary message. Here the significant mediators were Marx, Engels, and the Paris Communards of 1871. The direct action, class consciousness, and popular sovereignty that Marx and Engels found in the events of the Revolution and that were embodied in the establishment of the Commune eighty years later were the features that attracted Mao and other Communist leaders to the lessons of the French Revolution. Although the Commune—and through it the Revolution—quickly became a ritualistic relic in the sacred pantheon of Chinese socialism, generally devoid of real historical content or influence, Meisner shows that at three junctures from the 1860s to the early 1980s, the memory of the Revolution's legacy took on vivid and pointed political meaning in the hands of both revolutionaries and democratic reformers.

These concluding chapters demonstrate clearly a lesson implicit in all the others. Whether the Revolution's principles became part of the political culture, as in America, were used to combat authoritarian regimes, as in Eastern Europe, stimulated critiques of indigenous cultures, as in China and the Muslim world, or served as weapons against French colonialism, as in Haiti or Africa, the global ramifications of the French Revolution are pervasive and profound. The Revolution's impact has been strongly conditioned by the diversity of local circumstances, the mediating influences of historians and other commentators, and perhaps most of all by the mixed and often contradictory message of the Revolution itself. Yet the Revolution's power as metaphor and analogue still inspires theorists and political actors throughout the world. While it may be true that in the context of the political life of France, "the French Revolution is over," it would be most surprising if its encompassing legacy as measure, example, and point of contention ceased to be drawn on in coming decades. The dramatic and unexpected events of the late 1980s make it plain that the powerful ideals born two centuries earlier continue to maintain their grip on the modern consciousness. This book helps explain that remarkable fact.

# 1

The French Revolution
after two hundred years

JACK CENSER

Lively debates about the French Revolution and its impact filled scholarly journals and book reviews during the bicentennial period. Striking even to nonspecialists is the extent to which politics and ideas have displaced social and economic forces in most recent works. Also notable is the diversity of their authors. For many years, historians interested in the Revolution almost always looked to the French for leadership and direction, but during the last few decades, foreign scholars have begun to move into the limelight.[1] The following pages focus on six prominent representatives of this new generation who have offered general interpretations of the Revolution. Five of them are from England or North America—Lynn Hunt, John Bosher, William Doyle, Simon Schama, and D. M. G. Sutherland—François Furet is French.

To provide a context for the most recent scholarship, one still must turn to the classic works of Georges Lefebvre, because his successors continue to debate the tradition he created.[2] Lefebvre's overview most

In writing this chapter, I incurred a great many debts: to colleagues at the Max-Planck-Institut für Geschichte, to Keith Baker, Shaul Bakhash, Hans Erick Bödeker, and Lynn Hunt. My greatest appreciation goes to Jane Turner Censer, who helped me refine both my ideas and my prose. An earlier version of this chapter appeared in *The American Historical Review* 94 (December 1989): 1309–25, and is published here with the journal's permission. In revising for publication here, I benefited from the comments of Emmet Kennedy and Donald Sutherland at the Woodrow Wilson Center conference in November 1989. Of course, I take full responsibility for any remaining errors.
[1]For an excellent review of works on French history by Germans, see Jeremy Popkin, "Recent West German Work on the French Revolution," *Journal of Modern History* 59 (1987): 737–50.
[2]Georges Lefebvre's studies include: *Les paysans du nord* (Paris, 1972); *Questions agraires au temps du Terreur* (Strasbourg, 1932); *The French Revolution*, 2 vols., vol. 1: *From Its Origins to 1793*, trans. Elizabeth Moss Evanson, vol. 2: *From 1793 to 1799*, trans. John

often is labeled Marxist because class conflict lies at its core. He attributed the Revolution of 1789 to the separate actions of four distinct social groups: the nobility, the bourgeoisie, the urban working class, and the peasants. Though often considered the monarch's natural ally, the nobles were the first active opponents of long-term royal efforts to monopolize power and forced the calling of the Estates General. Encouraged by their example, the bourgeoisie escalated the conflict. According to Lefebvre, the middle class, bolstered by its strong economic position, wanted merit to replace the privileges of birth. As the battle against royal authority thus widened into an attack on privilege, it attracted still other social groups. Both the urban working class and the peasantry had long despised the decadent, snobbish aristocracy. Consequently, when in July 1789 the king's actions threatened the National Assembly, the people of Paris revolted in defense of the bourgeoisie. Later, fearful of an aristocratic counterattack, the peasants destroyed the contracts and records that underlay seigneurial authority. Eventually, the bourgeoisie succeeded in eliminating Old Regime privileges, an effort exemplified by passage of the Declaration of the Rights of Man and Citizen.

According to Lefebvre, even before 1789 ended, the initial alliance that made the Revolution had begun to disintegrate. It was replaced by a class struggle—mainly between the bourgeoisie and the urban workers. Angered by the self-interested bourgeoisie's domination of the National Assembly, the more egalitarian Parisian workers (especially the self-proclaimed sansculottes), with help from an unlikely partner, the middle-class Jacobins, fought for control of the Assembly. The summer of 1793 found the sansculottes allied with the Jacobins to advance a radical social and political program. Although Lefebvre credited the sansculottes with the Jacobins' ascendancy, he was reluctant to assign them responsibility for the Reign of Terror that followed. Instead, he blamed circumstances beyond their control, especially the warfare waged within the country and outside its borders.

To explain the fall of the Jacobins and the emergence of the more moderate Directory, Lefebvre turned again to notions of class conflict. The relationship between the Jacobins and Parisian workers deteriorated

Hall Stewart and James Friguglietti (New York, 1962–64); *The Thermidoreans and the Directory: Two Phases of the French Revolution*, trans. Robert Baldick (New York, 1964); *Napoleon: From Eighteen Brumaire to Tilsit, 1799–1807*, trans. Henry F. Stockhold (New York, 1969); *Napoleon: From Tilsit to Waterloo, 1807–1815*, trans. J. E. Anderson (New York, 1969); and *The Coming of the French Revolution*, trans. Robert R. Palmer (Princeton, N.J., 1947).

when the Jacobins, at least somewhat true to their class origins, refused to accede to the economic demands of artisan workers. Eventually, on 9 Thermidor (27 July) 1794, the middle class, through its representatives in the national legislature (the Convention), grasped power and held it through the Directory (1795–99). Maintaining authority was made difficult by continued opposition from the sansculottes and from revitalized royalists. This last group was dominated by former members of the nobility but included wealthy commoners who now longed for the return of the Old Regime. Also to the detriment of the prorevolutionary bourgeoisie, problems of war and poverty created enemies for their government among all social classes. When representatives of the middle class turned to the military for assistance, they inadvertently prepared the way for Napoleon, a soldier who acquired power by promising to implement the bourgeoisie's social agenda.

Lefebvre's detailed description of social struggles notwithstanding, his overall view of the Revolution was highly positive. The Declaration of the Rights of Man and Citizen, he declared, was a great milestone in history. Despite its bourgeois origin, this document, created during a period of relative social harmony, decreed a society open to all. Even when the Revolution later drifted into difficulties, Lefebvre did not lose faith in it. Although he disapproved of the bourgeoisie's narrow self-interest, he found its contribution to the development of capitalism important. The same mix of praise and apologia characterized his interpretation of the Terror.

Inevitably, Lefebvre's work produced controversy, which intensified during the mid-1950s. Although French scholars eventually joined the attack on Lefebvre's interpretation, Anglo-American historians, including Richard Cobb, Alfred Cobban, Robert Forster, and George V. Taylor, led the way. Later called "revisionists," most of these researchers accepted Lefebvre's emphasis on social causation but questioned his characterizations of the nobility, bourgeoisie, urban workers, and peasantry.[3] For the

---

[3]The more radical among this group, such as Cobb, also challenged Lefebvre's grounding of political behavior in class interests. Cobb's work pointed toward the political, but over time he retreated from offering any explanation at all. For instance, he portrayed the people of France as material beings interested in food, love, and fun. For them the Revolution's disruption of authority represented an unwelcome intrusion into their lives. From such a perspective, the Revolution lacked luster as an ennobling event. Cobban's famous *Social Interpretation of the French Revolution* was no more than an extended essay. Cobban also diminished the Revolution by depicting it as a chance occurrence, more an epiphenomenon than the inevitable outcome of massive social forces. Richard Cobb, *The Police and the People: French Popular Protest, 1789–1820* (Oxford, 1970); Cobb, *Reactions to the*

most part, the revisionists' work undermined Lefebvre's classic interpretation but failed to replace it with a new social explanation or an alternative
political account. Until recently, revisionism connoted attack more than
reconstruction.

Through the 1960s and 1970s, defenders of Lefebvre's perspective
continued to compete with the revisionists over how best to interpret the
Revolution.[4] In the last decade, however, Marxist historians have moved
in some new directions, most notably toward a concentration on cultural
history. Yet even this newest generation of Marxists works within
Lefebvre's general framework.[5]

This chapter focuses on work that is neither Marxist nor part of the
violently antirevolutionary writing that has appeared as part of the bicentennial, such as that of Pierre Chaunu.[6] Considered here are works reflecting a more general emphasis on politics and ideology that has helped
to divert the increasingly unproductive debate between Marxists and
revisionists into new channels.[7]

French Revolution (Oxford, 1972); Alfred Cobban, The Social Interpretation of the French
Revolution (Cambridge, 1965); Cobban, Aspects of the French Revolution (New York,
1968); Robert Forster, The Nobility of Toulouse in the Eighteenth Century (Baltimore,
1960); and George V. Taylor, "Noncapitalist Wealth and the Origins of the French Revolu-
tion," American Historical Review 72 (1967): 469–96. See also M. J. Sydenham, The
French Revolution (New York, 1966), and J. M. Roberts, The French Revolution (New
York, 1978). For a French revisionist, see Guy Chaussinand-Nogaret, La noblesse au
XVIIIe siècle: De la feodalité aux lumières (Paris, 1976).

[4]Albert Soboul, Lefebvre's successor as doyen of the Marxist school, spent countless hours
and pages refuting his critics. But he did not advance much beyond Lefebvre and, in many
respects, reified Lefebvre's stances. See Albert Soboul, A Short History of the French
Revolution, 1789–1799, trans. Geoffrey Symcox (Berkeley, 1977).

[5]Of particular note have been Michel Vovelle's investigations of popular mentalités, which
depend on imaginative uses of iconographic sources. Jean-Paul Bertaud, perhaps best
known for his study of the army, has contributed to the history of the press, while Jacques
Guilhaumou has borrowed from linguistics to explore the Revolution's intellectual framework. For important works, consult Michel Vovelle, The Fall of the French Monarchy,
1787–1792, trans. Susan Burke (New York, 1984); Vovelle, ed., Les droits de l'homme et
la conquête des libertés (Grenoble, 1988); Vovelle, ed., Les images de la Révolution française (Paris, 1988); Vovelle, La mentalité révolutionnaire: Société et mentalités sous la
Révolution française (Paris, 1985); Jean-Paul Bertaud, Les amis du roi: Journaux et jour-
nalistes royalistes en France de 1789 à 1792 (Paris, 1984); Bertaud, La Révolution armée:
Les soldats-citoyens et la Révolution française (Paris, 1979); Jacques Guilhaumou, La
langue politique et la Révolution française: De l'evenement à la raison linguistique (Paris,
1988).

[6]Chaunu and his followers view the suppression of counterrevolution in the Vendée as a
form of genocide and stress the tremendous financial and human costs of the Revolution.
Often, they portray the French Revolution as the precursor of brutal twentieth-century
leftist dictatorships, from that of V. I. Lenin to the regime of Pol Pot.

[7]The limited space of this essay precludes discussion in detail of the research of such other
notable exponents of this new trend as Keith Michael Baker and Patrice Higonnet. Although their studies resemble Furet's, each of these scholars makes notable contributions

Of all the major new overviews of the French Revolution, Furet's was the first to appear. Without question, he was the person most responsible for initiating a new explanatory paradigm. A full version of his schema appeared in *Interpreting the French Revolution,* published in France in 1978. Subsequently, he attempted to rehabilitate a number of nineteenth-century historians who offered alternatives to Marx.[8] During the bicentennial period, Furet once more has turned to work on the revolutionary decade, in the form of press interviews, colloquia, a new chronological overview, and two coedited books, one a dictionary of essays on vital concepts and the other a collection of the speeches given in the Constituent Assembly.[9] This most recent spate of work at least partially answers those critics who claimed that his brilliant hypotheses were unrelated to empirical efforts.

For Furet, ideas have the power that Lefebvre attributed to social class. Thus, in *Interpreting the French Revolution* he presented a story of competing ideologies. While particular interests may have been served by specific discourses, agendas in the political arena were set by belief systems or "political languages." Modes of speech—not interests—played the determining role. Furet began by describing (and defending) the prerevolutionary ideological status quo as a sort of traditional liberalism. Although revolutionaries criticized this philosophy for its production of a system of special privileges, Furet argued that they did not understand the benefits of such privileges. Under the Old Regime, he claimed, residency in a city or participation in a guild, just like the rank of nobility, served to protect individuals' freedom (here defined as a lack of oppression).

on his own. Higonnet's interest in America as well as France highlights a comparison at most implicit in Furet's corpus.

[8] *Interpreting the French Revolution* first appeared as *Penser la Révolution française* (Paris, 1978). Cambridge University Press published the English translation by Elborg Forster in 1981. This book and the articles that led up to it differ markedly from Furet's first overview of the Revolution, written with Denis Richet, which might be categorized as revisionist; *The French Revolution,* trans. Stephen Hardman (New York, 1970). For Furet's research on nineteenth-century historians, see *Marx et la Révolution française* (Paris, 1986); and *La gauche et la Révolution française au milieu du XIXᵉ siècle: Edgar Quinet et la question du Jacobinisme* (Paris, 1986).

[9] For sample articles on Furet, see the *Los Angeles Times,* 2 February 1989, and *Süddeutsche Zeitung* (Munich), 10–11 June 1989. The colloquia he organized met in 1986, 1987, and 1988 in Chicago, Oxford, and Paris, respectively, and volumes of the proceedings were published under the general title *The French Revolution and the Creation of Modern Political Culture* by Pergamon Press (London, 1987–89). The chronological overview is *La Révolution de Turgot à Jules Ferry, 1770–1880* (Paris, 1988); the two coedited books are, with Mona Ozouf, *Dictionnaire critique de la Révolution française* (Paris, 1988); and with Ran Halévi, *Orateurs de la Révolution française,* vol. 1, *Les constituants* (Paris, 1989).

Problems began when absolutist monarchs, eager to increase their authority, attempted to do away with such traditional protection. Although many privileges survived, the network of legal support—the parlements, municipalities, guilds, and manors—became isolated or limited. With traditional privileges under attack, French society became particularly vulnerable to the appeals of new political ideologies.

In this situation of flux, Rousseauian notions of equality, best explained in *The Social Contract,* emerged as the strongest competitor to traditional liberalism and its system of privileges. For Furet, this was not a promising development. Following Thomas Hobbes, Furet argued that absolute equality leads either to chaos or to dictatorship. During the closing decades of the Old Regime, Rousseauian ideas won the battle for the political heart of France, thanks largely to the actions of the king; for as Tocqueville had observed, thanks to the king's efforts at centralization, never had the French more resembled each other than in the years before 1789.[10] The increasing reality of equality encouraged wide acceptance of Rousseauism, even though its converts had little political experience and remained mostly philosophical, not practical, in their thinking. Following the lead of Augustin Cochin, Furet then described the flowering of a new social world, reflective and supportive of this ideology.[11]

Although this battle of ideas long predated 1789, it took the financial crisis and the resultant elections to the Estates General to settle the conflict. Those political contests were so organized by the monarchy as to mix traditional conceptions with the new Rousseauian notions of equality. On the one hand, various customary privileges, such as separate meetings of the estates, were allowed to continue. On the other, by linking the number of representatives to population figures and encouraging campaigns for votes, the monarchy recognized the principle of equal roles. As elections continued, the political process became increasingly egalitarian, with Rousseauists in charge.

Eventually, Furet argued, authority was for the first time formally entrusted to the people, with extraordinary results. In effect, royal power had ceased with the financial crisis in 1787, but it took two years for the people fully to appreciate what had happened. Then, in the midst of the

[10]For this position on the monarch's role and its effect, Furet depended on Alexis de Tocqueville, *The Old Regime and the French Revolution,* trans. Stuart Gilbert (1856; Garden City, N.Y., 1955), 77–81.
[11]Augustin Cochin, *Les sociétés de pensée et la démocratie: Etudes d'histoire révolutionnaire* (Paris, 1921); Furet, *Interpreting the French Revolution,* 164–204.

Revolution, with any actual exercise of authority believed to be the culprit for the ills of society, "language was substituted for power, for it was the sole guarantee that power would belong only to the people, that is, to nobody."[12] With politics reduced to a linguistic struggle and Rousseauian thinking dominant, politicians could no longer exercise power in the traditional sense. Although some resisted, in the end they were forced to compete in the arena of discourse. The most influential revolutionary leaders clearly understood that if they were to play the game of politics, they had no choice about its rules. Leadership passed to those who promised the greatest subservience to the people and the greatest equality. Once extreme notions of equality that denied individual differences dominated political discourse, the coming of the Terror seemed inevitable. Eventually, Furet went on, the Thermidoreans broke the tyranny of discourse and returned politics to competition among classes and political groups. Implicit in such a comparison of pre-Thermidor and post-Thermidor was Furet's negative evaluation of the Revolution.

In the years after the publication of his suggestive synthesis, Furet's fertile and active imagination led him toward revisions, most often incremental rather than general in nature. For example, Furet modified his initial critique of the legislators' inexperience so as to give more credit to their accomplishments.[13] Thus, he strengthened his argument without changing its essential emphasis on ideological struggle. And he has been equally successful in pursuing a new view of the monarchy. His early portrayal of a monarchy strong enough to undermine a society of privilege failed to account for the monarchy's inability by 1787 to keep itself alive except in name. Furet later explained that the attack on privilege eventually wounded the monarchy, an institution that, despite its own efforts to level privileges, also depended on this system of rights.[14]

In other areas, Furet made even larger adjustments without abandoning his general thrust. For example, he first declared that the elections of 1788–89 essentially settled the contest between traditional liberalism and Rousseauism, and he disclaimed interest even in Abbé Sieyès's views during the National Assembly. More recently, Furet extended the critical period of debate to include the late summer and autumn of 1789.[15] In

[12]Furet, *Interpreting the French Revolution*, 48.
[13]In the introduction to his book on the orators of the Constituent Assembly, coedited by Ran Halévi.
[14]Furet, *La Révolution*, 46–59.
[15]As late as 1987, he was still arguing that, in the elections, the Rousseauists had already triumphed. See François Furet, "La monarchie et la règlement electoral de 1789," in *The*

their work on orators, Furet and Ran Halévi argued that the transformation of the Estates General into the National Assembly on 17 June, the
abolition of privilege on 4 August, and the votes in late August and early
September (on the Rights of Man, the royal veto, and bicameralism)
constituted the "three great steps."[16] At each of these points, the two
sides confronted each other, and, Furet and Halévi concluded, the Rousseauists triumphed each time. In the end, an egalitarian world of isolated
citizens replaced the society of orders.[17]

Furet's newer publications also expand his presentation of the people.
Initially, he tended to portray the populace as faceless supporters of a
revolutionary dynamic moving inexorably toward radical equality. In
more recent studies, the people turn up at specific times and places, most
often to lend a hand to Rousseauist advocates. But, like all other interest
groups, the working classes act only through their choice of a discourse.
Language still dominates Furet's stage. The "key moment in 1789" happened not at the Bastille but at the Hall des Menus-Plaisirs, meeting place
of the National Assembly.[18]

Most recently, in newspaper interviews, François Furet calls the Revolution a great event that went astray. His intent here may be to distance
himself from conservative critics who suggest that the Revolution led not
only to the Terror but also to the unspeakably greater immolations of the
twentieth century.[19] Yet, for the most part, in scholarly talks and essays,
Furet does not alter his general theories about the origins of the Revolution or change his rather negative assessment of its outcome.

Like Furet, Lynn Hunt is interested in language, but she tends to focus
on subtle shifts in word usage and grammar rather than on the clash of
ideas. For Hunt, language and image serve as barometers of revolutionary
sentiment. In her pathbreaking work *Politics, Culture, and Class in the
French Revolution* (1984), Hunt scrutinized the everyday language used

French Revolution and the Creation of Modern Political Culture, vol. 1, Keith Michael
Baker, ed., The Political Culture of the Old Regime (Oxford, 1987), 375–86.
[16]Furet and Halévi, Orateurs, lix. On this shift, see also Ran Halévi, "La Révolution
constituante: Les ambiguités politiques," in The French Revolution and the Creation of
Modern Political Culture, vol. 2, Colin Lucas, ed., The Political Culture of the French
Revolution (Oxford, 1988), 69–85. This article is reprinted in English in Jack R. Censer,
ed., The French Revolution and Intellectual History (Chicago, 1989), 139–51.
[17]See also, for an article that applies Furet's general scenario to a specific context, that of
constitutional debates in 1789, Keith Baker, "Fixing the French Constitution," in his
Inventing the French Revolution: Essays on French Political Culture in the Eighteenth
Century (New York, 1990).
[18]Furet and Halévi, Orateurs, xxvi.
[19]See note 9 to this chapter.

to express the ideology of "democratic republicanism," which she found at the core of the revolutionary spirit.[20] Her concern was first to uncover and then to explain the underlying structure or grammar of the ideology. To do so, she turned to a range of theoretical formulations, particularly to hypotheses regarding theatricality. She also borrowed insights from the works of literary critics, anthropologists, and linguists. She used their theories to help her arrange and rearrange the content of revolutionaries' language, to uncover their basic values, the deeply embedded categories of revolutionary thinking. Revolutionaries' intentions, she argued, could be inferred from their symbolic efforts. Hunt maintained it was important to investigate as well the social backgrounds of her revolutionaries or republicans (terms used interchangeably) and did so in the second half of her book. Her intent was not to develop causal or hierarchical models of the relations among class, language, and belief but to locate, if possible, "a fit or affinity" between them.[21]

Hunt's interest in discourse analysis strongly shaped her overview of the French Revolution. Within revolutionary thought, she argued, there was no past, only a "mythic present," composed of belief in the nation and the revolution.[22] Propelled forward by fears of conspiracy, revolutionaries spoke and wrote first as if actors in a comedy, cheering their successes; then as if in a romance, struggling with good and evil; and finally, as if in a tragedy, watching things fall apart. In all three stages, their thought was envisioned as transparent or hostile to artificiality. It was also ever vigilant and always subservient to the people. Through the revolutionaries' use of symbols, they developed this litany of new beliefs.

But what political group was associated with such principles? Essentially, Hunt argued, it consisted of outsiders: individuals with education, wealth, and even connections, who, for reasons of religion, age, mobility, or external cultural and political ties, had not been thoroughly integrated into Old Regime society. For Hunt, this new political class gave "the symbolic forms of revolution . . . their motive force. Their newness to political affairs, their relative youth, and their position as relative outsiders had the effect of accelerating the development of the rhetoric and symbols of revolution." Yet—she warns those prone to statements of temporal causality—"the new men and the new political culture came into being together. In this case, it is fruitless to try to determine which came first."[23]

[20]Lynn Hunt, *Politics, Culture, and Class in the French Revolution* (Berkeley, Calif., 1984), 15.
[21]Ibid., 13.  [22]Ibid., 26–28.
[23]Ibid., 214, 216.

In terms of their focus on discourse and some of their specific findings, Furet and Hunt resemble one another. But Hunt's discussion of the revolutionary notion of a "mythic present" and her examination of the stylized emotional responses of the revolutionaries when events turned against them provided insights into mental fluctuations—psychological responses to revolutionary challenges—quite different from the critique that emerged from Furet's essentially political analysis of the effects of the language of equality. Although engaged like Furet in studying revolutionary language for patterns in political rhetoric, she also examined much deeper matters. And, unlike Furet, she tied these transformations of political views and subterranean mental structures to certain social groups, not to any eighteenth-century heritage. But, in her moral evaluation, she tended to move closer to Furet. For the most part, in *Politics, Culture, and Class,* Hunt played the neutral observer, impressed by the inventiveness of the Revolution. On occasion, however, she pictured the Revolution as a profoundly mixed experience associated with both political participation and authoritarianism.

In Hunt's more recent research,[24] she looks again at republican rhetoric, this time using feminist categories of analysis, in order to uncover a revolutionary grammar of gender relations. Once more, she invokes theory to help explicate texts. Where she had earlier relied, somewhat cautiously, on literary theory, she now boldly seizes upon Freudian conceptualizations, especially as formulated by René Girard, and begins to move toward an explication of the revolutionary unconscious.[25] Pervading revolutionary images, Hunt argues, were "unconscious fantasies about the familial order underlying revolutionary politics."[26] Particularly significant is the Freudian concept of the family romance of power. The king and queen are driven out and replaced by the band of brothers. "The revolutionary slogan of liberty, equality, and *fraternity* had a very distinctive meaning. In place of the one father-king, there are now many, equal brothers."[27]

Wishing to be free of their political parents, the revolutionaries imagined a different kind of family, dominated by the children—especially the

---

[24]Lynn Hunt, *The Family Romance of the French Revolution* (Berkeley, Calif., 1992).
[25]Lynn Hunt, "The Political Psychology of Revolutionary Caricatures," in *French Caricature and the French Revolution, 1789–1799* (Los Angeles, 1988), 33–40.
[26]Ibid., 36.
[27]Ibid., 39.

sons. But a family romance based on sons alone proved difficult to sustain, especially because

fraternity certainly did not mean that brothers and sisters were equal partners. . . . The elimination of the royal patriarchal couple did not automatically open the way for women to participate in public affairs; the proliferation of the female allegory was made possible, in fact, by the exclusion of women from public affairs. Women could be representative of abstract qualities and collective dreams because women were not about to vote or govern.[28]

Of great consequence is Hunt's shift of primary focus from revolutionary political discourse to profound changes in deep—even subconscious—mental structures still likely to be linked to certain societal supports. With this shift, she moves far away from the sort of issues that most interest Furet toward a consideration of *mentalités,* even of fundamental psychological states. Furthermore, while edging even closer here than in her book toward Furet's negative assessment of the Revolution, Hunt has specific misgivings very different from his. It is hard to appreciate the heroism of deeply misogynist revolutionaries whose releasing of the genie of revolution was, at best, an uncertain blessing. Thus, despite their somewhat different emphases, Hunt moves toward agreement with Furet on the problematic nature of the French Revolution.

Also critical of the Revolution but for quite different reasons are the authors of four recent narrative histories: William Doyle, D. M. G. Sutherland, Simon Schama, and John Bosher.[29] Although they do not constitute a formal school, these historians share a common background: a rejection of Marxist categories, an indifference to theory, a negative assessment of the Revolution, and some consensus about how best to understand it. They also have direct links to the revisionist critics of Lefebvre. Both Doyle and Sutherland earlier produced revisionist monographs.[30] Even though Bosher's and Schama's previous work did not

[28]Ibid., 39.
[29]J. F. Bosher, *The French Revolution* (New York, 1988); William Doyle, *The Oxford History of the French Revolution* (Oxford, 1989); Simon Schama, *Citizens: A Chronicle of the French Revolution* (New York, 1989); and D. M. G. Sutherland, *France, 1789–1815: Revolution and Counterrevolution* (New York, 1986).
[30]Sutherland, in his book *The Chouans: The Social Origins of Popular Counterrevolution in Upper Brittany* (Oxford, 1982) and in his numerous articles on the counterrevolution, disputes the Marxist belief that social strains between haves and have-nots led to counterrevolution. Instead, he focuses on the failure of the revolutionaries to provide relief for both rich and poor renters and on the way traditional communities resented the revolutionary intrusion into religious matters. Doyle, in *The Parlement of Bordeaux and the End of the Old Regime 1771–1790* (London, 1974), and his articles, "Was There an Aristo-

conform wholly to the revisionist mold, they have strong personal links to revisionism. Bosher was a student of Cobban; Schama, a disciple of Cobb, warmly thanks Cobban for inspiration.[31]

The books by Doyle and Sutherland closely resemble one another. In his *Oxford History of the French Revolution* (1989), William Doyle begins by describing the prerevolutionary formation of an elite composed of a unified bourgeoisie and the nobility. Distressed by the Maupeou coup of 1770–71 and convinced of the monarchy's despotism, the elite was encouraged by the financial collapse of the late 1780s to extract political concessions from the monarchy. At this point, the revolutionaries-to-be looked like idealistic reformers. Yet the tradition did not last. Although the reformers had proved a successful political combination, the process of elections to the Estates General divided the elite along class lines. Furthermore, the elections and the passions surrounding them had aroused the formerly acquiescent working classes—both rural and urban—and they pressed the bourgeoisie not only to insist on its demands but to go further and address some needs of the working classes.

In contrast to Lefebvre, who attributed the fall of the Old Regime to the accumulation of long-term grievances (the nobility against the crown and all against the aristocracy), Doyle argues that those wishing change before 1788–89 constituted a social amalgam of nobles and middle class and that the working classes became hostile to the status quo only during the revolutionary crisis. Thus, to explain the demise of the Old Regime, Doyle replaces Lefebvre's view of four fully formed prerevolutionary groups, each having a set agenda, with a reforming elite that lacked social cleavages and a quiescent poor. In his narrative, only late in 1788 do the four groups begin to emerge as formulated in the classic interpretation.

Despite accepting Lefebvre's view of the immediate revolutionary crisis of 1788–89, Doyle's construction of the subsequent years represents another departure. He shows various legislatures replacing the bourgeoisie as the centers of activity. And, in his account, the National Assembly (1789–91) created difficulties for its successor (the Legislative Assembly, 1791–92) by ill-advised actions that had unanticipated effects—particu-

---

cratic Revolution in Pre-revolutionary France?" *Past and Present* 57 (1972): 97–122; and "The Parlements of France and the Breakdown of the Old Regime, 1771–1788," *French Historical Studies* 6 (1969–70): 415–58, concentrates on the parlements. Instead of the tendency among Marxists to see the parlement as representing only the nobility in order to advance the narrow claims of that class, this author sees the French as viewing the parlement as a genuine bulwark of freedom against monarchical claims.
[31]Schama, *Citizens*, 906.

larly the settlement with the church. Such problems generated hostilities that cut across classes. The existence of a full array of enemies, inside and outside the country, stimulated the bellicosity of the legislature. Then, the war, and its failures, led to the political rift in the Assembly between the radical Jacobins and the more moderate Girondins and to the rise of the sansculottes as a political force. Together with the Jacobins, these Parisians installed a radical government. In this scenario, politics provides the motive force, with only the appearance of the sansculottes resembling their appearance in the classic interpretation. Sutherland, who shares many of Doyle's views, differs in emphasis of this point. He tends to stress the counterrevolution more than the war as the cause of the struggle within the political elite in Paris.

Doyle and Sutherland go on to provide new explanations of the Terror, the waning of radicalism and the collapse of the Jacobin regime in 1794. They emphasize general exhaustion as the cause of the retreat, in contrast to Lefebvre's stress on the social conservatism of the bourgeoisie. Further differences emerge regarding the classic view of Napoleon, which emphasizes a direct link between middle-class goals and his political rise and governmental efforts. Doyle concludes that the unpopularity of the Directory, the government established after the fall of Robespierre, led to the rise of Napoleon. Dominated by the executive, the Directory lacked a constitutional method to solve the many problems ailing France. Napoleon proved successful because he promised something to all those dissatisfied with the government, not just to a particular class. However, whereas Doyle views Napoleon as the efficient administrator, Sutherland depicts the dictator's rise as the result of governing officials' efforts to retain power. For Sutherland, the Revolution thus becomes a means of extending the radical centralization schema introduced by the monarch.

Largely dismissing class as a causal factor, Sutherland and Doyle usually substitute ideology for it in the period before 1789 and politics for it in the years after. In contrast to Lefebvre's systematic preference for social factors, these authors are more eclectic, empirical, and balanced. They are also markedly less theoretical and dogmatic. In the end, Doyle and Sutherland judge the Revolution more harshly than do Marxists such as Lefebvre. While some good issued from the Revolution, for most of the population, things were worse than before.

Those seeking a political narrative should consult Doyle; Sutherland is particularly rich in analysis. And each emphasizes different subjects. Sutherland draws on his own research in the provinces to show the Revolution outside Paris. Although Doyle knows the provinces well, his specialty is the war.

The narratives of Simon Schama (1989) and John Bosher (1988), like those of Doyle and Sutherland, constitute a pair with many features in common. Schama's special forte is literary skill. His massive book offers numerous close-ups of individuals, excursions into culture, images, and court gossip, and a remarkable stylistic virtuosity. Wit, word choice, and verve explain some of this work's appeal. This elegant work experiments linguistically and organizationally, in contrast to the more straightforward narratives by Bosher as well as by Sutherland and Doyle. Schama devotes almost half of his book to the Old Regime, pictured as a dynamic society led by a reformist government. He seems to find it somewhat inexplicable that anyone objected to the eighteenth-century French government and avers that no one had deep-seated grievances. Unexpectedly, from the social elite—both noble and common—complaints welled up. Those who railed against the Old Regime owed much of their thirst for change to observing the organizing, improving, rationalistic, and even liberalizing absolutist monarchy. While they contemplated change, they never envisioned the wholesale abolition of privilege. Still, weakened by the financial collapse, the monarchy fell. If only the monarch had been more tactful, muses Schama, things might have worked out differently.

For Schama, the months from fall 1788 to spring 1789 saw sharp transitions. While elite reformers remained committed to a restrained regime consistent with continued privilege or at least some kinds of inequality, a coherent competing group emerged in support of legal equality. Also members of the elite, these new entrants spoke an entirely different language of passionate hostility to inequality. The emotion and substance of their appeal played well to a populace that, according to Schama, instinctively and impulsively gravitated toward egalitarian—and thus antiliberal—economics and politics. Once drawn in, the lower classes gave way to their inherent anger and bloodlust. Such a complex mix of passion with popular participation and values, Schama argues, gave the Revolution even in 1789 both a radical and a bloody character. "The Terror," he recounts, "was merely 1789 with a higher body count."[32]

From its inception, then, Schama's Revolution, stemming from an alliance between the populace and the new breed of politicians, was steeped

[32]Ibid., 447.

in violence. The period after 1789 simply extended an earlier dynamic, with the vast majority of the revolutionary elite continuing to engage in passionate, egalitarian rhetoric and the populace, increasingly the Parisian sansculottes, responding with ferocity and violence. The willingness of politicians to compete and to outdo one another in crowd appeals apparently drove the Revolution to new heights. The radical Jacobins led by Robespierre were but the last and most histrionic of these politicians. Thus, the Revolution was propelled forward by an unholy fusion of ever more radical language with ever broader popular participation, until the Thermidoreans broke the spell.

Schama's explanation of the Revolution makes clear his estimate of it, for he links the Revolution to terror, anti-intellectualism, and antiliberal beliefs. If readers continue to doubt Schama's intentions toward the Revolution, they have only to consult two contrasting vignettes. Schama pictures Marie-Antoinette, after she was sentenced to death, as a gallant figure and doting mother. But he displays scant tolerance toward another prominent woman of the period, the revolutionary Théroigne de Méricourt, who had a nervous breakdown in 1793 and never recovered. In the last paragraph of his book, he proclaims, "Sympathy seems out of place here for in some sense the madness of Théroigne de Méricourt was a logical destination for the compulsions of revolutionary idealism."[33]

Some of Schama's themes reverberate in the pages of Bosher's *French Revolution*, but the two follow different tracks often enough that Bosher merits separate consideration. Enamored of Old Regime society and government, Bosher—like Schama—wonders about the source of the discontent of the noble and middle-class elite. Bosher argues that royal mistakes allowed such complaints, rather moderate on the whole, to erupt into an insurrection that a small measure of force could, and should, have stopped. Nonetheless, the revolutionaries gained power and, despite their unfortunate participation in an unworthy uprising, created a valuable enterprise. Although a bit vague on how Old Regime reformers instituted revolutionary change, Bosher appears to suggest that those in the opposition before 1789 gradually developed more advanced ideas. From this new position, they ushered in what he calls "the liberal interlude," ending privilege by making all equal before the law, a move Bosher clearly favors.[34]

To explain subsequent bloodletting, Bosher focuses on the radical

[33]Ibid., 875.   [34]Bosher, *French Revolution*, 133–57.

Jacobins—Robespierre, Danton, Marat, Hébert, and others from the social elite—who, after 1789, encouraged for their own ends popular political aspirations. In so doing, they opened the doors to the sansculottes,
whom Bosher characterizes as a violent group, imbued with antiliberal
political and economic habits. In 1793, the sansculottes' and the Jacobins'
lust for power overwhelmed the liberal legislators, who had managed
until then to maintain control. In Bosher's closing chapters, he edges
toward an overall evaluation of the Revolution in which he favors the
early liberalism but dissociates himself from its radicalization.

Although they differ on many specifics, Doyle, Sutherland, Schama,
and Bosher may be grouped together for good reason. First, like their
intellectual forebears, all reject Marxist accounts of the social origins of
the Revolution. Schama and Bosher are the most extreme in their avoid-
ance of issues of class; they also early express their antipathy toward the
sansculottes. Second, all four reject Lefebvre's optimistic assessment of
the Revolution. While early revisionists offered a highly qualified assessment of the Revolution's achievements, these new accounts are much
more aggressively negative. Here, Doyle is the most circumspect. Bosher,
while applauding the early Revolution and Directory, becomes angry
about the excesses at the height of the Revolution. Sutherland plainly
dislikes the drift of events; Schama condemns the entire affair. Cobban
and Cobb never went so far.

Third, these authors choose similar strategies to describe and explain
the Revolution. Politics takes center stage, and extensive political chrono-
logies fill their works. Yet they also consider social, political, intellectual,
and economic factors, a commonsense approach typical of historians for
whom theory is relatively unimportant. In particular, they make no attempt to deal with current debates about the relation of discourse to
reality. They simply accept that these factors coexist, one alongside the
other. Indeed, even when these authors disagree, they suggest only two
major lines of interpretation. Doyle and Sutherland agree on most matters all the way to Napoleon. And, despite serious differences, Schama
and Bosher offer similar interpretations of a number of issues, including
the vitality of prerevolutionary France, its political flaws, and its rather
unexpected revolution. The disagreements become even less significant
because of the originality of their shared viewpoint. They have virtually
no precedents in this century, although one can find resonance between
them and nineteenth-century critics of the Revolution.

Of course, they do disagree about the cause and the nature of the events of 1789. Bosher and Schama concur that prerevolutionary France was full of vitality and that the elite's criticisms were carping. For Bosher, a traditional elite simply grafted legal equality onto earlier goals and maintained a reformist tradition. Schama finds the Revolution fundamentally different from the Old Regime and quickly linked to violence. He attributes such developments to an alliance between the populace and a new breed of politicians. And, in dealing with the next two and a half years of the Revolution, Schama and Bosher extend and augment their views of 1789. Bosher notes the rise of radical politicians and the sansculottes but focuses on the efforts of the men of the assemblies to ward off attacks. Schama marks the change among revolutionaries as a class, ending with the Jacobins as merely the worst of the lot.

On events from mid-1792 until the Reign of Terror, whose importance as an era of violence remains unquestioned even by those (like Schama) who emphasize early extremism, the two agree again. They target the Jacobins, defined without reference to class, as the culprits in 1793. Bosher and Schama prove uncannily similar in their appraisal—and in their deep detestation—of the sansculottes. Both, in their analyses of the legal terror of the Year II, assert that the bloodletting flowed from the same unholy alliance of politicians and common people responsible for earlier turmoil.[35]

The recent proliferation of new interpretations, from Furet to Schama, is both exciting and bewildering. For almost every aspect of the Revolution, several competing approaches vie for attention. How can one select among them? They seem to share only a rejection of Marxism and a skeptical attitude about the accomplishments of the Revolution. And why are they so negative? While full answers to these queries require placing recent studies and their authors in political, personal, intellectual, and academic contexts, as well as the passage of time, preliminary comments are still possible.

The hostility to Marxism is not particularly difficult to explain. So much evidence undermines Lefebvre's interpretation that the authors of general syntheses pursue classic Marxist explanations only at great risk.

[35]While Schama and Furet agree as to the significance of language in the Revolution, they strongly disagree as to its content and source. First, Schama believes that by 1788 the language of egalitarianism was triumphant, while Furet depicts a struggle lasting well into 1789 between Rousseauists and traditional liberals. Second, Schama treats the discourse of egalitarianism not as simply a language the populace had to use but as an accurate expression of their viewpoint. In addition, Schama sees the Old Regime in far more positive terms than Furet does.

Explaining the common pessimism about the Revolution is more difficult. To be sure, many of the events of the years from 1789 to 1799 have since been condemned. But the vast scope of the Revolution, its moral uncertainties, and the complexity of the events and of interpretations to explain them suggest that this consensus also springs from shared subjective judgments. Both Bosher and Furet specifically note that dismay over modern popular revolutions led them in part to a new perspective.[36]

But not only political inclinations, seeping into historical judgments, bear responsibility. Traditionally, defenses of the Revolution have stressed its long-term political and economic effects. Several of the revisionists, by inclination empirical, were more interested in the immediate, short-run, and often negative impact of the Revolution. The emphasis on language in Furet, Hunt, and Schama—admittedly somewhat a political stance because it tends to reduce interest in social and economic questions— encouraged negative judgments, because authoritarianism appeared earlier in rhetoric than in deed. Sutherland's background as a scholar of the counterrevolution encouraged a sensitivity to its proponents. Finally, Hunt's measure of the Revolution along gender lines revealed another of its weaknesses. Thus, variations in approach as well as in ideology have helped to generate a chorus of negative views of the Revolution.

With so many crosswinds combining in these new studies of the Revolution, despite some similarities of evaluation, readers may easily end up more perplexed than enlightened. Such is the current state of play in a field long dominated by Georges Lefebvre's shadow. On the one hand, with such rich and detailed new alternative visions, it seems undesirable to favor one to the exclusion of others. On the other hand, it is likely that critics soon will begin just that task. Perhaps such an effort will reduce disorder while retaining the most profitable notions from the new scholarship.

In anticipation of such a thorough review, I would here like to mention those propositions that may prove the most enduring and at the same time indicate the kind of synthesis implied. Without a doubt, Doyle and Sutherland have produced the most comprehensive and least controversial of the accounts. Retaining those parts of the Marxist account that have survived challenge, they best replace the classic view. Additionally, their focus on the Revolution beyond Paris—especially the war and the counterrevolution—sets an impressive standard. Such concerns help to make sense of the seemingly ineluctable transformation of the political

[36]Bosher, *French Revolution*, x–xi; Furet and Ozouf, *Dictionnaire*, 13–16.

scene. And recent works on the *cahiers* and on the National Assembly, all of which suggest slow but steady change, further document the gradual slide toward radicalism.[37] Still, Doyle and Sutherland accept too uncritically the thesis of a despotic Old Regime. In contrast, Bosher and Schama envision this era as a period of great vitality, so effervescent that things got out of hand, although such excess was not necessarily inevitable. On the early revolutionaries themselves, Bosher has little to offer, as he is scarcely distinguishable from Doyle and Sutherland, and Schama's view ignores important distinctions among the politicians. Bosher's and Schama's treatments of the populace, flawed as they are by an almost obsessive dislike of the lower classes, are best left aside.

Finally, it seems to me that Furet and Hunt make important contributions to the reconceptualization of politics. Doyle's and Sutherland's treatments of the political center, while not incorrect, lack force. With the disappearance of class as an explanatory variable, the devastating splits among the revolutionary politicians are difficult to explain. The same may be said for the direction of policy after the great events of 1789. Both Furet and Hunt provide rationales: he for divisions among revolutionaries, she for the overall goals of the republicans. Perhaps these twin explanations—one mainly intellectual, the other more related to the revolutionary impulse—can be linked, although historians may be most comfortable with Hunt's earlier, and less theoretical, understanding of democratic republicanism. Her view of gender is dependent on modern theories that may not apply well to eighteenth-century revolutionaries. But, at the least, integrating the insights of Hunt and Furet into accounts such as those of Doyle and Sutherland provides the latter with a rationale for political action and divisions and the former with events that are needed to account for the development of ideas. This projected synthesis intentionally ignores Furet's characterization of the Old Regime, which to my mind overstates the role of Rousseau, underplays the importance of context, and is too insistent generally on problems. But I hasten to add that such judgments are preliminary comments on highly complex and skilled works of history. With more discussion and debate, these new riches will become easier to manage.

[37]George V. Taylor, "Revolutionary and Nonrevolutionary Content in the *Cahiers* of 1789: An Interim Report," *French Historical Studies* 7 (1972): 479–502; Roger Chartier, "From Words to Texts: The *Cahiers de doléances* of 1789," in Roger Chartier, *The Cultural Uses of Print in Early Modern France*, trans. Lydia Cochrane (Princeton, N.J., 1987), 110–44; and Timothy Tackett, "Nobles and Third Estate in the Revolutionary Dynamic of the National Assembly," *American Historical Review* 94 (1989): 271–301.

# 2

•ı•◦•ı•ı•◦ı•ı•◦•ı•ı•◦ı•ı•◦•ı•ı•◦ı•ı•◦•ı•ı•◦ı•ı•◦•ı•ı•◦ı•ı•◦•ı•ı•◦ı•ı•◦•ı•

## The French Revolution and the creation
## of American political culture

### LLOYD S. KRAMER

The French Revolution was the most influential international event in the
emergence of a distinctive American political culture during the 1790s.
Indeed, except for the two world wars, the cold war, and the Vietnam War
in the twentieth century, no *foreign* event has ever affected American
politics and culture as profoundly as the Revolution in France. The trans-
formative effects of the modern wars, however, resulted in large part from
direct and massive military involvements, whereas America remained at
peace and far removed from the revolutionary wars that divided Europe
in the 1790s.

Despite the vast changes in American politics, society, and military
power over the last two centuries, the French Revolution's impact on
America can be compared to the impact of modern wars on at least two
levels. First, like the world wars and the cold war, the French Revolution played a major role in helping or forcing Americans to define their
place in the world. In fact, the national political identity that took
shape in response to revolutionary events in late eighteenth-century
Europe has guided American politics into the modern era and contributed (among other things) much of the ideological rationale for participation in twentieth-century wars in Europe and Asia. This new national identity (which drew, of course, on long-established themes in
American culture) stressed that the United States had established a
uniquely successful and virtuous system of government that could either

I thank Eric Foner, Michael Hunt, and Donald Reid for their helpful comments on an earlier
draft of this chapter.

provide democratic examples for the Old World or suffer from the corrupting influences of European politics and diplomacy. In either case, the French Revolution helped Americans believe that their politics and culture were different from (and superior to) the politics and culture of Europe.

But the question of America's proper relation to Europe led to bitter political debates, which suggests the second level on which the events of the 1790s can be compared to twentieth-century American history. Like the Vietnam War, the French Revolution provoked exceptional internal disagreements about the institutions of American society, the meaning of patriotism, and the ideas of political leaders. In this atmosphere, the normal disagreements of political life took on intense ideological meaning, so that political opponents viewed one another as embodiments of profoundly different philosophies and cultural values. In short, the French Revolution transformed the new nation's first decade into one of the most divisive and ideologically charged periods in all of American history.

This essay analyzes the influence of the French Revolution in American society by examining its role in the emergence of America's early national identity and its contribution to the development of political and cultural themes that have reappeared often in subsequent American history. An account that considers the French Revolution's political and cultural impact in America must leave aside other issues, such as the Revolution's effect on international trade or domestic industrial development or territorial expansion. The French Revolution became a major event in American society because of its cultural meanings for people who knew very little about actual conditions in France. Lack of specific knowledge about France and great distance from revolutionary events made it likely that most Americans would assimilate the news from Europe into their own hopes and fears for the politics and culture of the New World. It is impossible to describe all of the complex nuances in the American responses to France's Revolution, but the cultural meanings that this event evoked in the United States can be approached in at least four overlapping spheres of influence: (1) political parties and the creation of political culture, (2) diplomatic policy and the separation from Europe, (3) nationalism and the definition of patriotism, and (4) religion and the rejection of the Enlightenment. The French Revolution entered all of these areas of America's early national history, contributing in each case to the emergence, extension, or redefinition of distinctive "American" institutions, policies, and ideologies.

POLITICAL PARTIES AND
THE CREATION OF POLITICAL CULTURE

Americans welcomed the first reports of France's revolutionary changes in 1789 with nearly universal praise, in part because the French seemed to be embracing American principles of self-government and in part because the Revolution began with relatively little violence. Among other encouraging portents, Lafayette's conspicuous participation in the events of 1789 suggested that France was now implementing the ideals that had guided America's own recent revolution; where French arms had helped America win its freedom from England, American ideas (as mediated by friends such as Lafayette) were now helping France win its freedom from centuries of absolutist government.[1]

This early American unanimity soon dissolved, however, as the more radical democratic ideas from France began to enter America's own political debates and as the American political elite divided into anti-French and pro-French factions. The French Revolution thus became a major cause for the creation of America's early two-party political system and the most important issue in the emergence of an active public culture. Debates about the French Revolution spread from Congress and cabinet meetings into the press, the streets, and local communities of America, thereby helping to create both the party rivalries and the popular political culture which many Founding Fathers had neither wanted nor anticipated.[2]

[1]See, for example, George Washington's letters to Lafayette, 14 October 1789, and to Catherine Macaulay Graham, 9 January 1790, in John C. Fitzpatrick, ed., *The Writings of George Washington*, 39 vols. (Washington, 1931–44), 30:448–49, 497–98.

[2]The French Revolution's impact on early American political life has been discussed from various perspectives in many well-known historical studies. See, for example, Vernon Louis Parrington, *Main Currents in American Thought*, 2 vols. (1927; reprint, New York, 1954), 1:327–402; Richard Buel, Jr., *Securing the Revolution: Ideology in American Politics, 1789–1815* (Ithaca, 1972); William Nisbet Chambers, *Political Parties in a New Nation: The American Experience, 1776–1809* (New York, 1963); Richard Hofstadter, *The Idea of a Party System: The Rise of Legitimate Opposition in the United States, 1780–1840* (Berkeley and Los Angeles, 1969), 74–128; David Brion Davis, *Revolutions: Reflections on American Equality and Foreign Liberations* (Cambridge, Mass., 1990), 29–54; and R. R. Palmer, *The Age of the Democratic Revolution*, 2 vols. (Princeton, 1959–64), 2: 509–46. Palmer's important synthetic study remains the essential starting point for study of the French Revolution's international significance.

Historians often trace the first political parties to the disagreements over Alexander Hamilton's economic policies, but the clearest ideological differences between Federalists and Republicans emerged in their interpretations of the French Revolution. Federalist leaders such as John Adams, Hamilton, and even George Washington began warning about the dangers of France's Revolution as early as 1790, whereas Republican leaders such as Thomas Jefferson, James Madison, and James Monroe generally supported the goals and many policies of successive French governments until Napoleon seized power at the end of the decade. Few foreign events have provoked such vehement disagreements within America's political elite, and perhaps no foreign event has revealed greater differences in the elite's conception of how American society should function. As Joyce Appleby has explained in a perceptive analysis of this era, the Federalists held a classical republican view of politics, which assumed that governments should be managed by elites, controlled through careful checks and balances, and removed from the direct influence of passionate, common people who form the broad base of social hierarchies. Republicans, by contrast, held a more democratic view of politics, which assumed that governments should be open to wider public participation, responsive to popular opinion, and influenced by political movements or voluntary associations of people who were outside official institutions.[3] In the political context and language of the 1790s, the Federalist views became linked with England, and the Republican views became linked with France. The French Revolution was thus the inescapable event that forced the two emerging parties to define their explicit political differences and to enter a heated battle for American public opinion.

Although the early anxiety over French developments could already be found in Washington's private fear (October 1789) that France's "revolution is of too great magnitude to be effected in so short a space, and the loss of so little blood,"[4] it was Vice President John Adams who launched

[3]Joyce Appleby, *Capitalism and a New Social Order: The Republican Vision of the 1790s* (New York, 1984), 6, 57–59, 61, 66–67, 73. The Republicans' conception of public participation of course did not extend beyond white males; they excluded women from political life, they mostly accepted slavery in the South, and they were often hostile to native Americans in the West. The opposition between Federalists and Republicans was therefore relative rather than absolute. Also, the emerging party rivalry reflected increasingly significant ethnic differences (New England Federalists feared the many recent immigrants who leaned toward the Republicans) as well as disputes over political theory. See, for example, Robert Kelley, *The Cultural Pattern in American Politics: The First Century* (New York, 1979), 109–40.
[4]Washington to Gouverneur Morris, 13 October 1789, in Fitzpatrick, *Writings of Washington*, 30:443.

the public criticism of actions and ideas that had gained revolutionary ascendancy in Paris. Adams wrote about the dangers of democratic revolutions in a series of articles called *Discourses on Davila,* which he published in a Philadelphia newspaper during the first phase of the French Revolution (1790). Reflecting on recent events, the Vice President offered some pointed advice for his American readers:

The increase and dissemination of knowledge, instead of rendering unnecessary the checks . . . [and] balances of rivalry in the orders of society and constitution of government, augment the necessity of both. It becomes the more indispensable that every man should know his place, and be made to keep it.[5]

This well-ordered, hierarchical system was precisely what the new French ideas seemed to challenge, but Adams insisted that Americans should not accept leveling assumptions from foreign countries. "Amidst our enthusiasm," he wrote, "there is great reason to pause and preserve our sobriety." The Federalist interpretation of the French Revolution thus emerged at an early date and stressed two essential themes: the danger of challenging social or political order and the danger of borrowing ideas from abroad. Adams drew an immediate and typical lesson from the Revolution when he concluded that "the balance of a well-ordered government will alone be able to prevent . . . dangerous ambition, irregular rivalries, destructive factions, wasting seditions, and bloody, civil wars."[6]

These somber warnings in 1790 by no means destroyed the growing American enthusiasm for France's Revolution. On the contrary, they did more to undermine the popularity of Adams than to reduce the popularity of French revolutionary ideas, and so other Federalist leaders were forced to join the public debate as the Revolution entered its radical, republican phase after 1792. Alexander Hamilton followed Adams into the newspapers with articles that suggested how "well-informed" and "sober-minded" people must see the French revolutionary wars (1793) as "repugnant" to the "true principles of liberty" and the Revolution itself (1794) as "an unexampled dissolution of all the social and moral ties." Indeed, the French Revolution had given way to "opinions so wild[,] so extreme [and] passions so turbulent[,] so tempestuous, as almost to forbid the hope of agreement in any rational or well-organized system of Government."[7]

[5]John Adams, "Discourses on Davila," in Charles Francis Adams, ed., *The Works of John Adams,* 10 vols. (Boston, 1850–56), 6:276.
[6]Ibid., 279.
[7]Alexander Hamilton, "Pacificus No. II" [3 July 1793], and "Americanus No. 1" [31 January 1794], in Harold C. Syrett et al., eds., *The Papers of Alexander Hamilton,* 26 vols. (New York, 1961–79), 15:62, 670.

Hamilton's public statements repeatedly stressed the problems in France, but his private comments showed that he was most concerned with the French influence in America. "The example of France," he wrote to Washington in the spring of 1794, "may be found to have unhinged the orderly principles of the People of this country and . . . a further assimilation of our principles with those of France may prove to be the threshold of disorganization and anarchy."[8] Similar assessments of the French Revolution and of France's dangerous influence in America appeared constantly in the writings of Federalist leaders throughout the 1790s and provided much of the ideological coherence for Federalist political campaigns. Defense of "orderly" government (as they defined it) required the defeat or repression of the French Republic's American advocates—a large group of enthusiasts who ranged from the uneducated fringe on the western frontier to the most articulate leaders of the emerging Republican party.

The Republicans found a radically different meaning in the French Revolution. Where Adams and Hamilton saw the collapse of order and the demise of true liberty, Jefferson, Madison, and Monroe saw the collapse of special privileges and the expansion of freedom. Jefferson's sympathetic (though not uncritical) view of France alienated him from Washington's administration and became a source of permanent political controversy. Critics would always remember that he had been in Paris in 1789 and that he had steadfastly defended revolutionary writers such as Thomas Paine; for most Federalists, Jefferson came to symbolize France and Jacobinism and the danger of Enlightenment ideas. Yet Jefferson's support for France was never as visible as the anti-French publications of Adams and Hamilton. He did not write newspaper articles on the Revolution (though he encouraged Madison to attack Hamilton in the press),[9] and most of his support for the Revolution appeared in his correspondence with friends. A famous letter to William Short, for example, deplored the loss of life in France but excused the deaths as an acceptable price to pay for the cause of liberty. "It was necessary to use the arm of the people," Jefferson wrote in January 1793, and " . . . a few of their cordial friends met at their hands the fate of enemies." These deaths would nevertheless be forgiven by a posterity that would long enjoy the liberty

---

[8]Hamilton to Washington, [14] April 1794, ibid., 16:270. Hamilton was urging Washington to avoid conflict with England.
[9]Thomas Jefferson to James Madison, 7 July 1793, in Paul Leicester Ford, ed., *The Writings of Thomas Jefferson*, 10 vols. (New York, 1892–99), 6:338. Madison responded with a series of newspaper articles in August and September of 1793.

for which some innocent people had unfortunately given their lives. "The liberty of the whole earth was depending on the issue of the contest, and was ever such a prize won with so little innocent blood?"[10] Jefferson's rhetorical question shows how far he had moved from Adams and Hamilton and Washington by 1793 and how clearly the identity of an opposition party was taking shape in the debate over France's Revolution. Despite the opinions of certain prominent government leaders, Jefferson wanted to assure Short that his own pro-French republican sentiments were "really those of 99. in an hundred of our citizens."[11] In other words, Jefferson recognized that a new sphere of opinion and political activity was developing outside the government and that much of this new political culture shared both his sympathy for the French Revolution and his aspirations for a democratic republicanism.

The new opposition party identified itself with the ideas and cause of the French Republic by stressing that America and France were "sister republics" in a world of despotic monarchs. Madison emphasized this link when he responded to a decree of the French National Assembly that had granted him honorary French citizenship. America was connected with France, Madison noted in a letter, because the two nations shared "the affinities of their mutual liberty."[12] In direct opposition to the Federalist emphasis on the differences between America and France, Madison argued that the two republics shared the same enemies and the same dangers. France's enemies, he explained in 1793, were "the enemies of human nature" and of America because France's revolutionary struggle promoted liberty on both sides of the Atlantic: "a miscarriage of it [the French Revolution] would threaten us with the most serious dangers to our present forms and principles of our governments."[13] Madison's comments point again to the striking Republican opposition to the Federalist views of France.

For Adams and Hamilton, the survival of America's government required French defeats, whereas for Madison, the survival of America's government required French victories. James Monroe, who went to Paris

[10]Jefferson to William Short, 3 January 1793, ibid., 154. Short was a U.S. diplomat in Europe who had criticized the Jacobins.
[11]Ibid.
[12]Madison to the Minister of the Interior of the French Republic, April 1793, in Robert A. Rutland et al., eds., *The Papers of James Madison*, 15 vols. to date (Chicago and Charlottesville, 1962–93), 15:4.
[13]Madison to George Nicholas, 15 March 1793, ibid., 14:472. Jefferson made the same point in a letter to Thomas Mann Randolph (7 January 1793) when he wrote "that the form our own government was to take depended much more on the events of France than any body had before imagined" (Ford, ed., *Writings of Jefferson*, 6:157).

as the American ambassador in 1794, agreed entirely with Madison. Addressing the French National Convention after the execution of the king, after the violence of the Terror, and after the coup that had deposed Robespierre, Monroe linked the United States and France in a speech that violated the entire Federalist conception of American political life. "Their governments are similar," Monroe assured the revolutionary convention; "they both cherish the same principles and rest on the same basis, the equal and unalienable rights of man."[14]

These various pronouncements on the French Revolution exemplify the contrasting ideologies of America's first political parties, but the development of rival political factions formed only one part of America's new political culture in this era. Political leaders were becoming much more self-conscious about their appeals to public opinion because the "public" was emerging as a more active force in American political life (recent debates over the new Constitution had shown much sensitivity to the nuances of public opinion).

The development of this new political culture in America can be compared to the creation of a "public sphere" in eighteenth-century Europe, which Jürgen Habermas has described in his influential book, *The Structural Transformation of the Public Sphere*. Habermas argues that a new sphere of public debate over politics and culture developed outside the institutions of absolutist government before 1789 in Europe and that the debaters in this sphere appealed for the support of "public opinion" through the critical rationality of their arguments. New institutions such as the press, literary societies, and coffeehouses became centers of a new public culture that was located somewhere between the domestic sphere of the household and the official sphere of government authority. This new public sphere broadened participation in public life and enhanced the communication, critical judgments, and social interactions that are essential for the existence of democratic societies. Habermas ties his concept of the emerging public sphere to a stage of capitalist development (the link might also apply in the American case), but I want simply to draw on his conceptual framework to stress the importance of an active "public sphere" for democratic political cultures and to argue that the response to France's Revolution promoted the rapid expansion of the "public sphere" in America.[15]

---

[14]James Monroe, "Address to the National Convention," [15 August 1794], in Stanislaus Murray Hamilton, ed., *The Writings of James Monroe*, 7 vols. (New York, 1898–1903), 2:13.
[15]Jürgen Habermas, *The Structural Transformation of the Public Sphere: An Inquiry into a Category of Bourgeois Society*, trans. Thomas Burger and Frederick Lawrence (Cam-

The mobilizing influence of the French Revolution in America's emerging public sphere appears in the remarkable development of the press, the numerous public celebrations of support for the French Republic, and the creation of local organizations that brought new "French" themes into American politics. These politicizing trends suggest that American culture was moving in the direction of Jeffersonian republicanism because they all contributed to a popular public sphere outside of official institutions—the sphere that Federalists distrusted as an arena of passions and disorder. Despite their dislike for much of this new public sphere, the Federalists also entered the new political culture through the press and through their campaigns for public office. But it was difficult to reconcile the elitist assumptions of Federalist republicanism with the new public sphere, and the Federalist party eventually lost its influence in a more democratized political culture.

America's public sphere depended (as in Europe) on the freedom and expansion of the press. By all accounts, the last decade of the eighteenth century was a period of spectacular growth in the printing and distribution of American newspapers; the number of publications increased from fewer than 100 in 1790 to more than 230 in 1800, and much of the space in these gazettes and journals was given over to news from France. Indeed, one study of the era concludes that the American press gave more attention to French news than to domestic news in the 1790s.[16] Many of the reports from Paris came by way of England, which may have helped the Federalist interpretation of events, but the press soon divided like the political leaders into pro-French and anti-French factions. This was especially true in Philadelphia, where Benjamin Franklin Bache's *Aurora* defended the French Revolution against the scathing criticisms of William Cobbett's *Porcupine's Gazette,* and where a large French émigré community supported or condemned the Revolution in publications that ranged widely across the political spectrum.[17]

---

bridge, Mass., 1989), 1–102. It should be noted that America's "public sphere" (like all others?) generally lacked the critical rationality of Habermas's "ideal-type" public discourse.

[16] On the growth of newspapers in this era, see Donald H. Stewart, *The Opposition Press of the Federalist Period* (Albany, 1969), 3–32; figures for the increasing number of publications appear on p. 15. On the prominence of French news, see Charles Downer Hazen, *Contemporary American Opinion of the French Revolution* (Baltimore, 1897), 248.

[17] For an introduction to the conflicts among Philadelphia journalists, see George Spater, *William Cobbett, The Poor Man's Friend,* 2 vols. (Cambridge, 1982), 1:53–109; on the French émigré press, see Frances Sergeant Childs, *French Refugee Life in the United States, 1790–1800* (Baltimore, 1940), 122–59.

The bitterness of the press wars reflected the passions of the revolutionary era in America's capital city. Bache believed the French example would help America achieve greater "liberty and equality," if only the new nation could survive the anti-democratic leadership of George Washington and the Federalists. Ceding nothing to Washington's lofty reputation, the *Aurora* regularly published the most outspoken attacks on the anti-French drift of Federalist policies.[18] Bache's vehement prose elicited equally violent responses from writers such as William Cobbett, who called Bache "the most infamous of the Jacobins . . . Distributor General of the principles of Insurrection, Anarchy and Confusion, the greatest of fools, and the most stubborn sans-culotte in the United States."[19] Cobbett's description of Bache conveys the polemical intensity that helped to spread the "French" debate from the press into the streets and taverns and churches of communities that were far removed from the political elite in Philadelphia.

The creation of the French Republic led to celebrations in cities from Boston to Charleston as American supporters of the new "sister republic" gathered to sing songs, drink celebratory toasts, participate in "civic feasts," and praise the ideals of liberty and equality. The celebration in Boston (24 January 1793), for example, began with a street procession of prominent citizens and children, moved to a great banquet in flag-draped Faneuil Hall ("Citizen Samuel Adams" presiding), and culminated in bonfires and fireworks. A large crowd in Charleston (11 January 1793) sang the "Marseillaise" before sitting down to a "grand fete" at Williams' Coffee House (250 participants). The Tammany Society celebrated the French Republic in New York (27 December 1792) by erecting a liberty pole and singing about the revolutionary battles: "May Heaven continue still to bless/ The arms of freedom with success, / Till tyrants are no more." Other celebrations took place in Providence, Philadelphia, Baltimore, Norfolk, Savannah, and elsewhere, contributing in each case to a public expression and understanding of political themes such as liberty, equality, and the rights of man.[20] The celebration of France's Revolution

[18]Benjamin Franklin Bache to Richard Bache, 4 February 1793, cited in Eugene Perry Link, *Democratic-Republican Societies, 1790–1800* (New York, 1942), 45; for more on Bache's criticism of Washington and the Federalists, see James Morton Smith, *Freedom's Fetters: The Alien and Sedition Laws and American Civil Liberties* (Ithaca, 1956), 188–203; and Stewart, *Opposition Press,* 609–13.
[19]Cited in Smith, *Freedom's Fetters,* 190.
[20]Accounts of the American celebrations of the French Republic appear in Hazen, *American Opinion of the French Revolution,* 164–73; quotation on p. 165.

became, of course, a celebration of America's own republicanism, which was now opened to new scrutiny and comparisons. It was not long before the interest in French principles helped to generate a new demand for greater democratization in America.

This demand emerged as the central theme of the new Democratic-Republican Societies that were established in more than forty towns during 1793 and 1794. As some of the first local political organizations and as early allies of the emerging Republican party, these Societies attracted immediate attention from the Federalist elite, and they have remained important for historians of early populist democracy in America. Loosely connected through a shared critique of official policies (e.g., Washington's Proclamation of Neutrality in the European war and Jay's Treaty with Britain), the Democratic Societies generally called for broader public influence in government affairs, more equality in social relations, and greater access to education. Most significantly in the context of 1793, however, all of the Societies strongly supported the French Revolution. Their membership came from both the artisan and professional classes, but the new revolutionary emphasis on equality inspired the Societies' members to address one another simply as "Citizen."[21]

The egalitarianism and the use of "French" ideas gave their opponents all the evidence they needed to believe that the Democratic Societies were "Jacobin" clubs that intended to bring the French Revolution to America, and it was in fact obvious that the Societies stressed the similarity between America's *true* political ideals and the French Republic. A typical resolution by the "Republican Society" of Ulster County, New York (1 January 1794) asserted that "the revolution which has been effected in France, is the proper touch-stone whereby to discriminate the friends of liberty, and that every man who is opposed to the regeneration of France, is, in principle, opposed to the Constitution of the United States, and would, were it in his power, saddle us with a monarchy or aristocracy."[22] All of the Democratic Societies proclaimed the bond of liberty and friendship between the "sister republics" and declared the universality of a shared republican cause.[23] The campaign for this cause, however, had to

[21]On the development, ideas, and activities of the Societies, see Link, *Democratic-Republican Societies*, 72–73, 108–9, 117, 149, and the introduction in Philip S. Foner, ed., *The Democratic-Republican Societies, 1790–1800: A Documentary Sourcebook of Constitutions, Declarations, Addresses, Resolutions, and Toasts* (Westport, Conn., 1976), 3–40.
[22]"Resolutions of Republican Society in Ulster County," 1 January 1794, in Foner, ed., *Democratic-Republican Sourcebook*, 236.
[23]See, for example, the Resolutions by Societies in Charleston and Pinckneyville, South

be waged in America as well as in Europe, and the specific American goals of the common cause were explained in the founding principles of the first Democratic Society in Philadelphia. The key purpose of the organization was "to cultivate the just knowledge of rational liberty, to facilitate the enjoyment and exercise of our civil rights, and to transmit, unimpaired, to posterity, the glorious inheritance of a *free Republican Government.*" Although this task called for actions from private citizens, it was by no means a private affair. "The public good is indeed its sole object," the Society noted in justifying its claim to a legitimate place in the public sphere outside of government.[24]

This claim to a permanent place in the political process clearly challenged the Federalist conception of proper, orderly government, especially since it was accompanied by so much enthusiasm for the French Revolution. Federalist editors and political leaders therefore launched an aggressive (even hysterical) counterattack on the "demagogues" and would-be "dictators" who threatened to bring Jacobinism to America in the guise of "democratic" clubs.[25] These denunciations combined with the Societies' own publicity to make the new "Democratic-Republicans" famous and extremely unpopular with almost everyone in Washington's administration, including the President. Indeed, George Washington took the lead in drawing attention to the danger of the Democratic Societies, which he condemned as "self-created" organizations, blamed for the Whisky Rebellion in western Pennsylvania, and castigated as the creation of the "diabolical" French ambassador, Edmond Genet. Like most Federalists, Washington believed the Societies were established by foreigners (i.e., Frenchmen) "to sow sedition [and] to poison the minds of the people of this country;" and nothing could be "more absurd, more arrogant, or more pernicious to the peace of Society, than for self created bodies" to meet "under the shade of night in a conclave" for the purpose of passing judgment on the policies of a duly elected government.[26]

Washington's charge that the Democratic Societies resulted from for-

Carolina (13 July 1793 and 7 April 1794), the declaration of the Massachusetts Society (13 January 1794), the toasts of the New York Society (20 March 1794), and the Resolutions of the Philadelphia Society (9 January and 10 April 1794), all ibid., 69, 77, 168, 258, 379, 393.

[24]"Principles, Articles, and Regulations," The Democratic Society of Philadelphia, 30 May 1793, ibid., 64.

[25]The quotations appear in a letter from Nathaniel Chipman to Hamilton, 9 [June] 1794, in Syrett, et al., eds., *Papers of Hamilton,* 16:468–70.

[26]Washington to Burges Bell, 24 September 1794, and to Daniel Morgan, 8 October 1794, in Fitzpatrick, ed., *Writings of Washington,* 33:506, 524.

eign influences was both true and false. It was true that America's democratic republicans supported the ideas and many policies of France's revolutionaries, but it was false to claim that Jacobin agents or French ambassadors had created the Democratic Societies. The French Republic's own diplomats in Philadelphia (Fauchet, La Forest, Petry) recognized that America's political clubs differed significantly from the Jacobin clubs at home, and they emphasized these differences in the letters they sent to Paris. Reporting on the notoriety of the Democratic Societies, the French representatives explained to their government (December 1794) that these so-called clubs were neither numerous nor large nor closely affiliated. Equally significant from the French perspective, the Societies admitted anyone who wanted to attend, they rarely met more than once a week, and their resolutions usually did little more than repeat what others had said in "town meetings," none of which resembled the Jacobin clubs in France. The French knew how a real Jacobin club met (often) and deliberated (with fervent revolutionary arguments), so they could see what the Federalists did not understand: the Democratic Societies were not the core of a revolutionary movement, they were not French, and they were not especially dangerous to the government. They nevertheless carried a certain influence because their resolutions were published "in all the gazettes from one end of the union to the other," which gave the impression of mass public support for ideas that "were only endorsed by the five to six hundred persons who make up the total [national] membership of all the Societies."[27] The French observers thus described the real significance of the Democratic Societies by stressing their contribution to the expanding contest for public opinion. Although they were never revolutionary in the sense of seeking the overthrow of America's constitutional government, the Societies played a prominent role in publicizing political debates and in extending the public sphere that was essential for a democratic political culture.

The French Revolution therefore helped to shape several of the most enduring characteristics of American politics. It provoked the political elites to define their contrasting visions of republican society and thereby develop the most permanent nonconstitutional feature of American poli-

[27]J. A. Fauchet, La Forest, and Petry to the French Commissioner of Foreign Relations, 15 Frimaire, Year 3 [5 December 1794] in Frederick Jackson Turner, ed., "Correspondence of the French Ministers to the United States, 1791–1797," *American Historical Association, Annual Report, 1903* (Washington, 1904), 500–502; quotation on p. 501. Fauchet replaced Genet as the French ambassador to the United States in late 1793; he was followed by Pierre Adet in 1795.

tics: the two-party system. Supporters of the French Revolution in the 1790s established the legitimacy of a political opposition and successfully rejected the Federalist conception of elite or classical republicanism. After this era, no political party could explicitly promote the idea of a hierarchical political system (for white males) or condemn the influence of the "common man" (though that influence would still be limited). But the emergence of political parties became part of a wider transformation in American political culture—the development of a new public sphere in the press, in public demonstrations, and in local political organizations. Both the parties and the expanding political culture were strongly affected by American supporters of the French Revolution who brought the new revolutionary language from Europe into the New World's distinctive traditions and debates. Many conservatives resisted these developments, however, and initiated the American tendency to blame reformist or radical agitation on "foreign influences." This fear of aliens and their ideas also developed in response to the French Revolution and contributed to the new diplomatic policy (isolationism), the new nationalism (patriotic nativism), and the new religion (Protestant revivalism), all of which stressed America's radical difference from Europe.

## DIPLOMATIC POLICY AND THE SEPARATION FROM EUROPE

The key statements of America's emerging diplomatic policy and ideology appeared in President Washington's Proclamation of Neutrality (22 April 1793) and in his famous Farewell Address (17 September 1796). Although historians continue to debate the genesis and implications of Washington's statements, one central theme seems indisputable: both documents responded directly to the revolutionary wars in Europe. This response is obvious in the Proclamation of Neutrality, which announced America's intention to remain "friendly and impartial towards the belligerent powers" (France and England),[28] but it is even stronger in the Farewell Address because the political meanings and consequences of Europe's revolutionary events had become more threatening to many Americans by 1796.

Modern analysts of the Farewell Address have moved the document from the realm of timeless advice into a specific historical context of bitter political rivalries and diplomatic disputes. They especially note

---

[28]George Washington, "Proclamation of Neutrality," 22 April 1793, in Fitzpatrick, ed., *Writings of Washington*, 32:430.

Hamilton's important role in shaping Washington's statements, which provided material for Federalist attacks on Jeffersonian republicans in the political campaigns of 1796.[29] Some historians have also emphasized that Washington never wanted America to withdraw from the world and that he envisioned an active, expansive role for America in international affairs.[30] These revisionist readings of the Farewell Address thus insist that it was not simply (or even primarily) an isolationist manifesto, but it is hardly surprising that generations of Americans drew precisely that isolationist meaning from the document. The central theme in the discussion of foreign affairs stressed that America should withdraw as far as possible from involvements in Europe. Dismayed by the "French" party at home and the revolutionary wars abroad, Washington pointed explicitly to the danger of sympathizing with other nations and to the advantage of America's geographical separation from the Old World. Whatever else one might say about Washington's address, it clearly offered prestigious endorsement for the idea that America differed profoundly from other societies and revolutions in the world—an idea that would flourish in America's subsequent diplomatic ideology.[31]

Although the Farewell Address is well known as a general statement about foreign policy, its message takes on very specific meanings in the context of the French Revolution. In the first place, Washington clearly distrusted those Americans who had embraced the French cause. "Passionate attachment" to a "favorite" nation, he wrote, "gives to ambitious, corrupted, or deluded citizens (who devote themselves to the favorite nation) facility to betray or sacrifice the interests of their own country without odium, sometimes even with popularity." Such attachments carried profound threats to America because "real patriots who may re-

[29]These themes appear, among other places, in Felix Gilbert, *The Beginnings of American Foreign Policy: To the Farewell Address*, 2d ed. (New York, 1965), 123–34; Alexander DeConde, "Washington's Farewell, the French Alliance, and the Election of 1796," *Mississippi Valley Historical Review* 43 (1957): 641–58; and Samuel Flagg Bemis, "Washington's Farewell Address: A Foreign Policy of Independence," *American Historical Review* 39 (1934): 250–68.
[30]Good examples of this anti-isolationist interpretation have been collected in Burton Ira Kaufman, ed., *Washington's Farewell Address: The View from the 20th Century* (Chicago, 1969). See the essays in this collection by Roland G. Usher, "Washington and Entangling Alliances," 53–62; St. George Leakin Sioussat, "The Farewell Address in the Twentieth Century," 67–81; and Kaufman, "Washington's Farewell Address: A Statement of Empire," 169–87. Kaufman's collection also includes excerpts from the works by Gilbert, DeConde, and Bemis, cited above, and the complete text of the Farewell Address.
[31]On the development of America's diplomatic ideology, with special attention to the American fear of "the perils of revolution," see the important synthetic study by Michael H. Hunt, *Ideology and U.S. Foreign Policy* (New Haven, 1987), especially chapter 4.

sist the intrigues of the favorite [nation] are liable to become suspected and odious, while its tools and dupes usurp the applause and confidence of the people to surrender their interests."[32] Few persons in 1796 could have missed the conspicuous references to "tools and dupes" (Jeffersonians, Democratic Societies) of the "favorite" nation (France, Citizen Genet).

This distrust of those who embraced foreign causes led directly to Washington's second theme, which called for America to have "as little *political* connection as possible" with foreign nations. Here, too, there was an anti-French implication, since America's only previous alliance had been formed with France (1778) and warmly welcomed by all American patriots at that time. The revolutionary wars in the 1790s, however, gave Washington a reason to emphasize America's difference and distance from the Old World. "Why forgo the advantages of so peculiar a situation?" he asked rhetorically. "Why quit our own to stand upon foreign ground? Why, by interweaving our destiny with that of any part of Europe, entangle our peace and prosperity in the toils of European ambition, rivalship, interest, humor or caprice?" The obvious answers to these questions rested upon the fundamental conclusion that Washington and many other Americans drew from the social and political conflicts of the French Revolution: "Europe has a set of primary interests which to us have none or a very remote relation. Hence she must be engaged in frequent controversies, the cause of which are essentially foreign to our concerns."[33]

In short, Washington issued a new declaration of independence in 1796, stressing that America's peace, liberty, and democratic government now justified a final, decisive separation from the controversies and politics of the Old World. This strong affirmation of America's separate destiny led to a prolonged withdrawal from European political affairs, until the twentieth-century world wars and the development of modern technology and commerce finally convinced America's leaders that their interests were in fact linked to Europe (especially after 1945). It was the French revolutionary upheavals, though, that helped to define an early American diplomacy and national identity in opposition to European politics and culture. This new national identity affirmed America's difference from the Old World and supported the enduring belief in American exceptionalism.

[32]Kaufman, ed., *Washington's Farewell Address*, 26–27.  [33]Ibid., 27–28.

## NATIONALISM AND THE DEFINITION OF PATRIOTISM

American nationalism evolved rapidly in the 1790s as Americans (like many early European nationalists) responded to the challenge of the revolutionary French Republic. The new nationalism appeared in both the politics and culture of American society, but it was especially prominent in the desire to differentiate the (good) American Revolution from the (bad) French Revolution, in the reaction to the famous XYZ affair, and in the passage of the Alien and Sedition Laws. All of these developments served to reinforce Washington's farewell advice on the dangers of European connections, and they all expressed the growing hostility to France. The Revolution in France provoked people to define the meaning of patriotism in America.

The widespread tendency to compare the American and French Revolutions contributed to national pride among France's supporters as well as France's critics. Democratic-Republican Societies, for example, frequently passed resolutions hailing the French Revolution as a flattering Old World acknowledgment of America's own political achievement. "The real importance of [American principles] . . . to the world was never justly appreciated," noted the Massachusetts Constitutional Society (1795), "until the French National Convention had erected an European Republic, in the same philosophical tenet."[34] Many Republicans simply assumed that France had taken the torch of liberty from American hands and that American light was now spreading into European darkness. But the theme of revolutionary continuity soon gave way to a more influential emphasis on revolutionary discontinuity, which has remained the prevailing American interpretation of the two revolutions over the last two centuries.

Although the insistence on revolutionary differences showed up repeatedly in the Federalist writings of the 1790s and also (by 1800) in the comments of many Jeffersonians, the statements of the young John Quincy Adams can be taken to summarize the perspective that would long enable Americans to praise their own Revolution while they condemned revolutions in other places. Writing the preface for his English translation of Friedrich von Gentz's *The Origin and Principles of the American Revo-*

---

[34]"Address from the Massachusetts Constitutional Society," 5 January 1795, in Foner, ed., *Democratic-Republican Sourcebook*, 261. The argument for links between the American and French Revolutions has received the fullest modern, scholarly statement in Palmer, *Age of the Democratic Revolution*.

*lution, Compared with the Origin and Principles of the French Revolution* (1800), Adams stressed that Gentz "rescues" America's Revolution "from the disgraceful imputation of having proceeded from the same principles as that of France." In fact, Adams argued, the revolutions embodied an "essential difference" that made the two events altogether opposed "in their *rise,* their *progress,* and their termination." And what was the difference? "A modern philosopher may contend that the sheriff, who executes a criminal, and the highwayman, who murders a traveller, act upon the same principles; the plain sense of mankind will still see the same difference between them, that is here proved between the American and French Revolutions. The difference between *right* and *wrong.*"[35] Despite what the theorists might say (i.e., French *philosophers* or Thomas Jefferson), America and France waged their revolutions in absolutely contrary directions: right versus wrong. This distinction became a central theme in America's emerging national identity, partly because it helped to deradicalize the new nation's own revolutionary tradition.

The same emphasis on America's difference from France's revolutionary government appeared in the angry response to the so-called *XYZ* affair. This famous diplomatic insult (1797–98) mobilized strong nationalist feelings in America because it seemed to show that the Old World power lacked respect for the New World nation. France and the United States drifted into a quasi-war after the Jay Treaty (1794) between America and England gave some commercial advantages to the English. The French retaliated by seizing American ships, and many Federalists began to anticipate a full-scale war with France. Hoping to defuse this widening conflict, President Adams sent special envoys to Paris (1797) for the purpose of negotiating compensation for the seized ships and a peaceful settlement of various diplomatic problems. The mission became a humiliating failure, however, when agents of the French foreign ministry brusquely told the Americans that their own government should compensate American merchants for the confiscated ships, that the United States must grant a sizable loan to the French government, and that the envoys

[35] John Quincy Adams, "Preface," in Friedrich von Gentz, *The Origin and Principles of the American Revolution, Compared with the Origin and Principles of the French Revolution,* trans. J. Q. Adams (Philadelphia, 1800; Delmar, N.Y., 1977), 3–4. Adams's emphasis on the differences between the revolutions continues to appear in modern scholarship. Patrice Higonnet, for example, argues in a recent book that "the two revolutions . . . developed as mirror opposites: the centrality of individualism that triumphed in the one [America] was badly shaken in the other [France]." See Higonnet, *Sister Republics: The Origins of French and American Republicanism* (Cambridge, Mass., 1988), 4.

would need to pay a large fee (bribe) to enter into more direct negotiations with the French foreign minister, Talleyrand.[36] These demands added up to a major assault on the American diplomats' national pride,
particularly since the request for money seemed to express the pervasive
corruption and arrogance of Old World societies. "We experience a
haughtiness," Charles Pinckney wrote from Paris, "which is unexampled
in the history and practice of nations."[37]

Most Americans shared Pinckney's anger when the U.S. government
published the envoys' report on the French demands (the French agents
were identified simply as *X, Y, Z*). Congressional leaders and newspaper
editors rallied patriotically to support belligerent new policies that included the creation of a Navy department, construction of new warships,
and expansion of the army. Jefferson complained privately to Madison that
the *XYZ* papers did "not offer one motive . . . for our going to war,"[38] but
the anti-French party dominated the public debate with the most famous
slogan of the day: "Millions for defense, but not one cent for tribute."[39] At
the same time, John Adams defended America's honor and national status
in defiant statements that carried the pride and sensitivity of a new nation.
"I will never send another minister to France," the President announced,
"without assurances that he will be received, respected, and honored, as
the representative of a great, free, powerful, and independent nation."[40] In
short, the new nation had been given French provocations for its first
military buildup, new reasons for affirming its national independence, and
further evidence of its own virtues in a world of corrupt governments. But
the corruption and radicalism might well come from Europe to America,
which meant that preparations for war abroad must be accompanied by
vigilance at home. The patriotic fervor of 1798 thus fueled an aggressive
campaign on behalf of native Americanism.

[36]Alexander DeConde, *The Quasi-War: The Politics and Diplomacy of the Undeclared War
with France, 1797–1802* (New York, 1966), 8–73; William Stinchcombe, *The XYZ
Affair* (Westport, Conn., 1980), 55–57.
[37]Charles Pinckney to William V. Murray, 30 October 1797, cited in Stinchcombe, *XYZ
Affair*, 58.
[38]Jefferson to Madison, 6 April 1798, in Ford, ed., *Writings of Jefferson*, 7:236.
[39]The phrase became a Federalist banquet toast and newspaper slogan; see DeConde,
*Quasi-War*, 93. The *XYZ* affair further weakened the Democratic-Republican Societies
that had already lost much of their prominence and influence after the Federalist campaign against them in 1794–96. Meanwhile, many Jeffersonians in the South had become
less enthusiastic about foreign revolutions because of the great slave revolt in Saint Do-
mingue.
[40]Adams issued this statement as he welcomed the American envoy John Marshall back to
the United States, 21 June 1798; cited ibid., 95.

During the late spring and summer of 1798, a Federalist majority in the U.S. Congress passed laws to restrict the naturalization of new citizens (extending residence requirements from five to fourteen years), to deport dangerous and potentially dangerous aliens, and to punish "seditious" statements or publications. This controversial legislation (the Alien and Sedition Laws) represented a concerted legislative attempt to define what it meant to be an American, and the definition tended to exclude precisely those people who showed the greatest inclination to support "French" ideas or Jeffersonian republicanism. Federalist leaders promoted these laws as the surest defense against foreign (French) influence in America,[41] thereby establishing a xenophobic strand in American political culture that would reappear in the various nativist movements of the nineteenth century and in the "Red Scares" of the twentieth century. Although no aliens were actually deported by President Adams, some French émigrés chose to leave the United States rather than to see how the laws might be implemented. The most direct punitive impact of the Federalist legislation, however, came in the arrests of Republican journalists under the provisions of the Sedition Law. Seventeen persons in America were prosecuted for violating a law that made it illegal to "write, print, utter or publish . . . any false, scandalous and malicious writing or writings against the government of the United States, or . . . to excite against [Congress or the President] . . . the hatred of the good people of the United States, or to stir up sedition within the United States."[42] All of the prosecutions (which produced eleven convictions) were directed against Republicans who had criticized Federalist policies or expressed "Jacobin" sentiments. The Sedition Law thus restricted the opposition press (or the new public sphere) and challenged the legitimacy of opposition parties by suggesting that both of these political developments were foreign-inspired, un-American activities.

The war fever and nativist hysteria of 1798–1800 gradually dissipated, partly because President Adams sent other envoys who managed to negotiate a settlement with France and partly because the Alien and Sedition Laws expired as Jefferson became President in 1801. Yet the conflicts of that revolutionary decade left permanent marks on America's

[41]Smith, *Freedom's Fetters*, 52, 94, 118; see also John C. Miller, *Crisis in Freedom: The Alien and Sedition Act* (Boston, 1951), 13–14, 34–35, 41–42.
[42]Smith, *Freedom's Fetters*, 187, 441–42. The full texts of the Alien and Sedition Laws are published as an appendix in Smith's book, 435–42; see also the comprehensive account of the various court prosecutions, ibid., 159–417.

national identity. The French Revolution eventually convinced almost all Americans (including Jeffersonians) that the United States was fundamentally different from Europe and that the typical European could not really be a good American. Patriotism in America was henceforth defined in opposition to foreign influence. "Who does not remember," wrote one Federalist in 1799, ". . . when Foreign Influence, like the golden calf, seduced multitudes from the worship of true liberty[?]"[43] The lesson of the decade for many conservatives pointed to the dangers of foreign ideas and foreign-born people, both of which were blamed for the expansion of Jeffersonian republicanism.

This scapegoating of foreign influences, however, did not impress French observers, who understood that Jeffersonian Americans were no less *American* than their Federalist opponents. The French ambassador in Philadelphia, Pierre Adet, in fact used Thomas Jefferson to describe the striking emergence of America's national identity in the mid-1790s. Writing about American politics in a report for the French government (31 December 1796), Adet stressed that Jefferson "is American and, for this reason, he cannot sincerely be our friend. An American is the born enemy of all European nations [*peuples européens*]."[44] Adet's stark analysis succinctly conveyed the central theme of America's new patriotism in the era of the French Revolution; his claim that no American could be a true friend of Europe simply reversed the emerging American claim that no European (with a few exceptions) could be a good American. Each side recognized that a new nation had established itself in America and that the Atlantic Ocean now divided cultural identities as well as continents.

## RELIGION AND THE REJECTION OF THE ENLIGHTENMENT

The French Revolution's impact on American society went beyond the emerging spheres of politics, diplomacy, and patriotic identity into the broader developments of religious and intellectual life that shaped a distinctive American culture. The influence of France's revolutionary events is less obvious in vast processes of cultural formation, and it is more difficult to isolate specific cultural events (equivalent to elections, treaty negotiations, laws) in which the "French" question plays an explic-

---

[43]Robert Treat Paine, Speech in Boston, 1799, cited in Hazen, *American Opinion of the French Revolution*, 298.

[44]P. A. Adet to the [French] Minister of Foreign Relations, 11 Nivôse, Year 5 [31 December 1796], in Turner, ed., "Correspondence of the French Ministers," 983.

it defining role. It nevertheless seems clear that the French Revolution was used in America to discredit the Enlightenment philosophical tradition and to justify a popular denunciation of European intellectual life. America's most significant cultural movement at the end of the 1790s was a great religious revival that transformed the following decade into the era of a Second Great Awakening. To be sure, this evangelical religion did not focus primarily on the rejection of European philosophes, and there were important differences between the New England clergy and frontier revivalists; but I want to emphasize an anti-European theme that ran through much of the movement and expressed negative reactions to the French Revolution.

The American clergy resembled other Americans in welcoming the early stages of France's Revolution. Indeed, many millennial sermons and publications in the early 1790s portrayed the French events as signs of a new era in world history—the long-awaited millennium of equal rights, liberty, and universal (Christian) republicanism. Although the "faith" of France's revolutionary leaders may have seemed obscure or alien to most American Protestants, the French attacks on despotism and the Roman Catholic Church offered assuring similarities to America's own political and religious traditions.[45]

After 1795, however, the clergy's support for the Revolution gave way to mounting criticism of the antireligious ideas and actions of the revolutionary regimes, and the millennial interpretations of many Protestant clergy suggested that France's Revolution had become the contemporary work of the devil or Antichrist. As most historians explain it, this shifting perspective resulted from the clergy's fear of an expanding deist movement in America which received much attention in the polemical arguments over Thomas Paine's *Age of Reason* (twenty-one printings of this work were published in the United States during the 1790s).[46] The political danger of Paine's book for many Americans arose from the implication that modern republicanism should be linked with religious radicalism or deism, whereas popular American republicanism had mostly

---

[45]Ruth H. Bloch, *Visionary Republic: Millennial Themes in American Thought, 1756–1800* (Cambridge, 1985), 150–63, 168–79; see also Michael Lienesch, "The Role of Political Millennialism in Early American Nationalism," *The Western Political Quarterly,* 36 (1983): 445–52.

[46]Bloch, *Visionary Republic,* 194–212; Lienesch, "Political Millennialism," 452–57; see also Henry F. May, *The Enlightenment in America* (New York, 1976), 173–76, 226; Donald H. Meyer, *The Democratic Enlightenment* (New York, 1976), 173–75; and Gary B. Nash, "The American Clergy and the French Revolution," *William and Mary Quarterly,* 3d ser., 20 (1965): 399–404.

developed through close connections with various forms of devout Protestantism. Paine's argument won some vocal adherents, but the clergy launched a powerful counterattack (especially in New England) which gradually extended the rejection of deism into a more general condemnation of the French Revolution. Drawing a gloomy, frightening portrait of deistic or atheistic French republicanism and its many sins, American religious writers emphasized that American republicanism rested on Protestant religious traditions and that the nation's future depended on evangelical Christianity.[47]

The most prominent spokesmen for this antideist campaign were Timothy Dwight and Jedidiah Morse, both of whom believed that America was besieged by a worldwide revolutionary, atheistic movement called the Bavarian Illuminati. Their information on this allegedly powerful conspiracy came mainly from Scotland in a book by John Robison (*Proofs of a Conspiracy against All the Governments and Religions of Europe* [1797]), but they found much local evidence of its influence among those Americans who continued to support "French" ideas or oppose Federalist policies.

Dwight was a Congregational minister and educator in Connecticut, where he became well known as the president of Yale College and the unyielding critic of "infidel" theorists. His sermons and published commentaries on contemporary history contained vehement warnings about the dangers of an Enlightenment philosophy that corrupted young people and led directly, in his view, to the disorder and violence of revolutions. Indeed, Dwight informed his readers (1798) that the French Revolution represented the culmination of an anti-Christian conspiracy that began with intellectuals such as Voltaire, d'Alembert, and Diderot and gained its vast power through the secret machinations of the Illuminati—that mysterious European organization whose ideas had eventually reached America. "About the year 1728," Dwight explained, "Voltaire . . . formed a systematical design to destroy Christianity, and to introduce in its stead a general diffusion of irreligion and atheism." This plan had achieved so much success by 1798 that Dwight worried about American sons who would become "the disciples of Voltaire" and American daughters who would become the "concubines of the Illuminati," unless the American nation severed all connections with French culture. "You are bound by

---

[47]Bloch, *Visionary Republic*, 213–16; May, *Enlightenment in America*, 263–77; Meyer, *Democratic Enlightenment*, 180–81.

the voice of reason, of duty, of safety, and of God," he wrote, "to shun all such connection with them, as will interweave your sentiments or your friendship, your religion or your policy, with theirs. You cannot otherwise fail of partaking in their guilt, and receiving of their plagues."[48] Although Dwight's account of French history lacked precision and evidence, his main point must have been clear enough for even the most uncomprehending Yale student: avoid French infidels like the plague.

Jedidiah Morse made the same point in equally well-publicized commentaries on the dangers of French influence in American society. He resembled Dwight in that he was also a Congregational minister (based in Massachusetts), a widely read author (his publications included the era's best-known books on American geography), and a strong believer in the existence of a vast atheistic conspiracy. Morse found evidence of Jacobin and Illuminati agents in America's Democratic Societies, and he stressed that the nation's "most precious and political interests" were "immediately endangered by *the hostile designs, the insidious arts and demoralizing principles of* . . . the FRENCH NATION." This danger appeared most conspicuously for Morse in the philosophical ideas that secret French agents were spreading throughout America. "If ever the time shall come when the *new philosophy* shall obtain ascendancy over public opinion," he wrote, "'America must drink the cup of Babylon.'" Faced with this danger from alien, subversive ideas, Morse urged Americans to monitor the actions of every French emissary and "to reject, as we would the most deadly poison, their atheistical and destructive principles in whatever way or shape they may be insinuated among us."[49]

Morse's warning about the "deadly poison" from Europe became part of a near-hysterical religious crusade to isolate and protect Americans from the secular philosophies that were inevitably traced to the writings and theories of European philosophers. "These principles are not only alienating our people from their government," wrote one of Morse's

---

[48]Timothy Dwight, *The Duty of Americans, At the Present Crisis, Illustrated in a Discourse, Preached on the Fourth of July, 1798* (New Haven, 1798), 10, 21, 23. For more comprehensive accounts of Dwight's views, see Kenneth Silverman, *Timothy Dwight* (New York, 1969), and Stephen E. Berk, *Calvinism Versus Democracy: Timothy Dwight and the Origins of American Evangelical Orthodoxy* (Hamden, Conn., 1974).

[49]Jedidiah Morse, *A Sermon Exhibiting the Present Dangers, and Consequent Duties of the Citizens of the United States of America, Delivered at Charlestown, April 25, 1799* (Charlestown, Mass., 1799), 12, 31–32; see also Jedidiah Morse, *An Address to the Students of Phillips Academy, Delivered July 9, 1799* (Charlestown, Mass., 1799), 12–13. For a detailed account of Morse's ideas, see Joseph W. Phillips, *Jedidiah Morse and New England Congregationalism* (New Brunswick, N.J., 1983).

allies, "but are secretly stealing into our houses and our seminaries. . . . Such is the tendency of the boasted principles of the age of reform and French philosophy; infinitely more terrible and more to be guarded against than all the power of their arms."[50] This kind of American attack on atheism, deism, and the Enlightenment began long before the French Revolution, but the anger and anxiety in such denunciations during the late 1790s suggest that the violence in Europe pushed many Americans to declare their cultural independence from Old World theories, much as Washington's Farewell Address declared the nation's political and diplomatic independence from Old World governments.

Although the clergy's condemnation of French atheism focused especially on the threat to Protestant Christianity, many Americans expanded the criticism of French philosophy from the sphere of religion to a more general warning about the dangers of all forms of speculative theorizing. The pamphlets and speeches of the 1790s already carried themes that would later become known as "American pragmatism," and they repeatedly drew distinctions between American common sense and European abstractions. Complaining about the "dark abyss of visionary speculation," Israel Woodward delivered a typical Independence Day oration (1798) in which he noted that *theories* are visionary,—we must appeal to *experiment*."[51] The reiterated theme here and in countless other orations stressed that America had built its government and society on the practical recognition of human nature rather than on ideas that could never be realized in practice. European thinkers knew how to destroy traditions, and yet they offered no realistic alternatives to what they destroyed. As Timothy Dwight explained the problem of infidel philosophy in his lectures at Yale, "its great object is to unsettle every thing moral and obligatory, and to settle nothing."[52]

This emphasis on the totalizing danger of the opposition (it disrupts "every thing") emerged as one of the most notable features in the writings of Dwight and others who used Manichaean perspectives to argue that

[50]Simeon Doggett, *An Oration, Delivered at Taunton, on the 4th of July, 1799* (New Bedford, Mass., 1799), 19; similar condemnations of French philosophy appear in Thomas Grant, *A Sermon Delivered at Flemington, on the 4th of July, 1799* (Trenton, N.J., 1799), 10; and in Elijah Parish, *An Oration Delivered at Byefield, July 4, 1799* (Newburyport, Mass., [1799]), 8–9.

[51]Israel Beard Woodward, *American Liberty and Independence, A Discourse Delivered at Watertown on the Fourth of July, 1798* (Litchfield, Conn., [1798]), 15.

[52]Timothy Dwight, *The Nature and Danger of Infidel Philosophy, Exhibited in Two Discourses, Addressed to the Candidates for the Baccalaureate, in Yale College* (New Haven, 1798), 50.

Americans must take nothing from secular philosophers, lest they risk a complete infection from the poison. Zechariah Lewis warned his audience at one of those sober Independence Day celebrations (1799) that the danger from abroad affected every aspect of civilized life. "In Europe, a vain and delusive philosophy, fraught with doctrines equally malignant in their effects on morals, government, and religion, has been laboriously taught and greedily imbibed," he explained in New Haven. "New opinions, dangerous to *every* interest, but flattering and fostering *every* passion and appetite of man, have been triumphantly advanced. *Every* former opinion, *every* standard of belief and of conduct, has been questioned, ridiculed, and trodden under foot." Lewis went on to list other threats that came with the "demoralizing principles" of the new philosophy and to emphasize the special responsibility of teachers to protect their students from an Illuminati philosophy that had already carried its deadly "infection" into the United States; there could be no compromise with ideas that threatened to "revolutionize *every* Christian country."[53]

American critics of the French Revolution thus joined their European counterparts in blaming many of its flaws on the baneful influence of the great philosophes, but the European critics would always face a more complex problem in trying to separate themselves from European intellectual and cultural movements that had produced the Old World's most famous modern writers. American critics, however, could advise their compatriots simply to avoid the European books and ideas that had apparently generated the evils of revolutionary violence—and the advice about theoretical ideas often expressed distrust of the persons (intellectuals) who produced them. The South Carolina Congressman Robert Harper, for example, summarized the argument against philosophes for his American colleagues in 1798. "Philosophers are the pioneers of revolution," he explained. "They advance always in front, and prepare the way by preaching infidelity, and weakening the respect of the people for ancient institutions. . . . They have always . . . eloquence enough, but very little sense. . . . They talk of the perfectibility of man, of the dignity of his nature; and entirely forgetting what he is, declaim, perpetually about what he should be."[54] Harper's description of philosophers therefore summarized at least three central themes that would carry the cri-

[53]Zechariah Lewis, *An Oration on the Apparent and the Real Political Situation of the United States . . . July the 4th, 1799* (New Haven, 1799), 16. Emphasis added.
[54]Robert G. Harper, *Observations on the Dispute Between the United States and France,* 4th ed. (Boston, 1798), 123. Harper gave his speech in Congress on 2 March 1798.

tique of the Enlightenment and the French Revolution into the wider development of American culture. His rejection of the philosophers' hope for human "perfectibility" reappeared constantly in the evangelical religious emphasis on human sin; his complaint about the philosophers' disrespect for "ancient institutions" reappeared constantly in the antiintellectual emphasis on the dangers or irrelevance of European theorizing; and his comment on the philosophers' lack of good "sense" reappeared constantly in the antiintellectual ridicule of subsequent political campaigns.

All of these criticisms of European philosophy and philosophers came together in the bitter attacks on Thomas Jefferson in the various political conflicts of the era. Jefferson remained the domestic symbol of French culture and politics for many Americans at the end of the eighteenth century, and the Federalist criticisms of his character, his ideas, and his policies commonly portrayed him as a Trojan Horse for the international "French" conspiracy. "It cannot be doubted," explained an editor who published Robert Harper's congressional speech on the dangers of France and philosophers, "that Mr. JEFFERSON returned to America from his European embassy, the agent of France, or something very much like it. . . . He is the head of the *philosophers* Mr. HARPER describes."[55] It is of course significant that Jefferson was elected to the Presidency, but his success did not owe much to his reputed status as a "French" theorist. In fact, judging from the Federalist literature of the day, Jefferson's French connection became his greatest political weakness and a target of opportunity in every political campaign. "It was in France," reported the Federalist pamphleteer Henry William Desaussure (1800), "where he resided nearly seven years, and until the revolution had made some progress, that his disposition to theory, and his skepticism in religion, morals, and government, acquired full strength and vigor. . . . Mr. Jefferson is known to be a theorist in politics, as well as in philosophy and morals. He is a *philosophe* in the modern French sense of the word."[56] Note the linkage of key concepts in Desaussure's argument (France, revolution, religious skepticism, theorizing philosophe), any one of which presumably made Jefferson unfit to be President.

Another Federalist writer, Joseph Dennie, stressed the French-theory-

[55] Ibid., editor's preface, p. 4.
[56] [William Henry Desaussure], *Address to the Citizens of South Carolina on the Approaching Election of President and Vice-President of the United States* (Charleston, S.C., 1800), 10, 15.

philosophe danger even more vividly in an essay on the philosophical origins of Jefferson's ideas (1798). "His abstract, inapplicable, meta-physico politics are either nugatory or noxious," Dennie complained. "Besides, his principles relish so strongly of Paris and are seasoned with such a profusion of *French* garlic, that he offends the whole Senate house. Better for Americans that on their extended plains 'thistles should grow, instead of wheat,' . . . than that a *philosopher* should influence the councils of the country, and that his admiration for the works of Voltaire and Helvetius should induce him to wish a closer connexion with Frenchmen."[57] Although Jefferson overcame such attacks to win two terms as President, it might well be argued that Dennie's critique of "philosophers" in government became the more permanent influence in American political culture.

In any case, the Federalist attacks on Jefferson entered a strong cultural current in America that would help sustain popular religion and a lingering hostility for European theorists throughout the nineteenth and twentieth centuries.[58] These broad, complex cultural tendencies in America after the 1790s can never be explained simply as a consequence of the French Revolution, yet they clearly gained much of their early strength in the American rejection of France's revolutionary policies and ideas. The French Revolution therefore contributed (at least as a negative referent) to the cultural development of a distinctive American inclination to build political campaigns upon the sanctity of religion, the distrust of intellectuals, the fear of alien ideas, and the danger of radical change.

## CONCLUSION: THE FRENCH REVOLUTION IN AMERICA

The French Revolution profoundly affected the early politics and culture of American society in two opposing directions: it helped to open American politics to wider political participation and debate, but it helped to close American culture to the influence and ideas of the wider world. No event played a clearer, defining role than the French Revolution in stimulating the development of a two-party political system and in helping to

---

[57] Joseph Dennie, "Miscellany," in *The Farmer's Weekly Museum* [Walpole, N.H.], 17 July 1798. Dennie's emphasis. The essay appears (with slight, later revisions) under the title "On Modern Philosophers" in a collection of Dennie's writings. See Joseph Dennie, *The Lay Preacher*, ed. Milton Ellis (New York, 1943), 171–74.

[58] The many dimensions of America's "post-Enlightenment" culture still call for comprehensive analysis, but see the brief discussion of this issue in Henry F. May, *The Divided Heart: Essays on Protestantism and the Enlightenment in America* (New York, 1991), 179–96.

expand an active, contestatory political culture of lively publications, street demonstrations, and local organizations. The cumulative force of these processes enlarged the "public sphere," discredited the Federalist conception of elite republican politics, and established the broader, democratic republicanism of the Jeffersonians as the reigning American political ideology. Indeed, the Federalists soon disappeared as a coherent political party.

Yet the Federalist hostility to the French Revolution entered widely into American culture, offering strong encouragement for Americans to close themselves to European influences. This powerful desire to separate from the Old World appeared in America's diplomatic withdrawal from European wars and in its affirmation of a new national identity. The overlapping theme in all of these developments emerged in the emphasis on America's *difference* from Europe. Instead of lamenting their distance from Old World centers of power and culture, Americans celebrated that separation as the surest protection of their virtue, their political achievements, and their cultural identity.

The French Revolution thus played an exceptionally large part in shaping early political and cultural tendencies that have remained at the center of American history since the 1790s: the recurring attempt to democratize and expand American politics (later to include black people, ethnic minorities, and women), and the perennial inclination to avoid or devalue or ignore the complexities of other cultures (later to include Asia, Africa, Latin America, and the Middle East). Patterns that developed or deepened in response to France's revolutionary events at the end of the eighteenth century have therefore continued to influence American political and cultural life to the present day and to shape the way Americans understand their place in the world.

# 3

## The French Revolution in relation to Poland and East-Central Europe

### JERZY W. BOREJSZA

By 1989, two hundred years after the French Fourteenth of July, the word "revolution" had become unpopular in Poland owing to its association with the Communist government. It is important to remember, however, that the word "revolution," signifying political upheaval meant to overthrow foreign rule and to regain national independence, had positive connotations within Poland for more than 150 years. For many Poles, the French Revolution served as a model for political action and as a source of antimonarchist ideas, particularly after the division of Poland among the three reactionary monarchies of the Holy Alliance. In addition, it set forth new methods for mobilizing the masses and carrying out armed warfare.

It is important to note that although this view was widespread, it was by no means universal. There were those who considered the French Revolution the embodiment of terrorism and antiliberal, antiintellectual attitudes. A conservative strain, present in Polish literature from the time of the eminent poet Zygmunt Krasiński (1812–59), saw the Revolution in a way similar to that in which Simon Schama describes it today in his *Citizens*. Revolution, according to Krasiński, is destructive, ruinous, and incapable of generating any positive cultural value. Even two hundred years after the Revolution of 1789, this vision is still present, at least subconsciously, in the Polish mind.

Nowadays, observers in Poland stress the Revolution's utopian slogans demanding absolute egalitarianism, dictatorship—even total dictatorship—and totalitarianism. As a result, the Revolution is no longer considered an event capable of ennobling and motivating the Polish masses. Yet it was just that for many Polish people between 1789 and 1919, when the

Revolution was a pivotal element in Polish political thought. In the years since the Bolsheviks seized power, insufficient attention has been paid to the fact that the Revolution of 1917 was very different from that of 1789. For example, it is seldom pointed out that the Bolshevik Revolution was antipatriotic, in contrast with the national and patriotic character of the revolution of the French. The Revolution of 1789 has lost its original meaning because it is now viewed from the perspective of the experiences of 1917 and the post-1944 period in Poland. As a result, perceptions of the French Revolution today have little to do with the actual events of two hundred years ago.

Yet when the word "revolution" made its original appearance in the Polish language, it had positive connotations precisely due to the events that took place in France in 1789. The French Enlightenment and the Revolution of 1789 introduced the term "revolution" into the vocabulary of both Polish journalism and Polish dictionaries. The famous lexicographer Samuel Bogumił Linde included the word in his *Dictionary of the Polish Language* published at the time of Napoleon I. (Curiously enough, this same Mr. Linde, not long before he referred to "revolution" in his dictionary, was carrying logs to the gallows to help hang traitors to the homeland during Tadeusz Kościuszko's Rising in 1794.)

After two hundred years, the French Revolution can be viewed in various ways. It determined the shape of the entire nineteenth century as we know it, that is, the period from 1789 until 1914. "Le grand 1789" gave rise to a whole new era not only in France but also in many other European countries. For example, in central and eastern Europe the ideas of 1789 were taken up as a whole some fifty years later during the "Springtime of the Nations." Poland, however, lost its independence just as the era of the French Revolution and of Napoleon came to a close in 1815. From the end of the eighteenth century until recent times—with only very minor intervals such as the period of the "Second Republic" (1918–39)—the struggle for independence has been Poland's chief objective. The French Revolution influenced this struggle in three ways: It became an example of political and military struggle, it offered a pattern for social revolution, and it provided an ideological model. Thus, the ideas and methods of France's political struggles have been more important in Polish thought than the Revolution's social program. Revolutionary France became a model for the Poles in fighting against a coalition of stronger enemies while relying exclusively on their own forces. This model was of great importance throughout the nineteenth century, whenever the Poles found themselves faced with the need to fight for independence against more powerful occupiers. Ironically, the fall of Poland was inseparably linked to the events of the French Revolution. As Georges Lefebvre tersely expressed it, "at the price of her independence, Poland helped save the Revolution." It is worth examining the events of these years in some detail to explain this paradox.

The onset of the French Revolution coincided with the attempts at reform that had been undertaken in Poland in 1788 by the so-called Four Years' Sejm (1788–92). This was the first Diet in the time of King Stanisław August Poniatowski, which was convened without the presence of Russian troops. It passed a bill enlarging the Polish army to one hundred thousand soldiers and it extended the franchise. An attempt was also made to eliminate control of Poland by Empress Catherine of Russia, as republican tendencies aimed at the recognition of the king as the symbolic head of the Res Publica appeared among the delegates. Most important, in 1791, the Four Years' Sejm passed the Constitution of the Third of May, the first written constitution in Europe and a document clearly influenced by Montesquieu and Rousseau. Although it still sanctioned the class system, the constitution nevertheless introduced profound changes. It restricted the power of great magnates for the benefit of the middle strata of the nobility. Voting rights were changed; the previous requirement of noble birth was replaced with that of having a certain financial status. The middle class was offered the opportunity to increase its social status. The division of state power began, and the constitution formulated a law guaranteeing parliamentary liability of ministers. A reform of the juridical system was also inaugurated.

In their work of 1793, *On the Institution and Fall of the Polish Constitution of the 3rd of May*, Hugo Kołłataj and his associates stressed that the constitution was meant to ensure "fraternity for the towns-people" and "justice for the countryfolk." Although it did not speak of equality, this first constitution, which was referred to in the preamble of the constitution passed on 17 March 1921, after Poland had regained independence in the First World War, put forth the slogans of liberty, fraternity, and justice. Thus, it is clear that the Constitution of the Third of May was an outgrowth of the revolutionary spirit of 1789.

Meanwhile, the Revolution in France underwent a bloody transformation—from the Girondins, to the terror of the Jacobin dictatorship, and finally, to the post-Thermidorian period—a sequence of events that had a profound effect on Franco-Polish relations. In 1791–92, the French envoy in Warsaw, Marie-Louis Descorches de Saint-Croix, was an outstanding spokesman for rapprochement between France and Poland. Unfortunately, the government in Paris did not respond to his suggestions. As the eminent Polish historian, Jerzy Łojek maintained: "A possible Polish-French alliance would have been of no real importance at that time. Poland and France would not have been able to come to each other's assistance, either in a diplomatic, or military way."[1] In any case, Stanisław August feared even the appearance of cooperation, because he was convinced it could provoke Catherine and, more significantly, could activate radical middle class circles in Poland.

In the autumn of 1792, Ignacy Potocki, Hugo Kołłataj, Józef Weyssenhoff, and Tadeusz Kościuszko formed a committee of Polish political émigrés that sought contacts who could help to promote a Polish-French alliance. The leaders decided to take advantage of the prestige of Tadeusz Kościuszko, who arrived in Paris with an offer to proclaim a revolutionary republic and to wage war simultaneously against all three of Poland's occupying enemies, on the condition that France provide military aid to the Poles. In spite of some Girondin and Jacobin interest, Kościuszko received no definite promises. The only time France actually relieved pressure on Poland was in the summer of 1792 when, as a result of the outbreak of a war between France and Prussia, the attention of the latter turned westward.[2] Prussian involvement on the western front was, however, short-lived; and its army once again increased its troop strength along the Polish border. On 23 January 1793, in Petersburg, Russia and Prussia signed a new treaty of partition that cemented the anti-French coalition.

Although the alliance with revolutionary France failed, its revolutionary example remained. The victories of the French made a great impression both on people in Poland and on Poles living in exile. They were fascinated by how effective the revolutionary methods were in moving the nation to make tremendous efforts, and were captivated by the French vision of a universal "war of the people against tyrants." When Kościuszko returned from France it was decided that, as leader of the uprising, he should seek dictatorial power. Kościuszko counted on the cooperation of a regular army made up of armed citizens from throughout the nation. Although the notion of a national militia had been a long-

---

[1] Jerzy Łojek, *Geneza i obalenie konstytucji 3 maja* (Lublin, 1986), 381.
[2] Ibid.

cherished ideal of Polish political thought,[3] this army was based on the principles of the American "minutemen" and the French *levée en masse*.

On 24 March 1794, Kościuszko promulgated the official Act of the Uprising in Cracow. He later added a separate proclamation concerning the peasantry. Criminal courts were established, which were authorized to impose the death penalty on adversaries of the uprising. In the courts as well as in local committees of law and order, townspeople were granted rights equal to those of the nobility. A peasant charge played a decisive role in the first victorious battle of the uprising, that at Racławice on 4 April. In Vilnius, power was immediately seized by advocates of more radical political and social reforms. This takeover was led by Colonel Jakub Jasiński, while in Warsaw the victorious insurgent movement was headed by a shoemaker, Jan Kiliński. The Warsaw municipal militia numbered almost twenty thousand men, and at the peak of the uprising the Polish army numbered seventy thousand men. The greatest similarity between the events in revolutionary Paris and those in Poland was the sight of public hangings in city squares. Although the guillotine was replaced by gallows, they were surrounded by the same elated, often armed, crowds. As Emanuel Rostworowski wrote:

The Polish "Jacobins" were given this name by their adversaries; in fact, they had no affiliation with the Paris clubs. They were usually groups of young enthusiasts who wanted to link the struggle for independence with the achievement of irreversible social and political changes. . . . Clearly their activities influenced the democratic character of the Uprising and governing institutions. Through their propaganda and literary works—numerous poems and songs—the "Jacobins" maintained a revolutionary atmosphere. They adopted the French slogan "La patrie en danger" and demanded the radical mobilization of all available forces, urging them to take over the possessions of rich individuals and institutions. Their hope was that terrorism would lead the Uprising onto the path of ruthless determination, thus eliminating any possibility of retreat.[4]

Care should be taken, however, not to exaggerate the historical analogies between France and Poland. The Poles adapted French patterns to their situation, they did not blindly imitate them. For example, in the summer of 1794, Tadeusz Kościuszko declared that he had no intention of stirring up a "French Revolution." Clearly, he was concerned with more than the appeasement of his patroness, Princess Izabella Czar-

[3]Emanuel Rostworowski, "Czasy saskie i Oświecenie," in *Zarys historii Polski*, ed. Janusz Tazbir (Warsaw, 1979), 362.
[4]Rostworowski, "Czasy saskie i Oświecenie," 366.

toryska. He was also in real earnest when he elevated the magnate Józef Maksymilian Ossoliński in order to show the Austrians his opposition to Jacobinism and the clubs and to assert that in accordance with his "gros bon sens" he would not deprive the nobility of their rightful leadership in the uprising.

Kościuszko's attitude toward political factions and events changed according to specific developments of the uprising. Following the Warsaw demonstrations and the hanging of alleged traitors on 28 June 1794, Kościuszko condemned all lynching and terrorism and spoke out against the escalation of the insurgent and democratic ideas of the uprising. He also removed Jakub Jasiński from command of the Lithuanian army. Nevertheless, because he feared possible uncontrollable reactions from the masses, he placed control of the criminal military court in the hands of the Jacobins. On 2 July 1794, he wrote to the Supreme National Council recommending, "You should take care not to show preference for the Jacobins, but rather to look out for the welfare of the whole nation."[5]

In some cases, Kościuszko restrained the activities of the Polish Jacobins, while in others, such as when he left Warsaw in the summer of 1794, he vested authority in them. In evaluating this behavior it is important to remember that a Polish Jacobin was not identical to his French counterpart. The same name stood for two different types of people. Using his characteristic gift for synthesis, Rostworowski wrote about the limits of Polish Jacobinism:

The growth of Jacobinism in Poland as well as the propagation of the slogans of left-wing insurgents were both limited in their extension. The climate existing in Warsaw was quite unlike that found in the provinces; in fact, the rich townspeople remained moderately and covertly royalist. In contrast, Warsaw was filled with unruly plebeians, who were flowing into the city and mingling with outcasts and people who had been persecuted by the [former pro-czarist] authorities. The 'Jacobins' were primarily recruited from amidst the nobility. They expressed their revolutionary zeal mostly by carrying out terrorism against traitors and by attacking the king—one of the Confederates of Targowica. They were, however, neither willing nor able to instigate an agrarian revolution directed against the nobility.[6]

The Kościuszko Uprising was put down in November 1794 by the combined forces of the Russian Army assisted by Prussians and Austrians. The Committee of Public Safety made no decision to assist the uprising even though French diplomats and some other French citizens

---

[5] Bogusław Leśnodorski, *Polscy jakobini* (Warsaw, 1960), 186–87.
[6] Rostworowski, "Czasy saskie i Oświecenie," 369.

living in Poland at the time, including Pierre Parandier and Casimir La Roche, sent repeated petitions. The latter regarded Kościuszko as a Polish Lafayette, which was in no way a recommendation to the Jacobins. Any movement that failed to abolish monarchy and was centered primarily in the nobility could not possibly be considered a revolution by Robespierre or Saint-Just. In addition, the character of Poland was alien to the French. Thus, it is difficult to imagine that any substantial assistance would have been forthcoming. Furthermore, secret peace talks between France and Russia were already under way. Many historians have maintained a very critical attitude toward the Kościuszko Uprising, not acknowledging the fact that Poland's dictator had to keep in mind the feudal character of his country.[7] Doubtless, the Girondins encouraged a revolt in Poland; yet neither they nor the Jacobins made any firm commitments of support. Precisely for this reason the mission to Paris of Franciszek Barss—a representative of the uprising—ended in failure.

Girondin and Jacobin policies toward Poland have been frequently criticized by distinguished historians, such as Alphonse Aulard, in France, or Szymon Askenazy, in Poland. One should not, however, ignore the fact that both factions were influenced primarily by *raison d'état*, the current interest of the state of France, and not by prospects of revolution in other European countries, or even a full-scale European revolution. In this sense there is a close analogy between the foreign policy of the French Revolution in 1789–94, and that of the Russian Revolution in the period 1917–22; both were forced to balance ideological visions against calculations of available force.

After the fall of the Kościuszko Uprising, Russia, Prussia, and Austria agreed on a new division of Poland, thereby completing the third and final partition. Nevertheless, there was one last-ditch, symbolic republican and Jacobinic effort, the so-called Franciszek Gorzkowski plot. In 1796–97, with the blessing of the Warsaw organization, Gorzkowski, an alumnus of Paris schools, organized a peasants' plot in Podole in an effort to prepare the masses for an armed struggle to abolish the power of the nobility and introduce a republican regime. The plot was uncovered by the Austrians, and Gorzkowski was imprisoned.[8]

[7]Henryk Kocój, *Wielka Rewolucja Francuska a Polska. Zarys stosunków dyplomatycznych polsko-francuskich w okresie Sejmu Wielkiego i powstania kościuszkowskiego* (Warsaw, 1987).

[8]Monika Senkowska-Gluck, "La conspiration de Gorzkowski, tentative de révolution paysanne en 1797," in *Région, Nation, Europe. Unité et diversité des processus sociaux et culturels de la Révolution française*, ed. Monika Senkowska-Gluck (Paris, 1988), 195–203.

In 1798, an Association of Polish Republicans was established in Poland, one of whose members was Kościuszko. Polish republicanism bore a definite resemblance to its French counterpart, but it also drew on the republican traditions of the noblemen's republic. After Bonaparte's coup d'état, Kościuszko had a falling out with the first consul, rejecting him as emperor. Nevertheless, thousands of Poles followed Bonaparte from the beginning until the bitter end. In contrast to the German-speaking countries, Spain, and some of the Italian states, within eastern Europe the reign of Napoleon I was seen as a continuation of the Revolution of 1789, and he was regarded by many as the principal link to the Revolution. As Goethe put it, Napoleon was "the revolution crowned." Thus eastern and southern Europe swarmed with admirers and followers of the first consul and emperor of the French. While the positive evaluations of the French Revolution and of Napoleon merged into a single impression, it must be stressed that although the Revolution was a real, living event in the consciousness of the elite, Napoleon himself was more a popular hero of the common man. Many Poles considered the period from 1789 (or at least that from Napoleon I) to 1870 (Napoleon III), which coincides with the period from the Legions of Henryk Dąbrowski to the battle of Sedan, a historical continuum. France appeared to be a patron—potential if not actual—of the Polish aspirations for independence. In this sense, Polish tradition differs significantly from that of western Europe. As Robert Mandrou wrote in the *Histoire de la civilisation française,* "The only country in Europe where national sentiment favored French rule was Poland. Divided by its neighbors in the first revolutionary wars, Poland at the time of Prince Józef Poniatowski was imbued through the Duchy of Warsaw with the new ideas, and was faithful to Napoleon until the battle of Leipzig."[9]

In 1797, Polish Legions were organized in Lombardy under the auspices of General Bonaparte. Their commander was General Henryk Dąbrowski, who announced that "France is fighting for the cause of the nations." The legionnaires wore French tricolored ribbons, bearing the colors of Lombardy and the inscription "Free Men are Brothers." In contrast with the revolutionary period when only a few Polish individuals such as Józef Sułkowski and Klaudiusz Franciszek Łazowski were

---

[9]Georges Duby and Robert Mandrou, *Histoire de la civilisation Française,* vol. 2 (Paris, 1984), 173.

involved, the legions were a mass organization. By the autumn of 1797 they numbered approximately eight thousand men. Altogether, some twenty-five thousand Polish soldiers passed through the ranks of the legions. The song composed for the Polish Legions in Italy in 1797 by Józef Wybicki soon became a national song, and later, in the twentieth century, it was raised to the honor of serving as the Polish National Anthem. For two hundred years the words of this song have proclaimed, "Bonaparte gave us the example of how to be victorious," making Poland's anthem, along with Corsica's, the only one that refers to the era of Napoleon.

The legionnaires sought the entry of the Napoleonic army into Poland. "Poles! Napoleon the Great marches with his troops three hundred thousand strong into Poland. Let us not fathom the secret of his plans," proclaimed Józef Wybicki's famous appeal of 3 November 1806. Napoleon always tried to capitalize on the Polish question, yet he avoided any concrete commitments. He never allowed anyone to "fathom the secret of his plans." "La Grande Armée" of Napoleon was welcomed warmly by the lower and middle strata of the nobility, by the patriotic circles of the middle class, and by that part of the peasantry that hoped to be freed from serfdom and labor service.

On 22 July 1807 the emperor signed a constitution for the Duchy of Warsaw, which had been established immediately following the signing of the Peace of Tilsit. Its political system was modeled on that of Napoleonic France. Article 4 of the constitution proclaimed, "Slavery shall be abolished. All citizens are equal before the law." The right to vote was given not only to the nobility, but also to part of the middle class. The townspeople were granted full rights to purchase land and to hold office in the administration. Article 11 abolished serfdom and gave the peasants the right not only to leave the land, but also to sue the landowners. Peasants were not, however, granted the right to own the land they had tilled. Labor service was retained despite the abolition of serfdom. The Duchy of Warsaw was governed by the Code Napoleon. This code guaranteed, among other things, the equality of the nobility and the middle class before the law. The Code Napoleon was in force on Polish territory until 1946. The *Code français de commerce*, which was introduced at the same time, lasted until 1933. Monika Senkowska-Gluck, who has written on Napoleonic institutions in Poland, emphasizes the extraordinary stability of these laws and quotes what Napoleon said to General Gourgaud on the Isle of St. Helena, "True greatness lies only in the enduring institutions men leave behind them."[10]

Military service brought citizens together as equals, a process in which the army of the Duchy of Warsaw played a significant role because it was very popular among the people. From 1806 to 1813, as many as two hundred thousand served in its ranks. In 1812, Poland made the largest contribution of manpower of all of Napoleon's allies, one hundred thousand soldiers. Although the emperor announced the beginning of the "second Polish war" at that time, the Duchy did not outlive the fall of Napoleon. In the battle of Leipzig on 16 October 1813 the newly nominated marshal of France, Prince Józef Poniatowski, died while covering the retreat of the French army.

Nevertheless, the fact that Napoleon addressed the Polish question had far-reaching significance. His interest invalidated the partitions of Poland. The very existence of the Duchy of Warsaw forced Alexander I to establish the Kingdom of Poland. At the same time, the Duchy undermined the feudal system on Polish territory. Napoleon, however, did not intend to create a sovereign Polish state; at most he envisioned Poland as a more significant political body within "Le grand Empire." Thus, although the memory of the achievements of Polish soldiers under Napoleon was for many decades an encouragement to armed struggle, it also discouraged Poles from counting on foreign assistance, particularly from France. Kościuszko advocated warfare relying solely on Polish forces, and the argument over whether to fight on one's own or to seek foreign assistance continued to rage among Polish politicians throughout the nineteenth century.

At the same time, there existed a Napoleonic myth, which held that the imperial liberator of the Poles would also be the liberator of the peasants. Walerian Łukasiński, a famous Polish conspirator who spent forty-six years in Russian prisons, wrote, "We have been told a million times and in various languages that Napoleon kept cheating Poles for his own benefit. Believe it if you will, but the Poles, who are those most directly affected, shall never believe it."[11]

The direct influence of the French upon Polish society, particularly because of the prolonged contact between thousands of French soldiers

---

[10]Monika Senkowska-Gluck, "Les institutions napoléoniennes dans l'histoire de la nation polonaise," in L'époque napoléonienne et les Slaves, ed. Stefan Kozak and Hanna Popowska-Taborska (Wrocław, 1982).
[11]Quoted after Andrzej Zahorski, Napoléon (Warsaw, 1985), 494.

and the Polish people during the Revolution and Napoleon's stay in Poland, has no equal in the history of any other East European country. Among the Poles there was a common impression that the French worker and peasant were free men who knew how to defend their rights. A popular nineteenth-century Polish saying captured this impression: "Francuz kiedy świśnie, wolność nam zabłyśnie" (when the Frenchman wields his sword, freedom will shine for us). The elites, both the Polish Jacobins and the generation that included Adam Mickiewicz, who was born in 1798, came to the conclusion that substantial changes in Poland, national independence, and social revolution were attainable only if linked with a European revolution accompanied by a French-Polish alliance.

Yet the majority of nineteenth-century Polish democrats did not associate revolution with the years 1793–94, that is, with the figures of Marat, Robespierre, and Saint-Just, but rather with the year 1789, that is, with the Declaration of the Rights of Man and Citizen and with the Constitution of 1791. They cherished the memory of Lafayette, Condorcet, and Sieyès, all of whom were supportive of Poland. By contrast, the Jacobins were remembered for their reluctance to get involved. Praise of the French Revolution was very often followed by a condemnation of French Jacobinism. In his work, *Human Kind,* Stanisław Staszic denounced the "extremities of the Revolution," "bloodthirsty Robespierres," and "ferocious Marats." Staszic's attitude is quite similar to that of Romanian politicians such as Mihai Kogălniceanu, who claimed that "quand les revolutions commencent, la civilisation finit."[12] In the twentieth century this position was further developed by the Romanian historian Nicolae Iorga.[13]

The only groups who claimed adherence to the ideas of Robespierre were the utopian socialists in exile in France and the members of the so-called Gromady Ludu Polskiego (The Assemblies of the Polish People) in England. This latter group belonged to that very small minority in Poland who criticized Napoleon. The Assemblies of 1836 wrote in one of their proclamations that "during the Revolution of 1793 Robespierre took the word 'fraternity' from the divine books and inscribed it in the book of human rights; thus he revealed the real essence of Christianity," while

[12]Quoted after Alexandre Zub, "L'impact du 'Grand 1789' dans l'espace roumaine: diffusion, adaptation, diffraction," in *L'image de la révolution française. Communications présentées lors du Congrès Mondial pour le Bicentenaire de la Révolution, Sorbonne, Paris 6–12 juillet 1989,* vol. 2, ed. Michel Vovelle (Pergamon Press, 1989), 872.
[13]See Stefan Lemny, "Nicolae Iorga, historien de la Révolution Française," *L'image de la révolution française,* 1220–28.

Babeuf "restored the true meaning of the words Liberty and Equality when he established common ownership."[14] The Assemblies of the Polish People showed a particular reverence for Philippe Buonarotti and also for James Bronterre O'Brien, a Chartist and English translator of Babeuf. O'Brien believed that the working class should adopt the ideas of the French Revolution and continue the process through the collectivization of land and capital.

The Assemblies of the Polish People, however, represented the views of only a few hundred people living in exile from 1830 to 1850. The Polish Democratic Society, composed of a few thousand members and far more influential in Poland, did not share this positive attitude toward the Jacobins. In its manifesto of 1836, the society referred to the principles of the French Revolution.[15] Many organizers of the Polish national uprisings came from this society. Those who organized, commanded, and participated in the Polish national uprisings of 1830, 1846, 1848, and 1863 are certainly included in Victor Hugo's characterization of nineteenth-century intellectuals as children of the revolution whose mother and father were the years 1789 and 1793.

The declarations of the Polish national uprisings contained many reminders of the French Revolution: the question of ownership; the slogans "liberty," "equality," "fraternity" written on banners and seals; the attitude toward revolutionary terrorism in both 1830 and 1863; and the jargon of Polish conspirators and insurgents. The Poles were particularly interested in the military traditions of the French Revolution, especially guerilla warfare and levée en masse. This interest is reflected in the works of Polish theoreticians of partisan warfare such as Karol Bogumił Stolzman and Henryk Kamieński. Jarosław Dąbrowski not only served as a general of the Paris Commune in 1871 but also became the commander-in-chief there for some time. Interestingly, the French Revolutionary concept of guerilla warfare was revived again in 1939 following the war in Spain. Poland was represented in that war in the person of Julian Brun-Bronowicz, a leading Communist. Under the pseudonym of Jules Leverrier he published a book in Paris entitled *La naissance de l'armée nationale 1789–1794*.

Nevertheless, by the end of the nineteenth century awareness of the

[14]Lidia and Adam Ciołkosz, *Zarys dziejów socjalizmu polskiego* (London, 1966), 1:124.
[15]Alina Barszczewska-Krupa, "Devises de la Révolution Française dans l'idéologie et politique de la grande émigration polonaise," in *L'image de la Révolution Française*, 2:1430–36.

French Revolution of 1789 was on the wane in Poland. Clear evidence of this is the fact that no mention of the Revolution is made in the ten volumes of works of Józef Piłsudski, who was a child of the nineteenth century and a leader of the Socialists. By 1905 both the Polish Socialist Party (PPS) and the Social Democracy of the Kingdom of Poland and Lithuania (SDKPiL) again referred to the experience of the Jacobins' struggle for power; however, these Polish Socialists were discovering the issues of the French Revolution through Russian translations and discussions because, in contrast to Poland, in Russia in the late nineteenth century interest in study of the history of the Revolution of 1789–94 remained widespread, which the publications of the Narodniki and Russian Social Democrats reflect.

As the Revolution of 1789 has receded into history, its influence on the political and social movements that it inspired has become more indirect. Although French revolutionary ideals are still found in the ideology, phraseology, and historiography of the elites, they no longer inspire the masses. Fernand Braudel was correct when he noted that as a revolution recedes into the past, its influence dwindles, its values lose their significance, and its repercussions die away.[16] In contemporary Poland, conscious awareness of the French Revolution is minimal. Although it is mentioned in essays and books, it is not present in the mind of the general public. It is impossible to say of Poland what François Furet says of France—that the Revolution not only explains our modern history, "it is our modern history."[17] Until 1870 the Revolution played a dominant role in Polish events; later, it became just one of the many foreign influences affecting the emergence of contemporary Poland. Finally, after 1918, the French Revolution actually faded into the background of Polish historical thought.

During the first two decades of postwar Polish history, from 1945 to 1965, the Jacobins were glorified perhaps to the point of exaggeration in the writings of the distinguished Polish historian Bogusław Leśnodorski. Following that period, an interesting work appeared by the sociologist Jerzy Szacki entitled *Counter-revolutionary Paradoxes: The Visions of the World in French Adversaries of the Great Revolution, 1789–1815*.[18] He

[16]Fernand Braudel, *Une leçon d'histoire* (Paris, 1986), 164.
[17]François Furet, *Penser de la Révolution Française* (Paris, 1978), 15.
[18]Jerzy Szacki, *Kontrrewolucyjne paradoksy: Wizje swiata francuskich antagonistów Wielkiej Rewolucji, 1789–1815* (Social philosophy of the French counterrevolution, 1789–1815) (Warsaw, 1965), 215.

attempted to present the counter-revolution as an effort to defend certain traditional values within the circumstances of the new order. Although this issue is currently a topic of study in French historiography, the monographs of Marxist historian Jan Baszkiewicz, who criticizes but defends Robespierre, arouse great interest today. Baszkiewicz claims that "Robespierre accurately evaluated the role of the bourgeois cadres within the Revolution, yet he was unable to grasp the historical consequences of the fact that the Revolution was indeed a triumph of the bourgeoisie."[19] He highlights the utopian character of the Jacobin program while showing the skill that the Jacobins demonstrated in the exercise of power. He also develops far-reaching comparisons between the French and the American Revolutions, although many Polish historians see far closer parallels between the Kościuszko Uprising of 1794 and the American Revolution.[20]

The fact that the French Revolution is still present in the minds of the elite is due principally to romantic literature, specifically to the works of Mickiewicz, Słowacki, and Krasiński, which are a canon in the education of a Polish intellectual. This literature addresses the key questions of the nineteenth century: republicanism, regicide, the identities of the people, of society, and of the nation, the rights of the majority in relation to minorities, and the masses' right of rebellion.[21]

In recent times, the theme of the Revolution has been used as a camouflage for writing the truth about contemporary Poland when censorship prohibited the direct portrayal of this truth. Such an approach is found in the dramatic productions of Andrzej Wajda, who twice presented to the Polish public Stanisława Przybyszewska's old drama about Danton. In the first production, he was still searching for the meaning of the Revolution and of Jacobin actions. Later, after martial law had been declared in Poland, Wajda produced a film in French based on the same play. In the film he depicted the Revolution in an atmosphere of gloom, focusing upon its senselessness. Here we see a significant change indicating how current Polish and European events influence an artist's vision of the past.

In 1969 an outstanding Polish historical writer, Paweł Jasienica, published *Reflections on a Civil War in the Vendée*, in which he openly and directly referred to the civil war that went on in Poland after 1944. Jasienica wrote:

---

[19]Jan Baszkiewicz, *Robespierre* (Warsaw, 1976), 291.
[20]Konstanty Grzybowski, *Refleksje sceptyczne* (Warsaw, 1972), 1:315.
[21]Cf., Maria Janion, Maria Zmigrodzka, *Romantyzm i historia* (Warsaw, 1978), 154–81.

The process of reform can never end. It constitutes the very essence of a worthwhile political program; that is to say, a program which has as its raison d'être the ongoing effort to reduce differences among people from all walks of life without exception.

There exists, however, one situation which is clearly contrary to these aforementioned assumptions. We refer to the case of a small group of people who—perhaps even in the name of the most noble cause—create and appropriate for themselves the exclusive privilege of control over the courts. In this situation millions of people are left with no civil rights. We can no longer accept the happy illusion which sees economic inequality resulting from relationships to the means of production as the only source of injustice.[22]

Jasienica juxtaposed "reforms" with "revolution" and held the former as absolutely superior to the latter. This point of view predominates in present day Polish thought. The watchword is evolution, not revolution.

### THE EFFECTS OF THE FRENCH REVOLUTION ELSEWHERE IN EASTERN EUROPE

Although many scholars maintain that the direct influence of the American and French Revolutions on the formulation of the programs and aspirations of the nations of Eastern Europe was minimal,[23] the two revolutions' indirect influence was immense. The French Revolution did have a far greater impact on Poland than on any other East European nation, but the rest of Eastern Europe was not unaffected by the spirit of 1789, even though it was much easier for French revolutionary slogans to reach the lands of the Habsburg dynasty than those of the underdeveloped and isolated Ottoman Empire. One of the results of the long, drawn-out wars between France and the Habsburg Empire (1792–97, 1799–1801, 1801–6, 1809) was ongoing contact between the multinational Austrian population and the French. Thus, the wars contributed to the awakening of the Hungarian, Czech, and Croatian nationalist movements, forcing the emperor of Austria to restrict his Germanizing policy.

The effects of the Revolution were felt in Hungary almost immediately. Together with events in Poland, particularly the promulgation of the Constitution of the Third of May, the Revolution strengthened the Hungarian revolutionary movement. In the spring of 1794, a network of clubs operated throughout the country. At the same time, an organization of

---

[22]Paweł Jasienica, *Rozwaz'ania o wojnie domowej* (Kraków, 1985), 126.
[23]Jerzy Skowronek, "Model rewolucji w myśli politycznij środkowowschodniej Europy w epoce napoleońskiej," *Przegląd Humanistyczny*, 1978, nr. 1.

Hungarian Jacobins was set up under the leadership of Ignác Martinovics. This former Franciscan and university professor turned Jacobin revolutionary, whose unique abilities were not in keeping with his weak character, sought to instigate a revolution in Hungary and to establish autonomy for Slovakia. But his organization was not strong. The plot was discovered, and Martinovics and other leading activists were publicly executed in May 1795 in Buda. Nevertheless, Ferenc Pulszky said, "Above all, we kept on studying the history of the French Revolution."[24] István Széchenyi's biographer emphasizes the extent to which this leader of the Hungarian national movement was brought up on the texts of the French Enlightenment, particularly those of the French Revolution.[25]

Yet, an analysis of the ideas as well as the political and social methods of Lajos Kossuth in the Hungarian Revolution of 1848–49 reveals that the influence of the year 1789 on the countries of eastern and southern Europe (Bohemia, Austria, Hungary, Moldavia, and Wallachia) should be measured principally by the events of the Springtime of Nations, not by the direct impact of 1789–94.[26] In the 1840s many Romanian politicians such as Nicolae Bălcescu, Constantin Rosetti, and Ion Brătianu, who were responsible for winning the independence of their country, pursued the study of the French Revolution with Jules Michelet and others. In Paris, they prepared for the role they would subsequently play during the years 1848–81, fighting for the independence of Romania as well as for reforms concerning nationalities and the social system.[27] By the middle of the nineteenth century, the influence of the movement for national liberation became more powerful within the territory of the Romanian duchies. C. D. Aricescu wrote about his studies in 1840 in Bucharest: "We read the biographies of Hus, More, Washington, Robespierre, of all martyrs for freedom."[28] In 1848, in a clear response to the French revolutionary actions of 1789, 1830, and 1848, a blue, yellow, and red national banner bearing the words "justice and fraternity" appeared in Romania.

It was not until the second half of the nineteenth century that Bulgar-

---

[24]Cf. George Barany, *Stephen Széchenyi and the Awakening of Hungarian Nationalism 1791–1841* (Princeton, 1968), 306.

[25]Barany, *Stephen Széchenyi and the Awakening*, 101.

[26]István Deák, *The Lawful Revolution. Louis Kossuth and the Hungarians 1848–1849* (New York, 1979).

[27]See Jerzy W. Borejsza, *Sekretarz Adama Michiewicza. Armand Lévy i jego czasy 1827–1891*, 2d ed. (Wrocław, 1977).

[28]Alexandru Dutu, "Mouvements de libération, mouvements nationaux et image de la France Révolutionnaire dans le Sud-Est de l'Europe 1789–1848," in *L'image de la Révolution Française*, 2:1427.

ians and Serbs began to be affected by the ideas of the Revolution. Scholars searching for revolutionary and Enlightenment texts found that some appeared in Bucharest or Jassy at the turn of the nineteenth century; however, there is no evidence of them in Bulgaria at that time. It is ironic that the spirit of 1789 reached these areas at a time when the glory of France, including revolutionary France, had already faded among the Poles, who had been estranged by the Russo-French alliance and by the French dismissal of the Polish Question.

Linear measurement of the popularity of ideas and programs that have endured for two centuries is impossible. The enormous collection of lectures concerning the bicentennial of the French Revolution of 1789 that has recently been published in Paris offers new data about the extension of French revolutionary ideas into Romania, Croatia, Dalmatia, and Bohemia at the turn of the nineteenth century. Two hundred years later, as articles, translations, police reports, and private correspondence from the years 1789 to 1848 in the countries east of the Elbe are collected, it is clear that the ideals of the French Revolution reached these countries and were adapted to their struggles for political liberation, national independence, and social reforms. The social programs and the civil rights being enacted in Eastern Europe today are largely based on the ideals of 1789.

# 4

# The French Revolution in Russian intellectual life, 1789–1922

## DMITRY SHLAPENTOKH

From the middle of the nineteenth century to the second half of the twentieth century, the French Revolution was one of the major topics in Russian intellectual life.[1] Despite the importance of the topic, however, no comprehensive monograph on the subject has been published. One explanation for this could be the way in which Russian history is viewed in the West. From the viewpoint of the majority of Western historians, Russian politics and history are distinctly different from those of the West. It is also implied that the majority of Russians have thought of

---

[1] This chapter does not pretend to cover the topic of the role of the French Revolution in Russian intellectual and political life in its totality. Clearly, no short writing could fully investigate so enormous a subject. In no other country did the French Revolution exercise such strong and enduring influence on the intellectual and political life. For this reason some aspects of the problem here are either completely omitted or touched on only briefly. For further details, see Dmitry Shlapentokh, "The French Revolution and the Russian Political Process in the Nineteenth and Twentieth Centuries," Ph.D. diss., University of Chicago, 1988.

The role of the French Revolution in Russian intellectual life has not been researched thoroughly and few works have been published on the topic. See, however, Boris S. Itenberg, *Rossiia i Velikaia frantsuzskaia revolutsiia* (Russia and the Great French Revolution) (Moscow: "Mysl'," 1988), which provides comprehensive information about the French Revolution's influence on Russian society from the Revolution's outbreak to the very end of the nineteenth century. Additional information on the French Revolution's role in the intellectual development of nineteenth-century Russia is in the bicentennial issue of *Revue des etudes slaves* (Tome LXI, 1989); in B. S. Alekseev-Popoy, "Znachenie opyta Velikoi frantsuzskoi revoliutsii dlia russkogo rabochego dvizheniia v period revoliutsii 1905–1906 gg" (Meaning of the experience of the French Revolution for the Russian Workers' Movement on the eve and in the course of the Revolution 1905–1906) *Frantsuzskii ezhegodniki* (1959); and in John Keep, "The Tyranny of Paris over Petrograd," *Soviet Studies* (July 1968). Hans Hecker's *Russische Universalgeschichtsschreibung: Von den "Vierziger Jahren" des 19. Jahrhunderts bis zur sowjetischen "Weltgeschichte,"* 1955–1965 (Munich and Vienna: R. Oldenbourg, 1983) provides information about the study of the French Revolution in Soviet Russia.

themselves mostly as a people with a distinct cultural and historical destiny. The ideology of Westernizers, that is, those who assumed that Russia, despite its uniqueness, belonged to the community of Western countries, has generally been seen as a fringe movement in Russian ideological development. It is not surprising that in the context of such an approach, the significance of images of the Russian past in Russian intellectual development was studied much more extensively than was the corresponding role of western-European history.

This study presents another approach, emphasizing that from the middle of the nineteenth century to the end of the Russian Civil War (1922), Western ideology was on the rise and that until the end of the 1920s, it rivaled the ideologies that stressed Russia's uniqueness. This ideological development was indicated by increasing interest in the French Revolution. By the end of 1920, however, interest in the French Revolution began to wane in Russian intellectual life, and it was images of Asian and Russian history that were employed in order to understand the country's political and intellectual development. This change corresponds to important changes in Russian intellectuals' perception of their historical destiny as being distinct from that of other European countries.

Since the middle of the eighteenth century, French culture dominated Russia's intellectual life, and the interest in France, especially the French Enlightenment, was quite strong. Catherine the Great (1729–96) corresponded with many French luminaries, including Voltaire.[2] The beginning of the French Revolution, especially the king's execution and the Reign of Terror, brought the fascination with France to an end, and made Catherine one of the implacable enemies of the new political order. Paul (1754–1801) continued the policy of his much-hated mother and, despite his sound relationship with Napoleon, strongly discouraged his subjects' interest in the French Revolution and suppressed any positive evaluation of the event.[3] Alexander I's ascension to the throne after his father's assassination in 1801 eased government control over intellectual life. Alexander's personal interest in the liberal ideas of the Revolution and the Enlightenment (he was educated, not by his conservative father, but by his grandmother) and the prolonged wars with Napoleon placed the French Revolution in vogue once again. It was at this time that young officers (many of whom participated in the Patriotic War of 1812) were inspired

[2] *Documents of Catherine the Great* (New York: Russel and Russel, 1971).
[3] George Lefebvre, *Napoleon: From 18 Brumaire to Tilsit, 1799–1807* (New York: Columbia University Press, 1969), 27.

by the French Revolution to organize secret societies and repeat it on
Russian soil. Their revolution, the palace coup of the Decembrists—the
tradition of the numerous palace coups that marked Russian history of
the eighteenth century also apparently influenced them—failed in 1825.

The next czar, Nicholas I (1825–55), was as harsh in his approach to
society intellectual life as Paul, under whose rule even the mere mention,
much less praise, of the French Revolution could lead to serious complica-
tions with the authorities.[4] Yet the harshness of the government's censorship was not the only reason society ceased to be interested in the French
Revolution. During this period, the pattern of Russia's political and social
development was distinctly different from that of western Europe. While
European countries experienced rapid industrialization and the rise of the
proletariat during the first half of the nineteenth century, Russia remained
a predominantly agrarian society. When Europe was engaged in several
violent revolutions that shook the European monarchies, the Russian
autocracy felt no threat. Even the Polish uprising of 1830, centered on
nationalism, had no effect on Russia itself.

All of these events inspired Russian intellectuals with the feeling that
Russia had a fate distinct from that of the West. Even those who regarded
Russia's future as similar to that of Europe, often referred to as "*zapadniki*" (which can be translated either as "Westernizers" or "Occiden-
tophiles") strongly believed that Russia would never precisely follow the
ways of western Europe. According to them, it was not a revolution of the
French type, but rather of the enlightened autocrat, that would and should
push the country toward modernization. The opponents of the *zapadniki*,
known as "Slavophiles," were even more definite in their assumption that
the French Revolution was not a scenario that could be repeated on Russian
soil. In their view, the French Revolution was due mostly to rather anti-
Christian elements of western European culture (they regarded Catholicism and Protestantism as a departure from real Christianity), with its
emphasis on violence and lack of moral restrictions in general. It is not
surprising that the French Revolution ignited little if any interest among the
outstanding intellectual figures of the second quarter of the nineteenth
century, who focused instead on Russian history, with Peter the Great
(1672–1725), emperor and reformer, figuring most prominently.[5]

[4]A. V. Nikitenko, *Dnevniki,* 3 vols. (Leningrad: Gosudarstvennoe Izdatel'stvo Khudozhest-
vennoi Literatury, 1955), 1:187.
[5]Nicholas V. Riasanovsky, *The Image of Peter the Great in Russian History and Thought*
(New York: Oxford University Press, 1985).

Nicholas's death opened a new period in Russian history that lasted until the beginning of the Revolution of 1905. During this time, Russia's political and social development seemed to continue to defy analogy with the West. The Russian autocrat was the only monarch of the great European nations whose power was not limited by any political institutions and was still similar in many ways to that of the Oriental despot. In sharp contrast to western Europe, especially to France, Russia still seemed to be immune from any major political upheaval, and the autocracy (at least as a political institution) had successfully repulsed the onslaught of the opposition. Russia's social development also retained its uniqueness. Russia continued to be a predominantly agrarian country, with the peasantry living under the umbrella of the medieval commune, which long before had ceased to exist in western Europe. Yet, Russia's differences with Europe were not as sharp as they had been under Nicholas I. The revolutionary movement emerged as a distinct phenomenon, and political terrorism began to pester the autocracy during the reign of Alexander II, the czar and liberator famous for his emancipation of the serfs and liberal reforms who was murdered by terrorists on 1 March 1881.

Industrialization also began to grow, together with workers' strikes. At the same time, the end of the nineteenth century marked the termination of Russian international isolationism, and autocratic Russia and republican France became allies. In short, while still different from western Europe, Russia apparently became more akin to France in its social and political life. As a result, various Russian intellectuals finally assimilated the French Revolution into Russian intellectual life. While in general rejecting the possibility that Russia could repeat the French scenario, they at least raised the subject.

For conservative Slavophiles of the last decades of the nineteenth century, the French Revolution was caused by certain traits inborn within Western civilization. Violence was one of the most important among these. Nikolai I. Danilevsky (1822–85), one of the preeminent Russian intellectuals of that time, elaborated these views in his book *Russia and Europe*. In Danilevsky's opinion, Russians and Westerners were as distinct as two different biological species, with a predilection for violence being one of the most fundamental components of the Western character. This trait, according to Danilevsky, explained why European history was nothing but a chain of wars and revolutions, the French Revolution being the best example. It also explained the nature of the Napoleonic Wars and provided the reason the French emperor had plunged into what seemed to be suicidal Russian expeditions instead of sharing world domination with the Russian emperor. At the same time, the "meekness" that was the essential element of the Russian character according to Danilevsky explains why the Russians were impervious to the influence of the French Revolution. The Russians also should have expected no gratitude from Europeans, whom Russia saved from French domination, and from this point of view, "one could only regret Russia's enormous efforts to direct this struggle [the French Revolution and the Napoleonic Wars], which in fact should concern it as little as the Taipeng Rebellion."[6]

Such an idea and approach to the French Revolution was espoused by other conservative Slavophile writers of that time, most prominently Tolstoy. In *War and Peace* for example, Napoleon, the manifestation of Western violence[7] and bellicosity, was clearly juxtaposed with the main Russian character, Platon Karataev. The latter demonstrated no violent propensities or even military valor, but rather was ready to suffer and, indeed, accepted his death in Christian fashion.

Lack of moral principles regarding sexuality was viewed by the conservative Slavophiles as the other root of the French Revolution, as another essential component of European history in general. Nikolai F. Fedorov (1828–1903) was among those who interpreted all of European history in terms of sexuality. (From this perspective Fedorov was a precursor to Freud and even more thoroughly anticipated Adorno.)[8] In Fedorov's view, the French Revolution provided much evidence for this interpretation.[9] At the same time, the sexuality of European culture was contrasted to Russian chastity. Fedorov believed that it was not sexuality, but parental respect, that defined the very essence of Russian culture. It was not accidental that Fedorov's grandiose apocalyptical project of the resurrection of "dead fathers" was to be initiated by the Russian czar, who was to unite mankind into a single empire—"family."

Similar ideas could be found on the pages of conservative periodicals. *Novoe Vremia* (New Time), one of the leading conservative vehicles of

[6]N. I. Danilevskii, *Rossiia i Evropa* (St. Petersburg: Tipografiia brat'ev Pateleevykh, 1885), 223.

[7]L. N. Tolstoy, *Voina i Mir*, 2 vols. (Moscow: Khudozhestvennaia Literatura, 1968), 2:15, 246–47.

[8]About Fedorov's life and teaching see: Stephen Lukashevich, *N. F. Fedorov (1828–1903): A Study in Russian Eupsychian and Utopian Thought* (Granbury: Associated University Press, 1977); George McCragen Young, *Nikolai F. Fedorov: An Introduction* (Belmont: Nordland Publishing Company, 1979).

[9]N. F. Fedorov, *Filosofiia obshchago dela: Stat'i mysli i pis'ma*, 2 vols. (Vernyi: Tipografiia Semerechenskogo Oblastnogo Pravleniia, 1906), 1:495.

that time, published a score of articles that explained the French Revolution as being the embodiment of European, especially of French, sexuality. (It is possible that the editors of the newspaper were under Fedorov's influence, since they occasionally published his writings.)[10] According to Fedorov, opposition to the Old Regime arose in eighteenth-century France because people were shocked by the depravity of the French upper class and because pleasing women required a lot of money, which increased the burden on the French populace. Debauchery also feminized the French elite, preventing them from defending their social position and their very lives. The aggressiveness of the French Revolution, the Reign of Terror, and the Napoleonic Wars was explained as the result of men's competitiveness in striving to attract beautiful French women, whose reign in Paris was unchallengeable.[11]

Various radicals, who were under the influence of Slavophilism to different degrees, were among those who dominated the oppositionist movement in the second half of the nineteenth century. To be sure, these radicals were fascinated with the French Revolution, which provided them with an operational model. Those who advocated spontaneous, grass-roots movements praised the French Revolution as the example of spontaneous popular action. Those who were called "Russian Jacobins" looked to the French Revolution as a first example of the strong revolutionary government that pitilessly crushed its enemies and led the citizenry in a proper direction.[12] All of them were eager to read the smuggled works of the radical and liberal historians of the French Revolution,[13] with their fulminations against Hippolyte Taine (1828–93), whose *Origines de la France contemporaine* they regarded as slanderous of the Revolution.[14] Yet, for all of the fascination the French Revolution inspired, it was similar to the upcoming Russian revolution only in external appearance and not in its social essence. And here, the approach to the French Revolution of Alexander Herzen (1812–70), the prominent Russian radical thinker and intellectual forefather of most nineteenth-century leftists, can serve as an example.

In his youth, Herzen was fascinated by western Europe and partic-

---

[10]*Novoe Vremia*, 14 October 1898.    [11]Ibid., 26 June 1892; 22 April 1899.
[12]N. S. Rusanov, *Iz moikh vospominanii* (Berlin: Izdatel'stvo Z. I. Grzhebina, 1923), 120; Franco Venturi, *Roots of Revolution* (New York: Alfred A. Knopf, 1960), 427.
[13]Rusanov, *Iz moikh vospominanii*, 120; Venturi, *Roots of Revolution*, 48; A. Borman, *A.V. Tyrkova-Vil'iams po ee pis'mam i vospominaniim syna* (Louvain and Washington: n.p., 1964), 25.
[14]*Revoliutsionnaia Rossiia*, 1 June 1903.

ularly the French Revolution, which made the West such a marvelous place to live. It was logical that Herzen did his best to escape Nicholas I's Russia, and in 1847 he crossed the border of the empire, presumably to treat himself in one of the European resorts. He never returned. As he later acknowledged, he entered Paris, the birthplace of the great European Revolution, "with trembling in his heart" and compared his feeling to that of pilgrims of the Middle Ages entering Jerusalem and Rome.[15] Soon, however, he became deeply disenchanted with the West in general and France in particular. He found that the heroic French Revolution, having decimated aristocracy, did not bring liberation. It replaced the aristocracy with the bourgeoisie, which was no less oppressive and did not have the splendor of the previous elite. The vicious circle of European revolutions (including those of France) was to Herzen the result of inescapable characteristics within Western civilization. European socialists, if victorious, would follow the same model and would establish a regime as oppressive as the previous one had been.[16] Russia would not and should not follow the example of the French Revolution in its entirety. Not only would Russian peasant communes secure for revolutionary Russia the Socialist regime in its purest form, but Russian character would keep Russian socialism from oppressing the populace. While many radicals disagreed with Herzen, they shared the conviction that Russia should look at the French Revolution critically and never forget the specifics of Russia's historical path.

For the majority of Russian intellectuals at the end of the nineteenth century, the French Revolution was an important subject that only demonstrated its basic irrelevance to Russia's historical destiny. Yet industrialization and, to a greater extent, political instability pushed a growing number of intellectuals, including the conservatives, to conclude that Russia was not much different from the West and that, consequently, the French scenario might emerge in Russia.

Fedor M. Dostoevsky (1821–81) in the last years of his life was generally considered to be a Slavophile. Although he viewed the French Revolution as one of a chain of grandiose cataclysmic events that would finally destroy Europe,[17] he did not see Russia as immune from the disaster. And

[15]A. I. Herzen, *Sobranie sochinenii v tridtsati tomakh* (Moscow: Izdatel'stvo Akademii Nauk, 1954–65), 5:141.
[16]Ibid., 11:239.
[17]F. M. Dostoevskii, *Dnevnik pisatelia za 1877* (Berlin: Izdatel'stvo I. P. Ladyshnikova, 1922), 227.

it was no accident that he appreciated works on the French Revolution, such as those written by Nikolai A. Liubimov,[18] professor at the University of Moscow and one of the editors of *Russkii Vestnik* (Russian Messenger), a leading conservative periodical. In Liubimov's view, the situation in Russia was ominously similar to conditions in prerevolutionary and even revolutionary France, and he drew direct parallels between Alexander II and Louis XVI. Vladimir Ger'e (1837–1919), the well-known historian of Europe (he was among the first to initiate teaching the French Revolution in Russian universities), disagreed with Liubimov at the beginning of his academic career but supported him later, after Alexander II's assassination. Like Liubimov, he duly employed Taine's *Origines* (the book played the same role in czarist Russia that Alexander Solzhenitsyn's *Gulag Archipelago* played in the Soviet Union) to demonstrate the horrors in store for Russia if the new Jacobins took control of the state machinery.[19]

The liberals and social democrats who formed their parties at the turn of the century were among those who had finally shaken off the last dust of the Slavophile vision of Russia's role in the world community and firmly believed that Russia was a part of the West. For them, the French Revolution became the focal point of political and philosophical discussions. And they became the dominant force in Russia's intellectual life in the epoch to come, beginning with the Revolution of 1905.

The Revolution of 1905 was the first Russian revolution of the European type, and one might argue that this event demonstrated that Russia was European, not much different from the West. Russia might lag behind in solving her problems, but how Russia solved them was Western in nature. Consequently, the French Revolution was not only relevant to Russia, but became the most popular subject in discussions among those who espoused the idea of a basic similarity between Russia and the West.

The Russian liberals became not only one of the leading intellectual forces, but also one of the most, if not the most, influential group in political life. (It was representatives of the liberal parties who occupied most of the seats in the first two meetings of the Duma, the Russian parliament.) Viewing the Russian monarchy as essentially similar to that of the French in the last years of the Old Regime, they debated the monarchists over how to prevent Russian Jacobins from taking power.

[18]B. Modzalevskii, "Dostoevsky o 'Brat'iakh Karamazovykh': Neizdannye pis'ma," *Bylos* 15(1919): 130–31.
[19]V. Ger'e, "Ippolit Ten v istorii iakobintsev," *Vestnik Evropy*, July 1895.

The issue that separated the monarchists from the liberals was whether the slackening of government control and reforms signaled the beginning of the end. The monarchists espoused ideas that can be likened to the domino theory. In their view, each political system (i.e., the French and Russian monarchies) had political forms that were more or less fixed. Attempting to change them would not improve the regime's stability but would lead to its collapse and usher in the revolutionary process that would inescapably pass through all of its stages.[20] The course of the French Revolution, during which monarchists, liberal Girondists, and then radical Jacobins themselves were decimated, was not, therefore, an aberration of the revolutionary process that could have been avoided by wise policy but was inevitable. The actual course of the French Revolution was the only one available, and there were no missed opportunities. The reforms, therefore, especially in the realm of politics, either should not be started or should be extremely limited. Furthermore, in this view, the French monarchy should have protected itself by employing harsh measures at the first sign of opposition. The monarchists were so fascinated by the repression that they were ready to praise Napoleon occasionally and even the Jacobins for the merciless destruction of their political rivals.[21]

Russian liberals had a different view. Having rejected the domino theory, they stated that the reforms could have saved the French monarchy and that not all stages of the Revolution were inevitable. Consequently, the French Revolution could have had a scenario quite different from that of its actual script. Maksim M. Kovalevsky (1851–1916), the well-known sociologist and historian, had elaborated these liberal ideas in his *Origin of Contemporary Democracy*, published before the Revolution of 1905.[22] The book was apparently modeled after Taine's *Origines*, yet reached different conclusions. For Taine the populace was the "lustful gorilla" that could be pacified only by repression. In Kovalevsky's view, the French monarchy and, later, the Girondists could have survived if only they had supported the populace's economic demands, especially those of the urban workers. Kovalevsky and his younger colleague, Ivan V. Luchitsky (1845–1918), pioneered the study of the agrarian relationship in

---

[20]V. Ger'e, "Iz proshlogo konstitutsionnykh voprosov o narodovlastii i svobode," *Vestnik Evropy*, May 1905.

[21]*Novoe Vremia*, 10 June 1907; 17 June 1907.

[22]Maksim M. Kovalevskii, *Proiskhozhdenie Sovremennoi Demokratii*, 4 vols. (Moscow: Tovarishchestvo tipografii A. I. Mamontova, 1895–97).

eighteenth-century France. (Thanks mostly to their efforts, the "Russian school" of the study of the French Revolution achieved prominence and even influenced contemporary French historiography.)[23] Luchitsky supported Kovalevsky's view that stressed the peasant's clamor for land as the main reason for the downfall of the French monarchy.[24]

Nikolai I. Kareev (1850–1931) and his pupil Alexander Onu, both professional historians and deputies to the Duma, stressed in their scholarly writings and in their public speeches, as did Pavel N. Miliukov (1859–1943), the leading figure of the Cadet party, that political reforms had been essential to the survival of the French monarchy and urged the Russian monarch, Nicholas II, not to imitate the ill-fated Louis's stubborn attempt to preserve the autocracy.[25] The French monarchy was not doomed to fall, and Mirabeau's plan to reconcile the king with the opposition could have been successful. Neither the Girondists nor even the Dantonists were fated to be destroyed. At several junctures the radicalization of the revolutionary process could have been arrested if the protagonists of the revolutionary drama had been wiser and had circumstances favored them.

While liberals and monarchists were engaged in a hot debate over what doomed the French monarchy and unlocked a Pandora's box of uncontrolled violence, the radicals of various political persuasions were in unanimous agreement that the French monarchy had had to be destroyed and that the Russian autocracy should share its fate. (Many of them were also convinced that Louis's execution was morally justifiable and hoped that Nicholas would suffer the same penalty for his crimes.) The vast majority of radicals did not share the Slavophile illusions of their radical, late-nineteenth-century forefathers concerning the essential uniqueness of Russia's historical destiny. In their view, Russia was definitely part of Europe, and Russia's revolutionary movement was just as clearly part of the European or world revolutionary process. The question, however, was what role should Russia play, and here, the French Revolution was extremely important in clarifying Russian revolutionary intentions. The opinions of Russian leftists were split.

The Mensheviks (literally "minority") were those who pulled away

[23]Albert Soboul, *Comprendre la Revolution* (Paris: Gancois Maspero, 1981), 301.
[24]I. V. Luchitskii, *Krest'iandkov zemlevladenie vo Frantsii nakanune revoliutsii* (n.p.: 1897).
[25]*Sbornik rechei deputatov Gosudarstvennoi Dumy I i II sozyva*, 2 vols. (St. Petersburg: Elektropechatnaia K. A. Chetverikova, 1908), 1:83; A. Onu, *Vybory 1789 goda vo Frantsii i nakazy tret'ego sosloviia s tochki zreniia ikh sootvetstviia istinomy nastroeniiu strany* (St. Petersburg: Tipografiia Stasiulevicha, 1908); *Rech'*, 8 May 1905.

from the radical wing of the Social Democratic party, the Bolsheviks (literally "majority"), in 1903. By 1912 they severed ties with the Bolsheviks completely. Strictly following a Marxist model, the Mensheviks assumed that contemporary Russia was on the threshold of a bourgeois revolution basically similar to France's. At the same time, and here they clearly differed with Marx, they did not perceive the revolutionary process as being inevitably international in its scope. The Russian revolutionary movement, even if initiated by the proletariat, might be quite isolated and receive no succor from its "class brothers" in the West. Consequently, in these situations the Russian revolution would be quite similar to the French in both its external form and its social goal, with the bourgeoisie taking the leading role. Those who would try to trespass on the bourgeois confinement of Russia's revolutionary movement could expect nothing but disappointment and the country's increased suffering as a result of their ill-fated experiment.

In the view of Evgenii V. Tarle (1875–1955), who began his career as a Menshevik and was exiled in the late 1920s and early 1930s before being accepted into the Soviet intellectual establishment, the French Jacobins tasted defeat in their attempt to organize the society's economy in a quasi-socialist manner. Having discussed the maximum law (which froze prices of major commodities), Tarle stated that it had been accepted because of the pressure of the starving Parisian populace and was upheld by the blade of the guillotine. Yet the market economy had its own implacable law, and eighteenth-century France was not ready for socialism either. A complete fiasco was the result of the Jacobins' economic policy, with goods disappearing from the stores and workers' dissatisfaction rising. This led to the Jacobins' downfall and the restoration of a pure market economy by the Thermidorians.[26] This "Thermidorian" account of the development of the Revolution would be quite popular among Mensheviks and other anti-Bolshevik intellectuals when applied to the Bolshevik Revolution.

According to the leading Menshevik intellectual and one of the founding fathers of the Russian Social Democratic movement, Georgii V. Plekhanov (1856–1918), the experiment of the Russian Jacobins could have even worse consequences. Having tried to impose state control over economic life, Bolsheviks promised to nationalize the land if they were victorious. In such a case not even a new edition of the French Thermidor,

---

[26]E. V. Tarle, "Istoriia odnogo sotsial'nogo eksperimenta," *Sovremennyi Mir*, no. 8, 1909.

but the Oriental despot, would be in store for the Russian populace.[27]
Plekhanov's predictions about the rise of Oriental despotism resulting
from a socialist experiment in Russia were surprisingly close to those
of the late-nineteenth-century conservative intellectual, Konstantin N.
Leont'ev (1831–91).

Bolsheviks under Lenin's leadership held a different view of Russia's
revolutionary process and to what extent it should be modeled after
France's. Certainly, Lenin had no illusions about special inborn characteristics of Russian culture (as espoused by nineteenth-century radicals),
yet he assumed that a Russian revolution would be different because the
French Revolution took place within a different historical context. The
crux of the difference was the rise of the industrial proletariat, which was
destined to be the major revolutionary force. In the course of its struggle
against the autocracy, the proletariat would inevitably clash with the
bourgeoisie who, having been frightened by the proletariat, would soon
drop out of the ranks of the revolutionary movement and join the reactionaries.

Thus, the struggle of Russia's Old Regime would be waged against the
Russian bourgeoisie, and a completely victorious revolution would place
the proletariat, allied with the peasantry, in control. The regime would be
socialist by its social composition and by its immediate goal. Yet it would
not be able to endure in a backward country with the industrial proletariat constituting only the smallest fraction of the population. Left on
their own, the Russian Jacobins would ultimately suffer their Thermidor,
that is, the restoration of capitalism. Here Lenin sounded very much like
many of the Mensheviks. Lenin believed that the Bolsheviks, unlike the
Jacobins, would attract powerful allies. Whereas eighteenth-century
France was surrounded by the reactionary, feudal regimes that opposed
the Revolution, twentieth-century Russia was surrounded by advanced
capitalist countries implanted with the ideals of socialist revolution.

Following Marx's visions of the revolutionary process, Lenin saw the
Russian Revolution as international in scope, that is, its initiation would
sooner or later have international repercussions.[28] In this situation, the
various European proletariats would extend their hands to the Russian
proletariat and rescue the regime from Thermidorian degeneration. Leon
Trotsky (1879–1940) held a view quite similar to Lenin's after 1905—

[27]G. V. Plekhanov, *Sochineniia* (Moscow: Gosudarstvennoe Izdatel'stvo, 1925), 14:68.
[28]Vladimir I. Lenin, *Polnoe Sobranie Sochinenii*, 55 vols. (Moscow: Gosudarstvennoe
Izdatel'stvo Politicheskoi Literatury, 1960[?]), 12:362.

that the worldwide revolution would begin with the incipient stage of Russia's revolutionary process. For this reason Trotsky rejected the French Revolution as the appropriate model for Russia's future.[29]

The collapse of czardom in February 1917 ushered in a new period of Russian history that continued to the end of the Civil War (1922). During this short period, Russia experienced two full-fledged revolutions and the Reign of Terror. Many of these events as well as the course of political development in general were strikingly similar to those of France. As a result, numerous Russian intellectuals not only assumed that the Russian Revolution was similar to that of the French in its political and social outlines, but also concluded that the Russian Revolution was a carbon copy of the events in France that occurred more than a century before. The number of intellectuals who held this view grew steadily during the period as more and more observers of the Revolution realized that a repetition of the French Reign of Terror was imminent. Consequently, they also concluded that Russia was not only a Western country, but more Western than any other country in the world. Many of the Russian intellectuals were filled with messianic fervor at the beginning of the twentieth century, but it was a more Westernized than Slavophilic type of messianism, although elements of Slavophilism could be discerned within their writings. These intellectuals believed that Russia should adopt certain ideas (e.g., freedom, equality, and brotherhood) that Europe had begotten but had abandoned long before.

The collapse of czardom led to a rising interest in the French Revolution among a broad section of the Russian population. Publishing houses released popular works and "red-bound histories of the French revolution" could be seen in shop windows of "fashionable" book shops.[30] They were "selling rapidly" and could be seen on the "tables of many politicians."[31] The Russian intellectuals as well as others were preoccupied with the question of to what extent the Russian revolutionary process would duplicate the French one, although the majority of the liberal and radical intellectuals were convinced that it would not happen.

Just after the czar was overthrown, Miliukov's *Rech'* (Speech) reas-

---

[29]Baruch Knei-Paz, *The Social and Political Thought of Leon Trotsky* (Oxford: Clarendon Press, 1978), 109.

[30]Philip M. Price, *My Reminiscences of the Russian Revolution* (London: George Allen and Unwin, 1921), 74.

[31]Pitirim Sorokin, *Leaves from a Russian Diary—and Thirty Years After* (Boston: Beacon Press, 1950), 39.

sured readers that while the Russian and French revolutions possessed formal similarities, they were "absolutely different phenomen[a]."[32] The two revolutions were similar only in a military sense. This was why Miliukov's public speeches were accompanied by the "Marseillaise,"[33] which almost became Russia's national anthem.[34] Alexander F. Kerensky (1881–1970), the radical prime minister of the ill-fated provisional government, shared Miliukov's view, and he made speeches to the soldiers at the front (Russia was at war with Germany at that time) "about freedom, enthusiasm, the republic, and peace, the fairy tale of the French Revolution."[35] At the same time, he stated firmly that he would be the "Marat of the Russian Revolution."[36] Lenin voiced a similar opinion, and while praising the Jacobins, he added that "imitation of good example does not mean copying it . . . . The Jacobins of the twentieth century would not guillotine the capitalists."[37] In other articles, he stated categorically that "the French Revolution had guillotined its enemies; the proletarian revolution would compel them to work for it."[38]

The intensification of political struggles and the spread of anarchy induced a rising number of Russian intellectuals to conclude that the Reign of Terror was looming on the horizon. Pitirim A. Sorokin (1889–1968), a leading right Socialist-Revolutionary, was quite contemptuous of those who, in the beginning of the February Revolution, assumed that it was destined to follow the cycle of the French Revolution. Later, however, he changed his mind, making the following entry in his diary:

I have begun to study more intensively the great French Revolution. How history repeats itself. Who are we but Russian Girondists? What will be our fate? Their own? What will happen to the Fatherland? Probably the same horror of bloodshed and destruction, without any of the military glory that followed France's political and social upheaval.[39]

[32]*Rech'*, 11 March 1917.
[33]Aleksei Tarazov-Rodionov, *February, 1917*, trans. William A. Drake (New York: Covici, Friede, 1931), 111.
[34]Prinse Cantacuzene, *Revolutionary Days* (New York: Arno Press and New York Times, 1970), 183.
[35]P. N. Miliukov, "Nicholas II (1894–1917): The Reign Concluded," in *History of Russia: Reforms, Reaction, Revolution (1855–1932)*, vol. 3 of *History of Russia: From the Beginning to the Empire of Peter the Great*, 3 vols. (New York: Funk and Wagnalls, 1968–69), 343.
[36]Meriel Buchanan, *The City of Trouble* (New York: Charles Scribner's Sons, 1918), 102.
[37]Lenin, *Polnoe Sobranie Sochinenii*, 14:307.
[38]Edward Carr, *The Bolshevik Revolution: 1917–1923*, 3 vols. (New York: Macmillan, 1963), 2:108.
[39]Sorokin, *Leaves from a Russian Diary*, 93.

Needless to say, the monarchists had no illusions about their fate, and in comparing their situation to that of the French monarchists, Russian monarchists were anxious to leave the dangerous Petrograd.[40]

In November 1917, the Bolsheviks, who turned out to be the Russian Jacobins, seized power. Quite a few of them, excited by their victory and the vision of their Bolshevik revolution spreading ideas of brotherhood and equality all over the world, rejected the idea of employing Jacobin-like methods to deal with their enemies.[41] At the same time, however, a growing number of Bolsheviks became convinced that an imitation of the French scenario constituted the only chance for them to survive. Trotsky was one of the Bolshevik elite who openly stated that a Jacobin terror would be launched in the near future and threatened to install a "remarkable machine which would shorten the human body by the length of its head."[42] The threat was taken quite seriously, and contemporaries reported that "above the grey mist of Petrograd in winter, terror and the guillotine hung like threatening swords." The public "discussed little besides the guillotine"[43] and in *Pravda* (Truth), a leading Bolshevik daily, venomous articles were reminiscent of Fouquier-Tinville,[44] the French prosecutor of the revolutionary tribunal. The images of the French Revolution that became known even to ordinary people incited the Russian populace to clamor for blood. The Petrograd garrison enjoyed enough erudition to threaten to start a "September massacre"[45] involving all enemies of the new political order. The sailors of the Baltic fleet, called by Trotsky "the pride and glory of the revolution" (he would be among the chief butchers the next year when the sailors challenged Soviet rule), hotly discussed the visibility of the French terror on the streets of the capital.[46]

By September 1918 the Reign of Terror was finally inaugurated, and the French Revolution, specifically the images from the French Reign of Terror, became popular as never before. The similarity of the events, at least in their external appearance, created a feeling largely among the

[40]Andrei Lobanov-Rostovsky, *The Grinding Mill: Reminiscences of War and Revolution in Russia, 1913–1920* (New York: Macmillan, 1935), 230–31.

[41]Simon Liberman, *Building Lenin's Russia* (Chicago: University of Chicago Press, 1945), 15; Israel Getzler, *Kronstadt 1917–1921: The Fate of a Soviet Democracy* (Cambridge: Cambridge University Press, 1983), 166; Bessie Beatty, *Red Heart of Russia* (New York: Century, 1918), 307.

[42]A. Gan (A. Gutman), *Rossia i Bolshevizm: Materialy po istorii revoliutsii i bor'by s Bol'shevizmom* (Shanghai: Tipografiia Russkogo Pechatnogo Izdatel'skogo Dela, n.d.), 234.

[43]Beatty, *The Red Heart of Russia*, 292–93.

[44]Ludvic Naudeau, *En prison sous la terreur russe* (n.p.: Librairie Hachette, 1920), 11.

[45]Sorokin, *Leaves from a Russian Diary*, 123.     [46]Trotsky Archive, T.-3448, f.1.

Bolshevik adversaries and major victims of the terror that they were
thrown back in time, and in their nightmarish vision the images of the
past blended with those of horrifying reality.

Bolsheviks, having compared themselves with Jacobins, were eager to
employ the examples of the French terror to justify their behavior. Lenin,
responding to the critics from the West, stated "the British bourgeoisie
had forgotten their 1649, the French their 1793."[47] V. V. Osininskii
(Obolenskii), scion of a noble Russian family and victim of Stalin's
purges, proclaimed his program of dealing with the regime's enemies. The
first group, and the most politically active, would be shot without further
ado; the second, pillars of class but less involved politically, would be held
hostage, and ten would be executed for every fallen Bolshevik; the third
would be destined for hard labor; the fourth would be "locked in the
camps." And if justification was desired, it was enough to remember the
leaders of the French Revolution who "paved their way to power with
corpses and reigned by means of terror."[48]

For the Bolshevik enemies the grim present was blended with images of
the past to the extent that people lost their feelings of reality. Isaac N.
Steinberg, left Socialist Revolutionary (SR) (Bolsheviks and left SR's were
bedfellows for a short period of time), and the Soviet minister of justice
were thrown into prison. "How shall one relate the grim emotions of a
revolutionary thrown into a prison of the revolution? I was experiencing
feelings of disbelief, of being in the midst of a fantastic nightmare mingled
with my consciousness of reality. Almost instinctively the weary mind
recalls the famous parallel of the French Revolution."[49] One of the young
Mensheviks, a certain Zepalov, experienced the same feeling of the past
blending with the present after reading Anatole France's *Les Dieux ont
soif* (The Gods Are Thirsty). Once he had a nightmare: "I thought I was
standing before the altar with my bride and I suddenly saw myself on the
guillotine with Mr. Vetoshkin (once a friend, but now a rabid Communist) as my executioner. I tried to kiss my bride and my mother, but he
thrust my head under the knife, crying out: 'The gods are thirsty!'"[50]

The end of the Civil War and the inauguration of a New Economic
Policy (NEP) marked a new period in Russian history and in Russian
intellectuals' perception of the French Revolution. Whereas the previous

[47]Lenin, *Polnoe Sobranie Sochinenii*, 37:59.   [48]*Pravda*, 8 September 1918.
[49]Isaac Nachman Steinberg, *In the Workshop of the Revolution* (New York: Rinehart,
   1953), 157.
[50]Sorokin, *Leaves from a Russian Diary*, 148–49.

period (1789–1922), when the scenario of the French Revolution had been employed with increasing frequency to understand the country's political reality, had been characterized by a steady Westernization of Russia's self-image, the new period was characterized by the opposite process; after the early 1920s (when the majority of Russian intellectuals compared contemporary Russia with Thermidorian France), the popularity of the French Revolution as a model for the country's political development began to decline steadily. At the same time, it was the history of Oriental despotism in its various forms (Russia's own history was incorporated in the Oriental model) that started to be employed to understand the country's political reality. The Oriental model was espoused by those who called themselves "Eurasians," and became dominant by the end of the 1920s. All of this indicated Russia's intellectuals' growing sense of their country's alienation from the West European community, and the sense that not a democracy, but an authoritarian or even a totalitarian regime was in store for Russia's future. From this point, the image of the French Revolution in the Soviet Union took a disturbing turn, one that deserves examination in a separate study.

# 5

## The French Revolution, people of color, and slavery

### ROBERT FORSTER

What did *liberté* mean to each of the three ethnic groups in Saint-Domingue (Haiti) in 1789—to whites, both wealthy and poor; to freedmen, both people of color and black; and to slaves, both Creole and African? And what did it mean to those in the National Assembly in Paris who had to make policy for the colonies? Was the Declaration of the Rights of Man and the Citizen applicable integrally to this complex racial society? If so, how could it be applied without disrupting the economy of the colony, which was so important to French prosperity, or fatally weakening the last overseas bastion in the path of British imperial expansion?

My purpose here is not so much to expose the timeless failures of human beings to disengage principles from interests but, rather, to elucidate and chart how deep conflicts about liberty, slavery, and color were brought to the surface by the events and watchwords of 1789. What tragic hesitation and ambivalence allowed the first three years of the French Revolution to pass by without a resolution of the issue of civil rights for people of color, much less for black slaves! The consequences of this irresolution, not to say resistance, were momentous for all three ethnic communities on Saint-Domingue. For revolutionary France, the loss was twofold—the eventual independence of its richest colony and also the forfeiture of its claim to be the Motherland of Liberty for *all* humankind.

The Society of Friends of the Blacks in Paris exhibited a certain naïveté. What a contrast to the Abolitionist Society across the English Channel! The French society failed to link principles with economic arguments about the appalling mortality of white sailors off the West African coast;

to mobilize witnesses among ship captains, surgeons, and civil servants to testify to the horrors of the slave trade; or to establish correspondents and branch clubs throughout France. All this Clarkson and Wilberforce had done so effectively in Britain. The planters of Saint-Domingue and the merchants of the French ports, not the *Amis des Noirs,* had learned these techniques only too well. It is a sad fact that the first well-organized lobbying campaign of the French Revolution was launched by the proslavery forces, and it was successful in delaying any legislation for the people of color until May 1791 and for the black slaves until February 1794. Events would take their own course in the colonies, but the delays and contradictory signals from the metropole played their role in crystallizing an already tense situation in Saint-Domingue.

Thomas Clarkson, the famous English Abolitionist, met with his beleaguered French counterparts in Paris in the summer of 1789. He was appalled by the propaganda of the merchants' lobbies, the Chambers of Commerce, and the Club Massiac; by the planters' pressure group and their delegation to the National Assembly; and by the decisive presence of both merchants and planters on the newly formed Committee on the Colonies, chaired by Barnave, one of the well-known Triumvirate of constitutional monarchists. These lobbies operated at all levels, including the most vulgar racial pamphlets and anonymous death threats (to Clarkson as well as members of The Society of Friends of the Blacks), the mobilization of delegations from the ports (often in the uniforms of the new National Guard), and a scurrilous misrepresentation of the goals and patriotism of the French abolitionists. Clarkson reported that their "public prints" were filled with malicious representations, "circulated industriously," depicting him as a wild man expelled from England who was attempting to "impose equality on the French Nation," or as a spy attempting to subvert the "noble constitution," presumably by preaching emancipation of barbarous Africans.[1]

More logically consistent economic arguments were employed in the planter-merchant discussions with the deputies, but these were no less forceful, even brutal. As Moreau de St. Méry put it: "No slaves, no sugar; no sugar, no colonies!" The port delegations had little difficulty demonstrating with facts and figures the economic value, indeed indispensability, of the "Pearl of the Antilles" to the Motherland. When Clarkson

---

[1] Thomas Clarkson, *The History of the Rise, Progress, and Accomplishments of the Abolition of the Slave Trade,* 3 vols. (New York, 1936), 2:250–51.

urged Mirabeau to canvass the deputies of the Assembly, he reported that every last one of them had been canvassed already by the Colonial Committee and that all had hesitated to support his motion. Lafayette made a second canvass and determined that only about three hundred deputies (of twelve hundred) would support a motion to abolish the slave trade "on principle," but that five hundred more might vote for it *if* England would also abolish the trade.[2] This same reservation was voiced in the English House of Commons in the debates of 1790–92.

Abolition was widely regarded on both sides of the channel as a kind of ruse by the imperial rival to gain the trade for itself. Lafayette, with customary naive good will, asked William Pitt if he would cooperate in this sublime endeavor, but the English prime minister could not promise a successful abolition bill in 1789. Even the English Abolitionist Society had politely declined an invitation earlier that year by the Friends of the Blacks to present a petition for abolition before the French National Assembly. Indeed, it might have weakened Pitt's case for abolition in Commons had it been known that the French were requesting it. Suspicion between the superpowers ran deep. What lay behind this apparently innocent "cause"? Indeed, for those who find Eric Williams convincing, Pitt's motives were not disinterested. Abolition would destroy the French, but not the British Empire.[3]

The merchant and planter lobbies had alerted the National Assembly and much of the French public to the issue of slavery where the Friends of the Blacks had failed. The newly formed Committee of the Colonies was fully aware of the emotions and interests involved. Barnave and Alexander Lameth, prominent members, at the outset supported abolition of the trade "in principle," but they were gradually persuaded by their merchant and planter colleagues, by former colonial administrators, and by a barrage of deputations that such idealism was premature and that to press the issue would surely alienate the whites on the island and inflame separatist tendencies. The American Revolution was fresh on the minds of everyone; Saint-Domingue had yet to produce a Benjamin Franklin, but in 1789 there was no lack of auditioners for the role of Samuel Adams. Prudence and national interest dictated that the white planters be reassured by a strong statement of support from Paris for their property rights and local customs, both of which of course included slaves.

[2]Ibid., 2:274–75.
[3]See Eric Williams, *Capitalism and Slavery* (London, 1987) and Roger Anstey, "Capitalism and Slavery: A Critique,"*Economic History Review* 21 (1968): 307–20.

Three issues before the Committee were closely related: (1) mercantilist regulations (*L'Exclusif*), vigorously contested by the planters but supported by the port merchants; (2) the abolition of the slave trade, opposed by both planters and merchants who now exhibited a remarkable harmony after years of bitter dispute over "Free Trade"; and (3) civil rights for the free people of color, opposed by both planters and merchants, but supported by the *Amis des Noirs* and also by a rival delegation of the people of color from Saint-Domingue led by Julien Raimond, an educated and wealthy quadroon who made an excellent impression among wavering deputies. The French merchants won the exclusive right to supply the island and market its exports. No doubt the Committee associated the *Exclusif* with the sovereignty of the National Assembly in matters of trade. The separatist influence of the Anglo-Americans, both in the economic and political spheres, had to be checked. This decision was not lost on the Assembly of Saint Marc which convened two months after the decree in Paris favoring the metropolitan merchants (May 1790).

The campaign against abolition of the slave trade reached a peak in the first two months of 1790. In the six weeks before the committee report was due, twenty-four addresses before the Assembly requested maintenance of the slave trade and not one petition from a French city asked for abolition or even for amelioration of the condition of the slaves in this critical period. The delegation from Bordeaux addressed the Assembly one day before the presentation of the committee report: "Five million Frenchmen exist only by dint of the [colonial] trade. To abolish slavery and the slave trade [note the link] means the end of the colonies." Yet despite the force of the economic argument (not unconnected with national pride), some deputies still hesitated. Begouën Demeaux, a committee member and merchant from Le Havre with property in the colony, who nonetheless was conscious of the moral dimension of the issue among many deputies, urged his colleagues to reach a clear decision:

I believe, Messieurs, that I can absolutely assure you of a favorable outcome to this affair [i.e., maintenance of the slave trade]. I tell you that the almost general intention of this Assembly is to find *a turn of phrase* which does not obviously contradict its principles.[4]

Barnave, chair of the Committee, shared this assessment. His report to the Assembly of 8 March 1790 was a masterpiece of brevity—and eva-

---

[4]Maurice Begouën Demeaux, *Mémorial d'une famille du Havre*, 2 vols. (Paris and Le Havre, 1982), 2:98. Emphasis added.

sion. "The National Assembly declares it had not intended to innovate in any branch of commerce of France with its colonies." The phrase, "slave trade" was not even pronounced. Mirabeau's rush to the rostrum does justice to the cause, but the shouts of his colleagues tell us more about the majority view. The president of the Assembly quickly closed debate, announcing that Barnave's report had been "approved almost unanimously" by the National Assembly. It probably had been.

The third issue, civil rights for freedmen of color, did not touch colonial trade directly and therefore was of less concern to the port merchants. The economic and metropolitan control arguments of the planters carried less weight here. Moreover, Abbé Grégoire, prominent member of the Amis des Noirs, was strategically placed as president of the Credentials Committee of the National Assembly to influence voting qualifications for freedmen of color. Julien Raimond, the mulatto spokesman, was very active, published numerous pamphlets, and even addressed the Assembly, which none of the six deputies of color were able to do. And Barnave, though now committed to maintain the slave trade, was more sympathetic to the *affranchis,* who after all already possessed property rights on the island. It seemed a logical extension of the principle of granting suffrage to the responsible property owners and taxpayers, the "active citizens" of the Constitution of 1791.

In preparation for future elections on Saint-Domingue, the Committee on the Colonies drew up the electoral procedures and the qualifications for voting. After several rewritings, Barnave presented his report to the Assembly on 28 March 1790. Article 4 read, in part, *"All persons 25 years old at least, owners of property, or if not propertied, domiciled in the parish two years and paying a tax, will meet to form the parish assembly.*[5]

Grégoire and Raimond were disappointed, not to say alarmed, by this wording. Like Barnave's earlier effort, the article seemed evasive. Raimond and the lawyer for the delegation of color had urged Barnave to insert the phrase "every man *without exception of color,*" but they had failed. More ominous for the freedmen of color was the reaction on the floor of the Assembly to Grégoire's request for explicit assurance that the "people of color" could vote. Charles Lameth immediately moved to close discussion of this "indiscreet proposition," and a majority of the

---

[5] Valerie Quinney, "Rights of Free Men of Color in the French Revolution," *French Historical Studies* 7 (1972): 552. Emphasis added.

Assembly supported the motion. The word "indiscreet" strongly suggests that Grégoire's proposal was considered an unwarranted intrusion into local practices and an insult to the white establishment on the island.

Barnave defended the wording on two grounds. First, he had been assured by the planters' delegation that the freedman of color had already voted in the first parish elections for the Estates General and that it was de facto practice on the island. This was untrue, and it is curious or perhaps suspicious that Barnave did not verify this assertion by the *colons*. Second and more important, Barnave said that local parish custom should decide the issue; for Paris to be too explicit on this complex matter "would cause trouble."[6] Barnave's Committee and, it appears, the majority of the National Assembly had yielded to the demands of the *colons* for local control of election procedures, no doubt in order to deflate white separatism. Local control of course meant white control. In the end, a kind of tacit bargain had been struck. The merchants retained their exclusive right to trade with the island (under the law at least); the planters *and* merchants had maintained the slave trade; the white planters had gained a large measure of local government in a critical area, race relations on the island.

The effect of these decisions early in the Revolution (March 1790) should not be underestimated. On one hand, they emboldened the whites on the island to maintain their "local customs." Even after the Saint Marc Assembly had been dissolved in the last forceful act of the royal intendant, the more moderate Assembly at Le Cap Français, though pledging loyalty to France, demanded an explicit guarantee of local (i.e., white) control over the status of the *gens de couleur*. The Assembly granted it in October 1790. At the same time, the freedmen of color attempted to interpret Barnave's text in their favor. Vincent Ogé, member of the unofficial delegation of color in Paris, was exasperated with their failure to obtain a hearing on the floor of the National Assembly and left for Saint-Domingue in the autumn of 1790. Clarkson, who dined frequently with the "deputies of color," described Ogé's state of mind before his departure:

We will no longer continue to be held in a degraded light. . . . We can produce soldiers on our estates as good as those in France. Our own arms shall make us independent and respectable. If we are once forced to desperate means, it will be

---

[6]Valerie Quinney, "Decision on Slavery, the Slave Trade, and Civil Rights for Negroes in the Early French Revolution," *Journal of Negro History* 55 (1970): 127.

in vain that thousands are sent across the Atlantic to bring us back to our former state.[7]

Ogé's anguished outburst reveals that he already envisaged the possibility of a forceful resolution of the issue of civil rights for freedmen of color. A few months later Ogé would launch his abortive revolt to obtain these rights, only to be captured and executed on the wheel at Cap Français in January 1791.

When Ogé referred to "our former state" he meant the treatment of freedmen of color (especially since the 1760s), and not treatment of slaves, which was quite another matter. Clarkson's dinner discussions with the six deputies of color in Paris gives an idea of their views on race relations, at least as understood by Clarkson. They said the slave trade was bad, not only because of its obvious cruelty, but also because it perpetuated "hateful distinctions" between the whites and themselves. The "infamy now fixed upon a skin of color (must) be done away with so that whites and blacks could meet cordially and look with respect upon one another." Did Clarkson understand the deputies of color to say respect for "blacks" or for "*gens de couleur*"? In any case, they stopped short of recommending immediate emancipation of black slaves. They said they were instructed to propose immediate abolition of the slave trade and an immediate amelioration of the state of slavery also, with a view to its final abolition in fifteen years.[8]

Julien Raimond was much less willing to propose even gradual emancipation of black slaves, and I do not think his reticence on this issue was only tactical. Raimond was very conscious of his education, wealth, and degree of whiteness. In one of his many pamphlets he seemed to take umbrage at being called a "mulatto." "If I were one, I should not blush about it, *but* I am the legitimate son and grandson of European fathers and landowners of Saint-Domingue. Can [even] Moreau de Saint-Méry say as much?"[9] Raimond wanted it known that he had only one black grandparent. Like many freedmen of color, the Raimonds had made their way over several generations of family networking in the region of coffee and indigo plantations in southern Saint-Domingue. The Raimonds had developed a coffee plantation with over seventy slaves and, as he said in a letter to his brother in 1793, "One could hardly suppose that I should want to ruin [by emancipation] at one stroke my entire family

[7]Clarkson, *The History of the Slave Trade*, 2:264.   [8]Ibid., 2:252–54.
[9]Mercer Cook, "Julien Raimond," *Journal of Negro History* 26 (1941): 153.

who possess . . . seven or eight million [livres] in property in Saint-Domingue."[10]

That Raimond was dedicated to the rights of the people of color can not be doubted. He sacrificed most of his personal fortune to publishing, lobbying, and traveling on their behalf. He was a master of contemporary political rhetoric and knew how important it was to convince his Parisian audience that he was a good patriot and anxious to keep Saint-Domingue French. The rights of freedmen were always embedded in the entire litany of revolutionary grievances: "Arbitrary power, ministerial despotism, remnants of the feudal regime, inequality between one citizen and another . . . abuse of the laws, the barbarous prejudices and humiliating customs which degrade humanity through us." Unlike Ogé, Raimond was very careful about flirtation with violence. As the "unfortunate victims of the aristocracy of whites," we might exercise the "right of resistance to oppression, but we have a distaste for violence against our fathers and brothers [whites] and still more against our Fatherland."[11]

In an almost Burkean manner Raimond argued that white prejudice against his people was an innovation since the 1760s, when a whole new generation of young whites arrived on the island to be faced with a growing number of prosperous mulattoes and freedmen. He reviewed the recent laws that had restricted the professional employment of people of color (in the civil service, law, medicine, many trades), and most resented the removal of the terms *Sieur* and *Dame* and even of Christian names and substitution of *the African idiom* in all legal documents to remind the people of color of their black origin. "It is not innovation," he wrote, "to restore our rights of thirty years ago."

In his appeal to the law, and in his sense of the broader issues of the Revolution in France and how to blend freedmen's rights with those of all French citizens, Raimond represented the group on the island that understood best what "liberté" meant as a tissue of human rights under law. Of course Raimond was not typical of thirty thousand *gens de couleur,* most of whom were black *nègres libres,* many freed without notarized documentation or even claiming freedom as maroons, the *soi-distant libres.* Raimond was a prosperous French-educated coffee planter, while most freedmen were artisans, shopkeepers, cattlemen, small proprietors, handymen, and "housekeepers," to employ the colonial euphemism. Yet all of the *affranchis* had property rights, which gave them an entry into the

[10]Ibid., 142.   [11]Ibid., 145.

European's world of legal paper and that unique Latin institution, the *notariat*.

In his recent thesis, John Garrigus explores this "notarial" world.[12] Let us turn from the crowded agenda of the Assemblée Nationale to the coffee and indigo plantations on the southern peninsula of Saint-Domingue. Here, from Cayes to Léogane was the stronghold of the island's mulatto population, where the *gens de couleur* in many parishes were equal in number to the whites, even by the "official" census. Wills, codicils, marriage contracts, death inventories, partnership agreements, sales, rentals, gifts in life, manumissions—the panoply of property registration and legitimation—was especially important to a group of property owners, large and small, whose legal and social status had been increasingly threatened since the end of the Seven Years' War. Given the scarcity of administrators, judges, and even priests outside of the two main ports, the notary played a much more important role than in the metropole. He had become a kind of justice of the peace who recorded depositions and settled disputes of contract or even of physical assault and verbal insult, especially common in this racial society. Garrigus shows that, whereas in any physical conflict or vocal dispute between freedmen and whites, the freedmen could rarely win, in the notarial world contracts were enforced and even a free mulatto might gain compensation in cash for having been beaten by a white.

This is not to say that contract law could completely compensate for a formal criminal law that prescribed imprisonment for a freedman who did not show sufficient respect to a white, and even death if he struck one. But the pervasive notarial apparatus did several things. It made the people of color aware that they had property rights, guaranteeing, for example, the execution of the will of a white father, the purchase of land, or the rental contract of slaves. Freedmen were very conscientious about notarizing their marriages, property titles, and manumission papers and with good reason. In criminal matters they learned that recorded depositions and the use of witnesses gave them hope of redressing grievances if only because a white offender might not want to go through the trouble of a legal procedure. There are cases of whites paying compensation to freedmen by private arrangement to avoid legal costs. In short, the freedmen were learning about the *potential* use of the law as a procedure that

[12]John Garrigus, "A Struggle for Respect: The Free Coloreds of Saint-Dominique, 1760–1768." Ph.D. diss., Johns Hopkins University, 1988.

followed its own rules free of arbitrary human action. They were also aware that this legal system was foreign to the island, at least to the slave world around them, and that the whites of Saint-Domingue and those of the metropole might not all share the same notion of law. No wonder the *gens de couleur* were little attracted to separatism in 1789. Raimond's protestations of the loyalty of the mulattoes to the French Republic even as late as 1798 was no ruse.

In Paris in 1789, the *citoyens des couleurs* called upon their long experience with French property law, assuring the National Assembly that they, too, were proud French citizens.

The Declaration of the Rights of Man revealed to them what they were worth, and their vision was immediately directed, not towards license and insubordination, as some have accused, but towards that precious liberty *assured them by the laws* and that they must share with you.[13]

Unfortunately, fine words about "precious liberty" were not enough. The spotty efforts of freedmen to participate in parish elections in 1789 had resulted in a series of lynchings for mulattoes and public humiliations for the few whites who supported them. These early atrocities went unnoticed in Paris, but the execution of Vincent Ogé and a large number of his followers at Cap Français in January 1791 did not go unnoticed. The Club Massiac blamed these "disorders" on the *Amis des Noirs* and renewed its lobbying campaign by an appeal to the port cities, a tactic so effective only a few months earlier. But this time the ports did not respond, while the petitions *for* the people of color gained a hearing in the Assembly. For many deputies, voting rights for freedmen did not threaten the slave trade or slavery; the two issues could now be kept distinct. Perhaps the "disorders" in the island could be defused by extending the vote to freedmen. Even many white planters had referred to the people of color as an "intermediary class," a kind of buffer between white and black slave.

Raimond blamed the whites in the island, but he was careful not to identify himself too closely with Ogé's abortive revolt except to say that Ogé had reason to revolt and that he shed a tear for him. Brissot, the future republican and Girondin leader, was less restrained. Ogé was a martyr to his cause. The issue of 1 May 1791 of his *Patriots Français* exploded:

[13]Dxxv 85, dossier 823, pièce 14, Archives Nationales, Paris, cited in Garrigus, "Struggle for Respect," 5. Emphasis added.

Ogé is dead . . . expired on the wheel . . . succumbed while claiming the Rights of Man [for the people of color] which the whites refused them. . . . At Saint Dominigue the heads of the defenders of Liberty roll down upon the scaffold.[14]

At last the Assembly faced the issue of civil rights for the freedmen without hiding behind the evasive language of Barnave's committee. The emerging "Left"—Brissot, Pétion, Grégoire, Robespierre—openly debated the old colonial hands—Malouet, Moreau de Saint-Méry, Barnave, Clermont-Tonnerre—who warned that hasty action could lead to secession and loss of the colony. Robespierre launched the rhetorical flourish he would regret three years later: "Perish the colonies if they must cost you your honor and your glory!"

The decree of 15 May 1791 did not grant all freedmen the right to vote. It stipulated that "Every man born of a free father and a free mother" could vote, which eliminated almost all free blacks and most free mulattoes since few had free mothers. Probably less than a thousand freedmen out of thirty thousand gained full citizenship by the measure. Nevertheless, the Rubicon had at last been crossed. The principle was established that color was not a bar to civil rights. With persistence of commitment, determined enforcement, and gradual extension of the new law it is possible, even probable, that the freedmen would have remained loyal to the metropole. Unfortunately, in the face of violent opposition among whites of the island to the May decree and the unexpected massive slave revolt three months later, the Assembly again wavered, and in September 1791 revoked the law of 15 May.

William Cohen, Seymour Drescher, and Daniel Resnick are surely right to emphasize a lack of commitment of the majority of deputies (and indeed of the French public at large) to racial equality if it threatened loss of Saint-Dominique. The valiant core of Amis des Noirs were too readily labeled an English import bent on weakening French presence in the world. "Prudent men" like Barnave, Lameth, Chapelier and many more among the five hundred La Rochefoucauld told Clarkson might vote abolition of the slave trade *if* the English would do the same were not mean-spirited people consumed by racial fear and hatred. Nevertheless, in the final reckoning they expressed their nationalism abroad more in terms of tangible muscle (trade figures, real estate, naval bases) than in the universal applicability of the Rights of Man. To be sure, the "regeneration of human kind" was a worthy ideal, but the "regeneration of

[14]Cook, "Julien Raimond," 147–48.

France" came first. Moreover, perfidious Albion had been a known element in world politics much before 1789, and English profession of abolition of slavery should not be taken at face value. In many French eyes, the
cause of the blacks was not enhanced by an English embrace. As William
Cohen demonstrates so well, this attitude would persist in the French
parliament well into the nineteenth century.[15]

Did the great slave revolt that began in August 1791 and lasted thirteen
years have anything to do with *liberté*? Of course, on a basic level it did.
To use Michael Craton's phrase, the slaves "tested the chains," and in this
unique case in Western history, they succeeded in breaking them.[16] It
would do injustice to their achievement not to call this "liberty." But it
was quite a different thing from the principles of law and "precious
liberty" espoused by Julien Raimond and the leaders of the people of
color. Surely it was different again from separatism, the "spirit of autonomy" of the white settlers of Saint Marc or of the racist sansculottism of
the *petits blancs* of Cap Français and Port-au-Prince. It was not even the
liberty of the *Amis des Noirs* in Paris, for even Grégoire thought the slave
revolt was a "disaster," and Raimond published a plan to restore the
rebellious slaves to their masters.[17] Only a tiny handful of Europeans or
people of color could approve of this kind of liberty—immediate emancipation of African slaves.

I use the adjective "African" on purpose. For the origins of the revolt
and the nature of its goals must be understood largely in African terms.
Jean Fouchard entitles his book on the Haitian maroons *Maroons of
Liberty,* and he insists that they are *black* maroons just as the majority of
*affranchis* were *black* (*négres libres*) and not mulattoes. For Fouchard, the
leadership, the catalyst for the slave revolt comes from the black maroons
who had already tasted the freedom of a community of runaways. We
need a work like that of Richard Price on the maroons of Surinam to learn
if the maroons of Saint-Domingue had developed an alternative Afro-
Creole culture. Other historians like Debbasch and Pluchon would argue
that most maroons were in the towns, not in the mountains, suggesting a
more Euro-Creole culture. This line of inquiry could be pursued, though I

---

[15]William B. Cohen, *The French Encounter with Africans: White Response to Blacks*
(Bloomington, Ind., 1980). See also Seymour Drescher, *Econocide: British Slavery in the
Era of Abolition* (Pittsburgh, 1977).
[16]Michael Craton, *Testing the Chains* (Ithaca, N.Y., 1982).   [17]Ibid., 161.

am not convinced that the key to the slave revolt lies with the maroons, African, Creole, or Euro-Creole.[18]

Let us turn back to demography. In the fourteen years before 1789 the slave population increased from 260,000 to 465,000. When we consider that death rates exceeded birth rates among slaves by about 2 percent per annum, we can say with certainty that by 1789 well over half the slaves of Saint-Domingue were African born. Now, how were Africans, known as "Bosalles" by the Creole slaves, normally socialized on the island? On the plantations it was customary to disperse the newcomers among the slave families (*ménages*) to learn to speak, cook, and work in the Creole manner. They also had to pray daily in front of the master, and after a year they were baptized, which for Europeans was a kind of rite of passage into Creole society and into the cane fields. It was the end of the "seasoning." Not all newcomers went directly to the plantations in the plains. More and more went to the *mornes* (bluffs) to clear land for coffee, but they too were mixed with Creole slaves in the labor gangs.[19] Some might be rented out to an entrepreneur or artisan in town, but most "seasoning" took place in the countryside.

Now, what happened when an avalanche of Africans arrived on Saint-Domingue in the 1770s and 1780s? Melville Herskovits, whose field-work on Haiti and life work on acculturation inspire confidence, suggests that the kind of interchange between Creole and African slave described above does not go only one way. It is a common Eurocentric notion that acculturation must proceed in favor of the dominant culture. In the case of Saint-Domingue in these years the probabilities of an African penetration of Creole customs and culture must have been especially high. Herskovits stressed that, even in the 1930s, the "tenacity of Africanisms" was marked in all sectors of Haitian society.[20] Moreover, he traced many of these Africanisms, religion especially, to a relatively small part of Africa, Dahomey (Benin). This brings us to voodoo and a very large literature which could take us far afield.

One does not, however, have to establish a precise link between voo-

---

[18]Richard Price, ed., *Maroon Societies: Rebel Slave Communities in the Americas* (Baltimore, 1979); Yvan Debbasch, *Couleur et Liberté* (Paris, 1967); Pierre Pluchon, *Histoire des Antilles et de la Guyane* (Toulouse, 1982).

[19]"Manuscrit d'un Voyage de France à Saint Dominique, à las havanne et aux Etats-Unis d'Amerique, 1789–1904," Ms. 1816, John Carter Brown Library, Brown University, 53–54.

[20]Melville J. Herskovits, *Life in a Haitian Valley* (New York, 1937), 292ff.

doo and the Haitian slave revolt, despite the alleged role of voodoo priests in the "blood pact" that presumably took place immediately before the massive burning of the cane fields in the Plain du Nord. More important is African culture taken as a whole and its relation to the white European culture on the island. Herskovits speculates on what the black image of the whites on the island must have been like. There was indeed a firm basis not only for separate identity but for moral superiority. Surely for a black slave, the voodoo deities offered more hope in this world than the white man's God.

Another aspect of the white man's (and freedman's) culture was the notarial world of registers and contracts discussed above. Both Father Labat and Moreau de Saint-Méry, excellent observers, noted that nothing struck the newly arrived African slaves more than the white man's ability to make paper talk. "What astonishes them the most in whites," wrote Moreau, "is writing, the communication of ideas, and they say that the Whites would have called the Negroes sorcerers if they had made this precious discovery."[21] It was this kind of sorcery that the voodoo loas were intended to ward off, like those whites who drank human blood by the barrel. How strange were even those free blacks who signed papers and gained a mule or a *nigrette* in exchange!

No doubt, the ratio of almost 20:1 of black slave to white freedman tempts one to speak as Michael Craton does about the Tobago risings in the 1770s: "The almost inevitable result was the slave revolt of the African type."[22] Craton is not usually glib, and he did not mean that numbers alone determined the revolt. One has to be impressed by the ability of a handful of whites to control and work hundreds of slaves on isolated plantations for almost a century on Saint-Domingue. No, something else had to happen. I suggest a growing cultural abyss, maintained in part by those "nocturnal meetings" the French could never suppress despite the myriad regulations against drumbeating, herbal medicine, amulets, and certain kinds of dress. Nor did the French understand the cultural import of something like the Calenda, the African dance that almost always accompanied the baptismal ceremony of African slaves.[23] Only later did whites draw a connection between an African dance and an act of revenge. Morange, a plantation manager at Le Cap in 1803 just before the

---

[21]Moreau de Saint-Méry, *Description de la partie française de l'Isle de Saint-Dominique,* 3 vols. (Paris, 1984), 1:79. See also Garrigus, "Struggle for Respect."
[22]Michael Craton, *Testing the Chains* (Ithaca, N.Y., 1982), 153.
[23]"Manuscrit d'un Voyage," 1:170.

end, wrote: "They are dancing the *vaudou*—an obscene dance to encourage murder—in two spots in town. We have just hung one of the principal actors. . . . This dance is a sinister prelude."[24]

The events of 1789 on the island were not irrelevant to the black uprising. But circumstances and even a certain litany of words and signs are not the same things as a revolutionary message or the acceptance of a Eurocentric notion of "liberty" among the slaves. Something sparked the revolt, but the combustible pile began to form in the 1780s in the decade of the sugar and coffee boom when the African slave imports passed twenty thousand a year. Raimond's "precious liberty under law" had little to do with that combustible pile.

Philip Curtin is right to stress the effect the conflicts among whites and between whites and freedmen in 1789 must have had on the blacks.[25] Most slaves could not read the Declaration of Rights of Man—more white sorcery?—but did they wonder about other visual artifacts of the Revolution? Morange was at Le Cap in October 1789 when the first news of the summer in Paris arrived. "The heads of the negroes are beginning to dilate here. The sight of the cockade gives them ideas. So does the news from France which circulates without discretion."[26] Three weeks later he evoked the rumor of the Good King and the bad master. "We have spoken so much about liberty for the negroes that finally the word has reached their ears. Many of them imagine that the King has granted them freedom and that their masters will not consent."[27]

Morange continued that the slave gangs were very restless, making outrageous remarks and that they could be controlled only by "fear of punishment." "We can not get the blacks to work and it is easy to see that if something breaks out on one plantation, it will be the signal for all the others."[28] The massive plantation revolt was still two years off, but white society was beginning to fissure, and the magic of white supremacy was fading. That is why the year 1790 was crucial, if not fatal, to white survival on Saint-Domingue.

In January 1804 Haiti became the first black republic in the history of the Americas and perhaps of the world. Its birth pains were staggering, and the legacy of racial war and a successful slave revolt was diplomatic

[24]Begouën Demeaux, *Mémorial*, 2:223.
[25]Philip D. Curtin, "The Declaration of the Rights of Man in Saint-Dominique, 1788–1791," *Hispanic American Review* 30 (1950): 157–75.
[26]Demeaux, *Mémorial*, 2:135. [27]Ibid., 2:137. [28]Ibid.

ostracism and economic hardship. A peasant society emerged slowly from the wreckage of war, one built on the slave plots of the Old Regime. The ex-slaves would not go back to the plantations even under the dragooning of a Toussaint-Louverture. Nor did they submit to Toussaint's and Dessaline's attempts to substitute Catholicism for voodoo. Their efforts seemed to confirm voodoo's potential for local and clan independence. The political legacy was more African than French, despite Toussaint's obvious taste for French administrative organization. As Herskovits suggests, a European option was not viable for the mass of ex-slaves. The choice would rather be between Ashanti-style centralization under an absolute monarch or a loose federation of clan networks and pastoral communities.[29] Either way, as the subsequent history of Haiti demonstrates, it would not be a government conducive to European notions of liberty under law.

Philosophical ideals about freedom and equality rarely operate in a vacuum. Here, the dimension of color and colonial status, economic interest and power politics, both national and international, greatly clouded thinking about the meaning of that shiny new ideal so much evoked in the revolutionary decade. Pierre Pluchon, in his excellent history of the French Antilles, boldly faces the issue of the French "regenerators" of 1789: "Was not the new ideology made by the Whites and for them only?"[30] Perhaps the greater tragedy, however, was that the Eurocentric notion of liberty under law that Julien Raimond had learned so well was not understood by at least a quarter of a million *African-born* slaves in 1789. We must deplore the hypocrisy of so many whites in Paris, their violent racism on Saint-Domingue, and even their failure to see their own economic and national interests clearly. Abbé Grégoire's "aristocracy of the epidermis" was also part of that Eurocentric culture. But we should also see tragedy in the political limitations of an Afro-Creole culture at this particular moment in the history of the Caribbean.

[29]Herskovits, *Life in a Haitian Valley,* 299.
[30]Pierre Pluchon, *Histoire des Antilles et de la Guyane* (Toulouse, 1982), 195.

# 6

‑‑‑‑‑‑‑‑‑‑‑‑‑‑‑‑‑‑‑‑‑‑‑‑‑‑‑‑‑‑‑‑‑‑

## Unfinished business: colonialism
## in sub-Saharan Africa and the ideals
## of the French Revolution

### CHRISTOPHER L. MILLER

Nous autres Français, nous avons la particularité d'être universels. [We French
have the particularity of being universal.]

Paul Valéry

François Mitterrand, in his speech commemorating and explicating the
French Revolution delivered at Versailles in June 1988, stated a simple
premise that is at the heart of the problem I wish to address here. He said,
"The Revolution made the Republic. The Republic cannot, without deny-
ing itself, forget what it is, where it came from, the thinking from which it
proceeds, the ideal on which it is based, the movement that it embodies.
For the Republic is not an empty form."[1] From a perspective encompassing attention to African history, this statement is charged with ambiguity:
To say that the Revolution and the succeeding republics of France have
straightforwardly "proceeded" from the ideals of the Declaration of the
Rights of Man, as the incarnation of those ideals, is to ignore what
happened and what continues to happen in relations between France and
Africa. The thought from which the Revolution proceeded has proved
from the beginning tremendously difficult to translate into foreign relations, particularly in regard to the Third World. Two problems present
themselves.

First is the obvious and explicit problem of slavery. No greater challenge was faced by the thinkers of the Revolution than that of living up to

---

[1]François Mitterrand, speech at Versailles, 20 June 1989, quoted in *Libération*, 22 June
1989, 39.

the ideal of liberty in regard to persons who had been considered as property. The failure of the Constituent Assembly to abolish slavery immediately, and its abdication of responsibility for suffrage and freedom within the colonies, was one of the great failures of the Revolution.[2] Siradiou Diallo, writing in the bicentennial issue of *Jeune Afrique*, says that the Revolution suffered from an "original sin" in its relations with Africans in particular.[3] Even after the Convention declared abolition on 4 February 1794, not all was solved in any definitive way. Slavery was simply reestablished by Napoleon in 1802, and the first nation to abolish slavery became the first to restore it. Abolitionism in France had to gear itself back up and struggle throughout the first half of the nineteenth century. So the first problem is slavery and the obstacle it presents to the implementation of revolutionary ideals.

Anna Cooper, in her thesis on the attitude of France toward slavery during the Revolution, rehearses this problem and concludes her study with a point that I would like to call into question. Cooper considers the reestablishment of slavery in the colonies—this *marche arrière* (back-pedaling) as she calls it—as a simple delay of fifty years, followed by France's coming to its senses and finally living up to its ideals; that is, the republic of 1848 "proceeds" from the ideals of 1789 and puts them into practice by definitively abolishing slavery. Cooper describes a simple mechanism of delayed implementation:

If the attitude of revolutionary France does not seem at first to have been sufficiently in agreement with its principles, we will see that these principles will triumph nonetheless, less than half a century later, because, as A. Cochin said, these principles are immortal. . . . France will regain slowly but surely the reasonable path of her thinking. Years will pass, but a man will come who, after Brissot, will let his eloquent words dedicated to the same cause be heard in a French Chamber. . . . Another revolution, the daughter and heir of the 1789 Revolution, will be necessary so that Lamartine can say: "Three days after the February revolution, I signed the emancipation of the blacks, the abolition of slavery, and the promise of compensation to the colonists."[4]

If the most obvious problem in the implementation of revolutionary ideals is thus finally solved in 1848, the second, more insidious problem

---

[2]See David Brion Davis, *The Problem of Slavery in the Age of Revolution, 1770–1823* (Ithaca: Cornell University Press, 1975), 28.
[3]Siradiou Diallo, "France-Afrique: l'héritage de 1789," *Jeune Afrique* 1489 (19 July 1989): 32.
[4]Anna J. Cooper, *L'attitude de la France à l'égard de l'esclavage pendant la Révolution, thèse pour le doctorat d'université* (Paris: Imprimerie de la Cour d'Appel, 1925), 128.

is left unanswered: that of colonialism and colonization. The quotation from Lamartine already shows this: Slaves will be freed, but colonial planters will be indemnified and left in place; the "right" of colonization remains unquestioned. How can this be reconciled with the ideals of the Revolution?

My aim in this essay is to explore a certain pattern of forced and dubious reconciliation between the ideals of the Revolution and France's nationalistic and imperialistic tendencies. The pattern is clear: the ideals of the Revolution, by the very fact that they are taken to be immutable and immortal, are pressed into service as justifications for various policies of domination and exploitation. In certain cases, the word *perversion* is not too strong to describe this misuse of the values of 1789. I am concerned here in particular with the idea that French colonialism passes for *the exportation of the ideals of 1789.*

This idea, as paradoxical as it may seem, served as the most compelling rationale for colonialism and continues to make itself felt in the post-colonial (or neocolonial) era, although it now wears new clothes. Two problems thus concern me: first, that the ideal of liberty, as it was translated into nineteenth-century contexts, became a banner of *liberalism* under which ardent republicans such as Tocqueville and Lamartine advocated colonial conquest and rule; second, that the nineteenth- and twentieth-century institutionalization of a colonial policy of "assimilation" was conceived of as the exportation of the ideals of 1789. These two developments represent further wrinkles in the triumph of the Revolution, beyond the question of slavery, into the complexities of imperialism, colonialism, and postcolonial culture in Africa. Particularly in the case of twentieth-century assimilation policy, this essay will show how the Revolution and its ideals have been used precisely as the "empty form" that Mitterrand says they cannot be: as images whose substance has been ignored. My itinerary will cover a variety of examples, spanning political and literary discourses, concentrating on Lamartine, Tocqueville, Ahmadou Mapate Diagne, and Léopold Sédar Senghor, without attempting to trace a complete genealogy or give a sense of actual causality.

I would like to begin by returning to Lamartine, who, in florid prose, describes his own role in the realization of revolutionary ideals. In the preface to his play "Toussaint-Louverture," written in 1850, Lamartine writes for himself what appears to be his own wishful epitaph on his role in history: "The February Revolution broke out. I then had the pleasure, rather rare for a statesman whom the people had improvised, to be at once the philosophical orator and the political executor of one of the most holy and memorable acts of this nation and this period, of a watershed in the history of the human race."[5] Lamartine goes on to say: "If my life had consisted only of that moment, I would not regret having lived." He then summarizes the state of affairs for which he was responsible in the following words: "The black man is free, the colonist is indemnified, competition is establishing itself, everyone is going back to work." Life goes on, and commerce remains undisturbed by this great social transformation, the end of slavery.

Lamartine had been for many years a passionate abolitionist. In his "Discours sur l'émancipation des esclaves" ("Discourse on the Emancipation of the Slaves"), delivered before the Chamber of Deputies in 1838, Lamartine invokes the ideals of the Revolution in order to shame the nation into seeing the evil of slavery. He asks the deputies if they are sure that

each of the Chambers that will succeed us will continue with this shameful anomaly of *a nation which before any other put philosophy and religion in its laws,* which spilled its blood without counting how many drops and torrents in the name of political reform and liberty, *which has made a sacred flag of equality,* which has sanctified, so to speak, the rights of citizens, and which would forget to such a degree human rights and dignity and would continue to cover up with a false liberty the most shameful degradations, the most infamous cruelties that can dishonor humanity?[6]

As political rhetoric, this is a masterful exercise in the application of an ideal. The Revolution of 1789 is held before the deputies' eyes as a model that they can either follow or fail; the current state of affairs—the unfinished business of the Revolution—hangs over them. But it should be noted as well that the germ of French nationalism is already present in this ethical appeal: France must consider its own identity as inseparable from *philosophie* and religion, but France is therefore glorified as a nation—if only it will live up to its claims. Nationalism and idealism are melded together in Lamartine's phrase, "a sacred flag of equality."

On the explicit question of abolition, Lamartine's passion does not lead him to any extremist positions. He, like so many others, is concerned that emancipation be "useful, normal, politic, without scandal or dan-

---

[5] Alphonse-Marie-Louis de Prat de Lamartine, preface to "Toussaint-Louverture," in *Oeuvres complètes* (Paris: Chez l'auteur, 1863), 32:6. Further references to this work, abbreviated *TS*, will be included in the text.

[6] Lamartine, "Discours sur l'émancipation des esclaves," 15 February 1838, in *Recueillements poétiques, poésies diverses et discours* (Paris: Pagnerre, 1863), 314. Emphasis in original. Further references to this work, abbreviated *DE*, will appear in the text.

ger" (*DE*, 348). Justice dictates that slaveowners be indemnified for their loss, and prudence requires that slaves be given an eight- to ten-year "apprenticeship" in freedom, during which time they will work *without wages*. The slave will help defray the costs of his or her freedom (see *DE*, 323). This is what Lamartine calls "une loyale émancipation" (*DE*, 320)—that is, legal, regulated, and nonthreatening.

Toward the end of the same speech, Lamartine turns the crucial corner, from a discourse of liberty (albeit limited and "gradual") to a discourse of veiled conquest. The moral imperative of abolitionism will become the flag of imperialism, all within Lamartine's thought. Finishing up his balance sheet on the costs of emancipation, he turns his attention to the world at large, and invites the Chamber to consider this:

Ah! Gentlemen, the opportunity has never been and will never be as fine for extinguishing slavery, not only in the colonies, but *in the entire universe*. Yes, gentlemen, thanks to events that were unforeseen, providential, independent of you and attributable to the political state of the world, you can cut off slavery in the world. You repress it, you take hold of it by the two extremities of Asia and Africa. . . . It is up to you. Say the word, declare the emancipation of blacks in your colonies, and slavery will be cut off everywhere. (*DE*, 324–35; emphasis added)

Leaving aside Lamartine's overlooking slavery in the United States—part of a general pattern of hyperbole here—we should be attentive to his underlying assumptions. In the same speech, he mentions that slavery *and polygamy* are disappearing in Constantinople. By implication, Western intervention will finish this dual task everywhere. His mention of polygamy in the same breath as slavery should give us a hint of the broader agenda, a program of social reform. This program is, in a word, the famous *mission civilisatrice,* of which Lamartine is one of the earliest and most articulate advocates.[7]

Speaking again in Paris two years later, at a banquet that brought together abolitionists from France, England, and the United States, Lamartine used rhetoric that clarifies the relation between idealism and imperial nationalism. Appealing to the union of the French and British movements, Lamartine stated, "England and France will remain united: we two together are the pedestal of the rights of mankind."[8]

Lamartine's nationalism here is the exception to the rule in that he is

[7]It is also well known that King Léopold of the Belgians exploited the slavery issue as a pretext for conquest of the Congo. (In the Tervuren Musée Royal de l'Afrique Centrale, near Brussels, there is a rotunda with a series of allegorical statues, including one called "Belgium Liberating the Congo.")

[8]Lamartine, "Discours sur l'abolition de l'esclavage," 10 February 1840, in *Recueillements poétiques*, 371.

appealing to international cooperation between two nation-states, each of which is construed as the embodiment of an ideal. There was always room in Lamartine's thought for healthy European cooperation and rivalry based on common goals. But what will endure after him will be the idea of France alone, above all others, as the standard-bearer of revolutionary ideals or, in late-twentieth-century language, of human rights. (There was an interesting echo of Lamartine in an exhibit at the Centre Georges Pompidou in the summer of 1989 entitled, "French and English, Languages of Human Rights.")

Lamartine did not say in 1838 exactly how the French Chamber of Deputies could effect a worldwide program of social reform—how they could eliminate slavery from every corner of the globe, and perhaps polygamy and other distasteful practices as well. The assembled deputies may all have been familiar with something Lamartine had written on the subject a few years earlier, a text that prescribed precise answers to these questions.

In 1832 and 1833, Lamartine had made the pilgrimage—nearly obligatory for the writers of Romanticism—to "the Orient," following the route established by Chateaubriand earlier in the century, clockwise around the Mediterranean from Greece to Spain. The voyage was literary in conception, and its culmination was naturally a book: *Souvenirs, impressions, pensées et paysages pendant un voyage en Orient*, published in 1835. At the end of the last volume, the future president of the Second Republic added what he called a "Résumé politique," summarizing his conclusions. It is a chilling document. By "the right of humanity and civilization," he writes, European powers must satisfy their natural need for expansion by taking over the "magnificent debris" of the Ottoman Empire, "so that the human race will multiply and grow there, and civilization will be expanded."[9] "Europe, united in the purpose of *conserving and civilizing the human species,* has incontestably the capability to *control the fate of Asia*" (*RP*, 330; emphasis added). The Empire will be amicably and peacefully divided between the European powers, who will

[9]Lamartine, "Résumé politique," in *Souvenirs, impressions, pensées et paysages pendant un voyage in Orient* (Brussels: J. P. Meline, 1835), 4:321. Further references to this work, abbreviated *RP*, will appear in the text. See my commentary in 23 December 1847 entry, ("Orientalism, Colonialism") of *A New History of French Literature*, ed. Denis Hollier (Cambridge, Mass.: Harvard University Press, 1989), 698–705. On Lamartine's voyage, see Edward Said, *Orientalism* (New York: Vintage Books, 1978), 177–81; on his intellectual relation to the east, see Raymond Schwab, *The Oriental Renaissance*, trans. Gene Patterson-Black and Victor Reinking (New York: Columbia University Press, 1984), 354–62.

exercise *"an armed and civilizing guardianship,* that each power will exert over its protectorate" (*RP*, 323; emphasis added); "There is not a cannon shot to be fired . . . not a violation of religion or custom to be authorized . . . " (*RP*, 330).

What Lamartine's "Résumé" sums up is the ability of European (and later, American) powers to have their cake and eat it too: to subjugate and exploit foreign lands for their own economic advantage, while justifying their actions on moral grounds such as the abolition of slavery and polygamy.[10] This is how the *mission civilisatrice* works. The kind of protectorate that Lamartine proposes is supposed to maintain republican ideals like freedom of religion ("All religions will continue to exist side by side, in openness and mutual independence" [*RP*, 325]), but it will nonetheless impose new strictures: "the protecting local law will recognize neither polygamy nor slavery, but it will not intervene in private matters such as family life or a person's conscience" (*RP*, 326). The contradiction between banning polygamy and claiming not to interfere in the structure of the family seems to escape Lamartine.

There is thus a crucial difference between Lamartine's attitude toward slavery and his stance on colonialism. On the one hand he liberates, on the other he subjugates; but within the terms of his discourse, both are moments of liberation. The curious thing is that the two impulses—the abolitionist urge and the desire for colonial expansion—both use the ideals of the 1789 Revolution as rhetorical fuel.

A similar pattern is found in Tocqueville. The author of *Democracy in America*, who "found himself in the democratic values that derived from the French Revolution,"[11] and who condemned slavery as an offense against natural law,[12] argued along with Lamartine that gradual

---

[10]The following passage from V. S. Naipaul's novel *The Bend in the River* (New York: Alfred A. Knopf, 1979) sums up this idea most eloquently: "The Europeans could do one thing and say something quite different; and they could act in this way because they had an idea of what they owed to their civilization. It was their great advantage over us. The Europeans wanted gold and slaves, like everybody else; but at the same time they wanted statues put up to themselves as people who had done good things for the slaves. Being an intelligent and energetic people, and at the peak of their powers, they could express both sides of their civilization; and they got both the slaves and the statues" (17).

[11]Tzvetan Todorov, Introduction to Tocqueville, *De la colonie en Algérie* (Paris: Editions Complexe, 1988), 10. Further references to this work, abbreviated *CA*, will appear in the text.

[12]Tocqueville, *Ecrits politiques 1*, tome 3 of *Oeuvres complètes*, ed. Andre Jardin (Paris: Gallimard, 1962), 330. Further references to the two volumes of *Ecrits politiques*, abbreviated *EP 1* and *EP 2*, will appear in the text. *CA* (see previous note) consists of excerpts from the *Ecrits politiques*, and I shall refer to *CA* when the passage is to be found in this more accessible volume.

emancipation—generation by generation—would be impractical and dangerous (*EP* 1: 49–54). Like Lamartine, Tocqueville is concerned with maintaining the economic and social order:

France, gentlemen, does not desire to abolish slavery in order to witness the painful sight of shattered whites leaving the soil of the colonies and blacks digressing back into barbarism. France does not intend only to grant liberty to men deprived of it, but to build civilized, industrious, and peaceful societies. . . . It is thus necessary that the home country, after granting compensation to the colonists, act upon the slave via firm and prudent legislation, to familiarize him first then bend him *to the painstaking and manly ways of liberty.* (*EP* 1:59; emphasis added)

In other words, abolition will *perfect* colonialism by ridding it of an anomalous and dangerous moral flaw. Once slavery is abolished, the social order of the colonies will remain largely the same, with French law firmly "bending" former slaves in the direction required for the smooth operation of the economy.

The idea of liberty as a derivative of the French Revolution motivates Tocqueville's arguments, as it motivated Lamartine's. In the following passage from an article Tocqueville published in 1843 (quoted by Todorov in his introduction to *CA*), we see a similar blend of idealism and nationalism, the notion that France must live up to the values it "invented" in 1789:

These notions of liberty and equality which everywhere today are shaking or destroying forms of servitude—who spread them throughout the universe? This unselfish and yet passionate feeling of the love of mankind which has suddenly made Europe attentive to the cries of slaves—who propagated it, directed, and enlightened it? *It is we, ourselves.* . . . This has been not only our glory, but also our strength (*EP* 1:88). . . . *It is we* who are the true authors of the abolition of slavery (*EP* 1:125; emphasis added).

In this insistence on the first person plural, one sees the crucial hinge between the ideal and the practical or national dimensions of Tocqueville's thinking. Because France embodies an ideal, France can only do good by advancing its own self-interests in the world: idealism and nationalism will both be served.

Thus, the apparent contradiction, which Tzvetan Todorov addresses in his discussion of Tocqueville's works on Algeria—the contradiction between revolutionary values and colonial conquest[13]—does not trouble

---

[13]"De Tocqueville se reconnaît dans les principes démocratique issus de la Révolution française; . . . il n'est pas évident que la conquête coloniale puisse être justifiée au nom de ces mêmes principes" (Todorov, Introduction to *CA*).

Tocqueville himself. Once France is understood to be a force for moral good, and so long as France's ideals are not put into question, France can behave as it wants. Hence there is a smooth transition in Tocqueville's writings, a simultaneity between his idealistic antislavery and pro-democracy positions and statements like the following, which have been brought to light by Todorov in a new edition of Tocqueville's writing on Algeria:

One can only study barbarian peoples with guns in hand. (CA, 152)

I do not doubt that we can erect a great monument to the glory of our mother country on the coast of Africa. (CA, 53)

Domination [is not] the goal that France ought to set forth; it is the necessary means to achieve peaceful ownership of the coast and colonization of a part of the territory, a real and significant goal. (CA, 69)

Burning harvests, emptying silos, taking hold of unarmed men, women, and children . . . these are in my opinion *unfortunate necessities*, but ones that any nation that will go to war with the Arabs will have to face. (CA, 77; emphasis added)

As far as I am concerned, I believe that all means must be used in order to devastate the tribes. (CA, 77–78)

It was [in Algiers] that the plow of our colonial effort was first put to the earth; *it is there that we must prove that we can colonize Africa*. In Algiers as elsewhere we can only establish ourselves by taking territory away from the tribes. . . . It is an extreme measure, but *according to the customs of that country*, it is not unjust. (CA, 100; emphasis added)

As with Lamartine, the glance south and east (toward Algeria and the Middle East) seems different in character from the glance west to America. Although Tocqueville rejects Lamartine's characterization of "the Orient" as a dead body or a black space,[14] and although Tocqueville seems more aware of the problems involved in colonization, the two look on the East in remarkably similar ways, as territory for France to dispose of. Particularly in the case of the author of *Democracy in America*, who said in that famous work that he saw in conquest "the greatest and most irreparable calamity for a people,"[15] and who disapproved of Americans' covetousness of Indian lands, the contradiction is startling. Todorov paraphrases the logic of Tocqueville's stance in the following manner:

[14]"Il existe . . . plus de force qu'on ne l'imagine dans cet empire ottoman, dont M. de Lamartine disait hier, dans son beau langage, qu'il avait vu de ses yeux et touché de ses mains le cadavre" (this being the argument Lamartine makes in his "Résumé politique," discussed above) (Tocqueville, *EP* 2: 259–60).

[15]Tocqueville, quoted in Todorov, *Nous et les autres: la réflexion française sur la diversité humaine* (Paris: Seuil, 1989), 234. Henceforth abbreviated *NA*.

Liberty and equality among individuals are inviolable principles; but the situation is different when you are talking about states and peoples: domination of others, illegitimate when applied to individuals, becomes acceptable as soon as one is dealing with groups. . . . Tocqueville, who denounces the possession of one man by another, has no objection to one state possessing another. (NA, 226–27)

In Todorov's analysis, nationalism, as Tocqueville's motivation and justification, is liberalism translated to the international sphere: "Liberalism proclaims the right of the individual to do what he wants . . . nationalism does the same for states" (NA, 229).

Todorov's analysis is astute until he reaches his conclusion, that Tocqueville "set up a radical divorce between morals and politics" (NA, 234). This is true on the level of our retrospective reading, but not on the level of Tocqueville's explicit logic and discourse, in which both sides are justified as forms of "enlightenment." The "unethical," colonizing Tocqueville speaks the same language as the "ethical," abolitionist one: precisely the thing that justifies colonialism as "the superiority of a people's enlightenment," namely, that of the French people.[16] A similar moral position is evident in President William McKinley's rhetorical question about the American annexation of the Philippines: "Did we need their consent to perform a great act of humanity?"[17]

The most troubling aspect of reading Tocqueville is not that there is a contradiction between ethical and unethical positions, but that Tocqueville *takes both to be ethical:* contradictions can be resolved, but the mix of liberalism—the values of 1789—with colonialism here is more like a conundrum than a contradiction. It is no surprise to find the unethical along with the ethical when one is reading history, but the real problem is that, in regard to colonialism, the ethical and the unethical wear the same clothes and speak the same phrases; and this is at least partly how colonialism advanced itself: as a program for the exportation of *values.*

It is true, however, that Tocqueville envisions no systematic program for inculcating values in the Arab population. The value—the "enlightenment"—of European civilization will simply surround the

[16]"Il faut bien s'imaginer qu'un peuple puissant et civilisé comme le notre exercé par le seul fait de la supériorité de ses lumières une influence presque invincible sur de petites peuplades à peu prés barbares . . . " (CA, 49). "Nous sommes plus éclairés et plus forts que les Arabes. . . " (CA, 51).
[17]Quoted in Raymond F. Betts, *Uncertain Dimensions: Western Overseas Empires in the Twentieth Century* (Minneapolis: University of Minnesota Press, 1985), 48. This chapter was written before the American invasion of Panama in December 1989, but the parallel should not go unmentioned.

Arabs, who will perhaps remain immune to it. The Arabs will be taken as they come and left as they are, so long as they submit to French rule. His detailed proposal for reforming the colonial system in Algeria, in fact, resembles the ideology of Indirect Rule that will be promulgated in British Nigeria by Lord Lugard in the early twentieth century:

We are governing the population. . . . By the intervention of the native chiefs whom we only oversee from afar; the population . . . obeys us without knowing us. (*CA*, 156)

Different native civil servants, established and recognized by us, administer under diverse names the Moslem population; these are the intermediaries between the population and us. (*CA*, 166)

For the present, it is not in the direction of European civilization that they should be pushed, but rather toward the civilization that is their own. (*CA*, 172)[18]

Thus, although Lamartine and Tocqueville advocate domination and colonization, they do not yet envision the wholesale exportation of values and inculcation of them among non-European peoples. That plan— which is far more ambitious—will come later, after the scramble for Africa in the late nineteenth century. Only after the European powers have succeeded in carving up the territory will distinct cultural-political policies emerge. At some point in the early twentieth century, differences between French and British policy took on the coherent shape of opposed ideologies: Indirect Rule for the British and assimilation for the French.

Lord Lugard, the ideologue of Indirect Rule, wrote: "The French system proceeds on the hypothesis that the colonies are an integral part of France, and their inhabitants Frenchmen."[19] Although this is an exaggeration, and although the idea of assimilation was more of an ideal than an actual policy, as an ideal and as an instigator of culture, it exercised tremendous influence and continues to do so in the former French colonies. Assimilation could be summed up as the notion that French civilization is the best civilization, but it is not exclusive to any race or even nationality. Frenchness can be taught and learned; the royal road to civilization is the French language, whose actual materiality is taken as an embodiment of values and skills. The subliminal message of assimilation

---

[18]Cf. Frederick, Lord Lugard, *The Dual Mandate in British Tropical Africa* (London: Frank Cass, 1965): "There is no desire to impose on the people any theoretically suitable form of government, but rather to evolve from their own institutions, based on their own habits of thought, prejudices, and customs, the form of rule best suited to them, and adopted to meet the new conditions." (213).

[19]Ibid., 228.

is: You can be equal to me, provided that you become identical to me. In the political history of the French colonies, this provided a mechanism by which Africans could gain participatory rights like voting. But assimilation as a blanket policy was unworkable.[20] On the conceptual level, assimilation did not allow for local difference or ethnic autonomy; there was one system for all, and that was thought to be a liberal policy. But in terms of practical politics, a pronouncement by the governor-general of French West Africa Joost van Vollenhoven is symptomatic of the other side of this universalism: "Only the [French] *commandant du cercle* commands; only he is responsible. The native chief is but an instrument, an auxiliary."[21]

We are on a trajectory here that has taken us from eighteenth-century ideals to nineteenth-century intentions: what happens when these intentions are translated into colonial reality in early twentieth-century sub-Saharan Africa? The short answer is that we find a consistent echo of rhetoric from 1789 within the discourse of African colonialism.

Hubert Deschamps, in a fascinating and amusing article called "Et maintenant, Lord Lugard," published in 1963, reflects back on his own career as a colonial administrator and university professor, and makes some startling assertions about assimilationist policy in contrast to Indirect Rule:

Lord Lugard, I have been your enemy. . . . Assimilation . . . responds to deep and constant tendencies within the French people, trends with two-thousand-year-old origins, yet revealed so perfectly in the classicism of the 17th and 18th centuries. . . . The first colonial efforts of France were of this mind. The extension of the kingdom, the conversion of the savages, the absence of racism—these were the touchstones of these efforts.[22]

Deschamps goes on to explain that Colbert's mercantilism and slavery ruined this good beginning. But in the eighteenth century, universal ideas like Descartes's "man in himself, identical everywhere" gain ascendancy and allow ethical thought to apply itself to the entire world: "Spiritual and sentimental assimilation attacks slavery and tyranny[;] in the Revolutionary Republic, these ideas triumph" (297). He then asserts that universalist assimilationism was drowned out in the nineteenth century by an increasing insistence on particularist differences among peoples, in a

[20]See Michael Crowder, *Senegal: A Study of French Assimilation Policy* (London: Methuen, 1967).
[21]Quoted in Betts, *Uncertain Dimensions*, 68.
[22]Hubert Deschamps, "Et maintenant, Lord Lugard," *Africa: Journal of the International African Institute* 33 (October 1963): 294, 296.

word, racism; Gobineau certainly exemplifies this pattern. But the point of Deschamps's article is to describe how, in the 1930s, he conceived of assimilation as progress:

> Raised in the republican tradition of the left, and a militant socialist, I was hardly favorable to the chiefs and kings [and thus Indirect Rule was unappealing to him] . . . *Assimilation* and *universalism* were thus confined to refuge in this part of the Left which, not holding power, criticized its methods and doctrines. Colonization seemed to me justifiable, according to Jaurès' words, as the "duty to proceed, by degrees, toward the unification of the human race." . . . [And, imagining a trial in the Court of History, Deschamps sets up two opposing sides, Indirect Rule, on the one hand, and, on the other,] assimilating tendencies of the French people, as vague and sporadic as have been their actual application in the colonies . . . their task for immense rational constructions . . . the romantic vision of France the liberator. . . . To sum up these ideas in one symbolic image, I would say that it is Assimilation, in other words, the Revolution of 1789 tiptoeing into Africa slightly late. (298–300)[23]

Although Deschamps argues that assimilation was "only rarely the official colonial doctrine of France," a cult and culture of assimilation—using references to the Revolution of 1789 and the myth of a liberating France—has asserted itself within francophone Africa and within French discourse about Africa. A discourse of enlightenment and progress was the key to the success of colonialism; a misguided idealism, referring to either the *mission civilisatrice* or to national prestige, seems to have held the floor in the debate on colonialism. (Economic arguments never seemed to hold water.) France could think of itself as colonizing and liberating at the same time.[24] Deschamps makes a point in passing that serves as our entry point for considering two African perspectives on assimilation and liberal values. He states that in Africa, "The French

[23]Ibid., 298–300. Deschamps's attitude toward this is ironic; he depicts himself and other "assimilateurs" as having been slightly naive: "Les assimilateurs de bonne foi (c'étaient surtout des gens de gauche) ont cru dans la simplicité de leur coeur que le temps des nationalismes était passé et qu'on allait, comme en U.R.S.S., vers la formation de grands ensembles préludant à l'unité mondiale" (303).

[24]This does not mean that economic motivations were absent, only that they were more rarely stated out loud and more difficult to support. Cf. Henri Brunschwig, *Noirs et blancs dans l'Afrique noire française ou comment le colonisé devient colonisateur (1870–1914)* (Paris: Flammarion, 1983): "Ce type de colonisation pacifique assurerait à la langue et à la culture françaises un rayonnement universel et la France, plus libérale et plus désintéressée que ses rivales, conduirait les populations qui accepteraient sa tutelle à quelque système d'assimilation ou d'association qui respecterait la liberté, l'égalité et la fraternité" (27–28). For a general comparison of colonialism and revolutions in a political science context, see Richard Jeffries, "Revolution in Black Africa," in Noel O'Sullivan, ed., *Revolutionary Theory and Political Reality* (Brighton, U.K.: Harvester Press, 1983), 158–72.

language became the means of intellectual emancipation and the path to unity" (304). Leaving aside the ideological problems in that original statement—which are obvious—I would like to look briefly at the original text of the francophone African tradition in fiction, Ahmadou Mapate Diagne's *Les trois volontés de Malic,* published in 1920, as an example of the "Trojan Horse" theory of language learning.

*Les trois volontés de Malic* is the first published piece of fiction in French written by a sub-Saharan African. Ahmadou Mapate Diagne was a Senegalese teacher and former secretary to Georges Hardy, to whom Diagne refers in the story's dedication as "the Architect of Education in West Africa."[25] Hardy and Diagne were engaged in the same enterprise, that of translating France's abstract mission of *tutelle* (guardianship; cf. Lamartine) into literal education. A comprehensive system of education had been recognized as a necessity by the French as early as 1855, when Louis Faidherbe set up the first "Ecole des fils de chefs" (School for Sons of Chiefs), more commonly known as the "Ecole des otages" (School of Hostages). The sons of the elite were to be inculcated and curried as "potential auxiliaries of the French."[26] In fact, using an astute strategy of resistance, the chiefs often sent their slaves' sons instead.

*Les trois volontés* was apparently commissioned by the Paris publishing house Larousse for eventual use in colonial schools: it is a tool of literacy teaching, *alphabétisation.*[27] But literacy is not given, here or elsewhere, as a neutral "technology of reason"; it bears within it—like a Trojan Horse—ideological messages. The message of *Les trois volontés* is of loyalty to France and reorientation of Senegalese society according to the new priorities of colonialism.

Malic is a young boy living in a Wolof village. Great excitement is stirred by the construction of the town's first *école française* (of course there has been an *école coranique* for as long as anyone can remember, but it will now be superseded): "These singing workers, this *Toubab* (white man) who supervises them, have nothing which can frighten little children" (*TV,* 2). Malic wishes that he could make friends with the newcomers, run errands for them, fetch them water, tools, and so on. His eagerness is shown to be culturally ingrained: the chief of the village "had preferred the friendship . . . of the good 'Commandant Faidherbe' . . . to

---

[25]Ahmadou Mapate Diagne, *Les trois volontés des Malic* (Nendeln: Kraus Reprints, 1973), 1. Henceforth referred to as *TV.*
[26]Henry S. Wilson, *The Imperial Experience in Sub-Saharan Africa since 1870* (Minneapolis: University of Minnesota Press, 1977), 40.
[27]Robert Cornevin, *Littératures d'Afrique noire de langue française* (Paris: Presses Universitaires de France, 1976), 133.

that of an unfair and bloodthirsty Damel. He took the side of the French because he was sure of their good intentions" (*TV*, 3). One of the old men states, "The whites bring only peace" (*TV*, 4). A meeting is convoked, at which the French commandant proclaims the advantages of French literacy: your children will become "diligent, honest, just, and good" (*TV*, 6)—if they learn French. The French language within the colonial system of education is thus advertised as a bearer of values, values that are useful to the colonial order.

Malic learns to read and write, and this immediately puts him in a superior position. In a scene that can only be described as ridiculous, Malic explains what writing is to a group of old men, who "laugh like children": "The three old men are as touched as they are filled with wonder, and they are speechless. Their eyes are fixed, they reflect. They ask themselves how this little Malic learned how to distinguish the little marks which resemble the feet of flies" (*TV*, 16). This is implausible at best, in a context where Islam had introduced writing a long time before; but the lesson here, addressed to the school children reading the text, is about the acquisition of power. Malic acquires power and prestige automatically through his association (not yet assimilation) with the French. He has begun an inexorable participation in the system of "progress."

One day, Malic gives a history lesson to the old men. He surveys the relationship between the French and the Wolof, culminating in Faidherbe's conquest in the nineteenth century. What Faidherbe is said to have done is not surprising in this context: he "freed trade and liberated the people of Senegal. He established peace in the country and allowed all honest and hardworking men to attain affluence" (*TV*, 23). Faidherbe is one of those larger-than-life figures in French history books: he presents himself as the model of the anthropologist-governor. He spoke Wolof, informed himself about customs, and married an African wife. But his role in history is actually more ambivalent: he was the founder of the famous *tirailleurs sénégalais,* African sharpshooters under French command, employed against other Africans in campaigns of conquest. He created "a tradition of French military imperialism in the Sudan," even if circumstances such as the Franco-Prussian War of 1870 did not allow him to lead sweeping campaigns. His control of territory "was asserted only within cannon range."[28] Nonetheless, he occupies the position of liberator in *Les trois volontés de Malic.*

Liberty is of course the central issue here. It finds its most paradoxical

[28]Wilson, *The Imperial Experience,* 41.

and significant expression—in any text that I have seen—toward the end of *Les trois volontés*. Malic, supposedly completely on his own, has decided that he wants to become a blacksmith. No "career" decision could be more problematic in the Wolof or Mande spheres of West Africa, in which smithing, wood carving, and oral performances are considered spiritually dangerous tasks, to be carried out only by hereditary groups often called "castes." The school teacher accedes to Malic's decision, seeing in it "the desire to work arduously" (*TV*, 24), but the old men of the village are appalled. Malic as a "freeman" simply cannot "work like a *gnegno* (artisan)" (*TV*, 25). Malic's choice places him at the dividing line between African culture, with its traditions, and French colonialism, with its need to recruit and maintain a cadre of faithful workers. This sets up the dramatic climax of the story, another history lesson given by Malic to the old men:

In the days that followed, little Malic resumed teaching his three old pupils as he had before. Now, one evening when he had summarized for them the history of France, which he like to compare to that of Senegal, the young "professor" concluded with this:
"It is no longer the moment to speak of origin or caste. Men are no longer distinguished by anything but their work, their intelligence, and their virtues.
"We are governed by France, we *belong to that country where men are born equal*." (*TV*, 27; emphasis added)

Here, then, is the central paradox: the Declaration of the Rights of Man is invoked within a colonial structure that seems to render it invalid, or at least highly ironic. How can one group "belong" to another if "all men are born equal"? Significantly the allusion to the Declaration skips one essential word: *free*. (The Declaration states: "Men are born and remain *free and equal* under the law.") That absent detail is a sign of what has happened to the values of the Revolution within the discourse of colonialism: the heart has been cut out.

Yet the body keeps marching on. While Diagne's *Les trois volontés de Malic* is an extreme example, it is not an aberration within this context. Ideologically, the earliest authors of the francophone African tradition were literally employees of the colonial regime, and their works often showed their indebtedness.[29] I would like to take as my last author in this sequence perhaps the best-known poet of the francophone tradition, Léopold Sédar Senghor. Senghor's ideology and poetry of negritude are

[29]See Guy Ossito Midiohouan, *L'idéologie dans la littérature négro-africaine d'expression française* (Paris: Harmattan, 1986), 60–79.

not my object here; rather I would like to discuss one of his most recent publications, which recasts and reorients the question of the French Revolution.

The last chapter of Senghor's most recent book is called "La révolution de 1889 et la civilisation de l'universel."[30] The concept of the civilization of the universal is one that Senghor takes from Teilhard de Chardin; it is his vision of a cultural millennium in which discrete, *essential* identities such as negritude will all be assumed to a universal level. The thesis statement of this chapter is the following: "I would like to demonstrate that, since the Revolution of 1889, the peoples of the earth, willy-nilly, have been in the process of building the Civilization of the Universal" (CQ, 204).

Why 1889? The choice is strange and revelatory. There is an obvious allusion to the Revolution of 1789, but it is not openly discussed. What Senghor calls the Revolution of 1889 is a figure of speech for literary and artistic modernism, which he sees as the bridge between Europe and Africa; in Rimbaud he sees negritude, in Picasso he sees negritude, in anyone associated with Parisian *art nègre* he sees negritude. Senghor explains his choice of 1889 as the year of a crucial change by pointing to the publication of two works: Henri Bergson's *Essai sur les données immédiates de la conscience*, and Paul Claudel's first play, *Tête d'or*. These are surprising signs of a revolution. Senghor explains:

Here and there, one saw the first major and convincing reactions to the *Cogito, ergo sum*, to discursive rationalism as well as to materialist positivism. Starting with his first theatrical work, Claudel brought a breath of fresh lyric poetry to French drama: the breath of his hope for the absolute. As for Bergson, who found his way back to the spiritualist sources of Greek philosophy, to the *theoria*, he restored intuitive reason to the place it had had in Egypt and in Africa, where Plato had found it. (CQ, 210)

Senghor's reasoning depends on a complex genealogy of culture and race which owes much to Cheikh Anta Diop and to Gobineau as well. Everything goes back to ancient Greece, but Greece in turn owes the flame of its culture to Egypt and to Africa as a whole. Therefore, any moment in the history of the West that fully realizes its debt to Greece and to Africa will be a moment of accession to universality. In the sweep of Senghor's thought, historical differences and political tensions are completely abstracted under the weight of universal categories; the West and

---

[30]Léopold Sédar Senghor, *Ce que je crois: négritude, francité et civilisation de l'universel* (Paris: Bernard Grasset, 1988), 199–234. Henceforth abbreviated CQ.

the rest achieve a state of union that leaves them indistinguishable: "If 'Western civilization' [one wonders what these quotation marks mean] has lasted so long—almost 1000 years, from the Holy Roman Empire to the taking of Constantinople—it is because it had attained for the first time a kind of universality. . . . Africa was not absent" (CQ, 208). But the universality of Western civilization—its participation in a worldwide logic of spirituality and intuition—was lost, according to Senghor, during the Renaissance, crushed by the Cogito. This state of affairs lasted well into the "stupid 19th century," with its discursive reasoning and its realism. The Revolution of 1889 restored France to its rightful heritage of universality.

Thus, it is of no consequence to Senghor that Bergson and Claudel have nothing to say about Africa. In both authors Senghor found a spiritualism that was wholly compatible with his vision of African culture, with negritude. The relationship with Claudel is one that Senghor explored at considerable length in his essay "La parole chez Paul Claudel et chez les Négro-Africains"; he explained the convergence as an effect of Claudel's rediscovery of an "ancient Celtic temperament (characterized by great emotive and imaginative power)."[31] The invocation of Bergson also falls into a general category of "irrationalism" which harmonized with the Art Nègre movement of the early twentieth century—all of these things being closely associated and interconnected in Senghor's mind.[32]

Senghor's perspective is thus somewhat different from what we have seen before. The Revolution of 1789 and its declaration of rights has nothing to do with his vision of liberation. His nearly obsessive insistence on the primacy of the cultural over the political and his system of European cultural references, including Bergson and Claudel, lead him to occlude the obvious political and historical factor that brought Africa and Europe "together"—colonialism. Thus, he makes no mention of the material precondition for his Revolution of 1889, the condition without which it would be meaningless as a bridge between Africa and France: the "Revolution" of 1885 that was the Conference of Berlin. There would be no "convergence" or "symbiosis"—in other words, a benign version of colonialism—if the European powers, under the perfidious leadership of King Leopold of the Belgians, had not carved up the continent and proceeded to colonize it for the first time in a systematic way.

[31]Senghor, in Liberté III: Négritude et civilisation de l'universel (Paris: Seuil, 1977), 385.
[32]See Jacques Louis Hymans, Léopold Sédar Senghor: An Intellectual Biography (Edinburgh: Edinburgh University Press, 1971), 48–52.

The central mystery in Senghor's thinking is the centrality of France, expressed most insistently now through his support of the francophone movement. *Francophonie* is in many ways the heir to the myth of *la France libératrice*. France and the French language are given supreme status precisely because they are "universal." Centrality is at once asserted and obscured by this gesture. Since *francophonie* embraces and even embodies negritude and everything African, there is no worry about cultural imperialism in the use of French.[33] France remains the key to the universal, as it has been since Lamartine and Tocqueville and even before. Thus, Senghor concludes *Ce que je crois* in this way:

At the Third Francophone Summit which will take place in Dakar in May 1989, the heads of state will give the organization its political framework. This was suggested by the French Academy delegation at Quebec. To be more specific, its Constitution will be "à la française," again because it will be built on a Universal scale. (*CQ*, 234)

In this statement, the identification between France and universality makes more sense if one assumes that Senghor is referring to unconditional ethical injunctions within a constitution: guarantees of rights, and so on. Ethical statements indeed tend to claim universality: "Thou shalt not kill," not "Thou shalt not kill here and now." Taken in this sense, the identification between France and human rights is of course legitimate as an ideal that the French state must try to live up to.

But the pretensions that are rapidly gathering around the concept of *francophonie* seem more problematic and more familiar in the context I have been evoking: the idea that *francophonie* will introduce an entirely new idea of culture;[34] the idea that French is "médiatrice et non pas impératrice" ("a mediator, not a dictator," that is, central but not oppressive);[35] the idea that *francophonie* is, in Senghor's words, "a spiritual community, a noosphere around the earth";[36] the idea that *francophonie* is "an ideal that ignores borders and neglects political separations"[37] (to

[33]For Senghor's views of *francophonie*, see also Chapter 4 of *CQ*, "Francité et francophonie."

[34]"Il faut constater l'apparition d'une 'culture francophone' resultant d'un profond bouleversement de l'essence contemporaine de culture elle-même . . . une culture qui prend son essor non d'une unité, mais d'une diversité première" (Xavier Deniau, [President of the "Association francophone d'amitié et de liaison"], "Donne son avis sur la culture francophone," *Soleils et francophonie* 1 [June 1989], 7).

[35]Xavier Deniau, *La francophonie* (Paris: PUF, 1983), 5.

[36]Léopold Sédar Senghor, "La francophonie comme culture," in *Liberté III: Négritude et civilisation de l'universel* (Paris: Seuil, 1977), 80.

[37]Xavier Deniau, "La dimension francophone dans la politique française," *France-Eurafrique* 25 (May–June 1974): 4.

which one could reply: "Precisely!"); the idea, promulgated by the Haut
Comité de la Langue Française in 1977, that "francophonie" is a sort of
school for human "fraternity"[38] (again, liberty and equality seem to take
a back seat). This kind of *francophonie* is the legitimate heir to the discourse of colonialism.[39]

The common denominator throughout these examples has been the
conceptualization of France. In April 1951, a newspaper called *La dépêche africaine* and identifying itself as "organe *républicain* indepen-
dant" published an editorial entitled "La France et sa mission civilisatrice
dans l'Union française" ("France and Its Civilizing Mission in the French
Union). The editorial celebrates the reappearance of the paper after a
hiatus caused by the war and the Occupation, and it sets the agenda for
the new French Union. The editors state: "France does not oppress, she
liberates." And they explain, in a passage that echoes the logic of Senghor
and others, why France is to be considered not so much a nation with
particular and limited interests, but the embodiment of principles. The
reasoning depends on the editors' use of the French Revolution as an
image:

The Declaration of the Rights of Man was not an improvisation of a moment
of civic fervor, but the result of a painstaking working out of National History;
the Constituent Assembly has constructed it *for all of humanity and not only
for France. They have declared the Rights of Man and not the Rights of the
French.* It is one of their claims to glory. That is why we must recognize that,
doctrinally speaking, France's political ideas regarding its overseas territories are
the most generous, ideas which best understand the native because they are
inspired by the most elevated and the most noble doctrine of the emancipation of
men.[40]

The editors then quote Leon Gambetta, who in 1892 spoke of reciprocity
in the colonial encounter as a consequence of 1789: "The French Revolution will above all have this glory and this honor, of having substituted in
human affairs the idea of contract for the idea of exploitation and arbi-
trariness."

But we have seen that the translation of the ethics of the Revolution of
1789 into sub-Saharan Africa has been a tricky process. Ethical impera-

---

[38]Quoted in Guy Ossito Midiohouan, "Le sottisier francophone," *Peuples noirs, peuples
africains* 59–62 (September 1987–April 1988): 181.
[39]For a more detailed discussion of *francophonie* and its literary ramifications, see Christopher L. Miller, *Theories of Africans: Francophone Literature and Anthropology in Africa*
(Chicago: The University of Chicago Press, 1990), 181–201.
[40]*La dépêche africaine* 1 (30 April 1951), 1, emphasis added.

tives were not simply implemented; in examples we have seen, they were hijacked and abused. In Tocqueville and Lamartine, they appeared as a smokescreen over imperialism; in Diagne's *Les trois volontés*, the translation of ethics reached a climax of paradox as the colonized echoed a discourse of fake liberation that proved his defeat. In Senghor's chapter, the terms seem to have been altered but the underlying pattern conserved.

This pattern has of course not gone unnoticed or uncriticized in Africa. Twenty years before the editorial in *La dépêche africaine*, another, very different newspaper called *Le cri des nègres* published an editorial on the Colonial Exposition of Vincennes, which they call "this extravagant manifestation of murderous, thieving imperialism": "We thank especially all those who . . . helped us unmask the hypocrisy of those who claimed and still claim to go to the colonies in order to bring them 'Civilization'." At the bottom of the page, under the title "What They Don't Show at the Vincennes Colonial Exposition," there is a picture of decapitated Africans, escaped prisoners who were executed. This is a strong dose of demystification, a reminder that the "revolution" of colonialism had its own guillotines.

It takes a writer of the fortitude of Mongo Beti, the Cameroonian novelist, to call the whole structure into question. Writing in the journal he edits, *Peuples noirs, peuples africains*, Beti denounces *francophonie* as a fraud and announces a rather dubious solution, simply switching sides to English: "English is today, more than French, far and away more the language of liberty, which is to say, of creativity."[41] And in the preface to this special issue on *francophonie,* the editors write: "Besides, francophonie rhymes with hegemony" (6). They see *francophonie* as France's way of "leaving and staying at the same time, *liberating and dominating,* loving and hating, praising and denigrating . . ." (4; emphasis added).

The real intellectual stumbling block here had in fact been resolved even before the Revolution, but in theory only. Diderot, in his additions and corrections to the Abbé Raynal's *Histoire . . . des deux Indes,* thought his way beyond the contradiction between abolishing slavery and practicing colonialism. Whereas Raynal himself had "left the principle of colonization intact," Diderot "resolutely negate[d] the right of colonialization."[42] But Raynal's work, amended by Diderot and transformed from

---

[41] Mongo Beti, "Seigneur, délivre-nous de la francophonie," *Peuples noirs, peuples africains* 59–62 (September 1987–April 1988): 106.
[42] Yves Benot, "Diderot, Pechmeja, Raynal et l'anticolonialisme," *Europe* 41 (January–February 1963): 149, 153.

a reformist into a revolutionary document, was not republished anytime between 1820 and 1951; the business that Diderot had foreseen, that of decolonization, was left unfinished. The French colonial system instead built itself over a myth of the Revolution, while suppressing the truth that Diderot had understood: you can't dominate and liberate at the same time.

# 7

The French Revolution and the Arab world

ELBAKI HERMASSI

In considering the impact of the French Revolution on the Arab world, it is possible to hold two entirely contrary views at the same time, depending on how one views and defines the Revolution. Thus, if the Revolution is seen as a unique event occurring at a particular time and place, the inevitable conclusion must be that the Arab world did not experience this event; nevertheless, if by "the Revolution" one understands a worldwide historical phenomenon[1]—which is, in fact, this author's view—one may then argue that it had an impact that, though indirect, was highly significant.

As a worldwide historical phenomenon, the French Revolution set its seal on a new type of society and gave rise to a vast expansionist movement. Practically all the concepts of political and cultural life, of power, authority, community, and justice, were influenced; for example, the word "civilization" itself took on a completely new meaning.

Originally, "civilization" implied a slow evolutionary process, and at least at the beginning, it occupied a secondary position compared with the catchwords of the Revolution. When the pace of the Revolution became more moderate in the late 1790s, however, "civilization" became a slogan that was to spread all over the world and serve as a justification for expansionism. When Napoleon undertook his Egyptian campaign, he addressed his troops in these words: "Soldiers, you are engaging in a conquest whose consequences will be incalculable for civilization." Instead of a long-continuing process, civilization was henceforth seen as something already existing and fully developed. To quote Norbert Elias:

[1] Elbaki Hermassi, *Third World Reassessed* (Berkeley and Los Angeles, 1980).

127

Gone is the former interest in the problem of "civilization" seen as a process: The conviction of one's superiority and of the superiority of one's national civilization serves to justify conquering and civilizing nations in thus elevating themselves to the status of a "superior caste" in vast areas outside Europe.[2]

The historians of the Arab world are almost unanimous: It is Napoleon's expedition to Egypt that marks the beginning of modern history in this region, and it was through Napoleon that the catchwords of the French Revolution began to make headway there. The new ideas were to have an immense influence among senior state officials, scholars, and the first of the intellectuals to be produced by the Revolution. It was a turning point that, in the first place, fully recognized the irreversible superiority of the West in the world—a superiority that could be resented or admired but that could not henceforth be ignored. In the second place, it marked an exceptional point in history, when the will to discover, study, and admire the outside world for once prevailed over the temptation to put up barriers and employ defense mechanisms. Raif Khouri caught the feeling of wonder of this first generation,[3] and Louis Awadh, in even more enthusiastic terms, wrote that in Napoleon we find "the first minister, the first Constitution, and the first Parliament."[4]

## THE MODERNIZATION OF THE STATE:
### A REVOLUTION FROM ABOVE

It will naturally be borne in mind that concurrently with the French Revolution the Ottoman bureaucracy initiated a series of reforms and set in motion a modernization program. The French Revolution was to contribute to this process by encouraging the Arab provinces themselves to take charge of their own modernization. This was particularly the case with Muhammad Ali, the Viceroy of Egypt from 1805 to 1849 and Ahmad Bey, who governed Tunisia from 1837 to 1855.

Initially, reforming the state meant above all reorganizing and reequipping the army along European lines. However, it soon became apparent that military reform was totally impossible in the absence of a system of education capable of training the necessary officials and technicians, and without an adequate budget. Modernization required tax reform and, above all, an increase in economic production. Consequently, Egypt, Tu-

[2]Norbert Elias, *La Civilisation des moeurs* (Paris, 1972), 72.
[3]Raif Khouri, *La Pensée arabe moderne: l'impact de la Révolution française sur son orientation politique et sociale* (in Arabic) (Beirut, 1943).
[4]In Anouar Abdel Malek, *Idéologie et Renaissance nationale* (Paris, 1969), 260.

nisia, and the central Ottoman government carried out a revolution from above. The aims of each government, whether its efforts succeeded or failed, were to make up for lost time and strengthen its own position, while at the same time ensuring continuity.

In the immediate term, this modernization of the state was to clash head on with both the age-old customs and the acquired privileges of the population. Up until the nineteenth century Arab society had only had the most distant relationship with the government. With the modernization movement, governments constantly sought to extend their control and to intervene more extensively in nearly all areas of the life of the community. With the codification and systematization of the activities of society, local autonomy received a fatal blow, and the former system of authority, embodied by the tribal chiefs and the religious leaders, gave way to an increasingly centralized administration. The reform of the state brought with it a number of advantages: in order to increase revenue the state counted on economic growth.[5] However, the traditional "patrimonial" state had a clear advantage over the reformed state: by recognizing the authority of the tribes, corporate organizations, and religious brotherhoods, the "patrimonial" state appears, in retrospect, to have been more relevant to the Arab world of the time. The anticipated economic expansion did not materialize.

The high cost of the new reforms, in the absence of economic growth and in the face of foreign pressure, led each new state to go back on its own policy and dangerously increase the tax burden, which gave rise to rebellion among both the rural and the urban masses. With regard to the Maghreb, Laroui clearly shows that at the very time that the state was growing richer by introducing new agricultural methods, developing communications, and intensifying trade, it was becoming politically and socially weaker as a result of internal conflicts. Rebellion initially broke out among the rural communities, but it soon spread to the cities and small towns as a consequence of the crisis that affected the artisan class and trade in the wake of the abolition of monopolies and customs barriers.

In his exemplary study of the Ottoman reform movement and the policy of the "notables," Albert Hourani makes it clear that the objective of the reforms in the Arab Near East, apart from rationalization and uniform centralized administration, was to strengthen the position of

[5]Abdallah Laroui, *Islam et modernité* (Paris, 1987).

those in power. The aim of the relationship that Muhammad Ali sought to establish with Europe was to create a new framework in which Europeans could operate, always and solely through him, not only as ruler but also as the principal merchant and the main intermediary between the rural cultivator and the European market.[6] Invariably it was the majority of the population that paid the price of change, the beneficiaries being—apart from the governing elite—minorities, foreign merchants, and European consulates. While the Muslim merchants, contrary to the general trend, still managed to maintain their position in Damascus, "in Baghdad it was the Jewish and Armenian traders who prospered; in Aleppo, it was local Jews and Christians, and in Jeddah, the Europeans as against the Adrani merchants."[7]

Since it proved impossible to carry out fully the planned Ottoman reforms (*Tanzimat*, 1837–76), local notables were able to survive and even consolidate their position. In a situation where the population was increasingly brought into contact with state officials and given the newly imposed legal, taxation, and conscription regulations, these local leaders were able to play their role of intermediaries and thus strengthen their control in both town and country. In the final analysis, however, as Hourani explains, they generally took up a position against reform.

This was not merely out of prejudice or through conviction, but because the general direction of reform was contrary to their interests: the political conception underlying the *tanzimats* was that of a direct uniform relationship between the government and each of its citizens, and this was incompatible with both the privileges of the Muslim notables and their role as intermediaries.[8]

## TOWARD A CONSTITUTIONAL STATE

Alongside the modernization of the state apparatus and as if in reaction to its objective limits, the emphasis gradually shifted during the second half of the nineteenth century toward improvements in the political system. Here, we are witnessing a change from the practical empirical approach of bureaucrats and army officers to a new world of thought inspired by the first intellectuals educated under the influence of

[6]Albert Hourani, "Ottoman Reform and the Politics of Notables," in William R. Polk and Richard L. Chambers, eds., *Beginnings of Modernization in the Middle East: The Nineteenth Century* (Chicago, 1968), 65.
[7]Ibid., 61. See also Donald Reid, "Arabic Thought in the Liberal Age: Twenty Years After," *International Journal of Middle Eastern Studies*, November 1982, 541–57.
[8]Polk and Chambers, *Beginnings of Modernization,* 63.

Muhammad Ali and Ahmad Bey. These men were to reflect on the state of
Islamic and Arab societies, the grandeur and decadence of civilizations,
and the underlying circumstances of the Arab awakening.

Let us examine first of all how these men came to know France and
Europe in the period after the Revolution. Tahtawi (1801–71) was the
imam of the first Egyptian educational mission sent to France by Muhammad Ali in 1826. During his five years in Paris, Tahtawi acquired a wide-
ranging culture and was particularly influenced by the ideas of 1789 and
the theories of Saint-Simon. He took a passionate interest in the revolution of 1830, which he witnessed personally. In his book *Takhlis al-Ibriz
fi Talkhis Barís* (The Purification of Gold; or, A Brief Survey of Paris), first
published in 1831 and subsequently republished three times during the
century, Tahtawi provided Arab readers with their first view of Western
civilization, as it appeared in Parisian life.

The book is full of information about the way the French live, their
manners, life-style, and administrative and political institutions. The author dwells at length on the public services, schools, universities, parks,
and hospitals, which have no equivalent in his country. He describes in
minute detail the constitution, institutions, and political mechanisms that
guarantee freedom of opinion, association, and belief. He also mentions
the vitality of the Parisians, the quality of their way of life, and the
presence and participation of women "in public life, on an equal footing
with men."

There is a clear tendency on the part of the author to see similarities
and draw comparisons. He maintains that Montesquieu is for the French
what Ibn Khaldun is for the Arabs; freedom of expression has its basis in
the *Shari'a,* and what has no precedent is not in conflict with the *Shari'a.*

French laws are not derived from holy books, but taken from other rights, most of
which are political . . . ; they are called French rights, that is to say, the rights of
the French toward one another . . . from which one can see how the human mind
has judged that justice and equity are factors making for the prosperity of king-
doms and the tranquility of those who respect them . . . justice being the foundation of civilization.

Thus, after noting similarities and parallels, it is on the basis of practical
efficiency that Tahtawi argues his case.[9]

The continuation of his argument is closer to "political radicalism."[10]

[9]See Anouar Abdel Malek, *Idéologie et Renaissance nationale,* for a translation and analysis of the text.
[10]Ibid.

The French can be divided into "two groups: royalists and libertarians." The author's analysis of the differences unequivocally shows where his preference lies:

The royalists are for the most part priests with their disciples, while most of the libertarians are philosophers, scholars (*ulama*), learned men, and the vast majority of the people. The first group attempts to help the people. Among the second group there is an immense sect which would like to see power entirely in the hands of the people and [thinks] that, as a general rule, there is no need for a king. However, given that the people cannot be both the governors and the governed, they have to delegate those whom they choose from among them to form the government, which is the government of the republic.[11]

Tahtawi then traces the political history of France since the Revolution. He distinguishes among three different types of government: absolute monarchy, which he openly rejects; a republic, which he clearly favors; and constitutional monarchy, to which he finally comes around. His explanation of the revolution of 1830 leads him to exalt the role of representative parliamentary assemblies and to justify violent revolution against a royal power guilty of having flouted the rights of the people. The installation of Philippe-Egalité as "King of the French" provides him with the opportunity for a harsh attack on the monarchy of divine right, together with a plea for constitutional government.

Tahtawi's study of parliamentary institutions leads him to introduce for the first time into Arab political thought the notions of "right" and "left," to explain the concept of "*mort civile*" (deprivation of all civil rights), to describe the rights of man and of the citizen, to explain the separation of powers, and to emphasize that only a constitution (the "Charter"), based on a social contract, not granted by the sovereign, is the basis of civilized society.[12]

Anouar Abdel Malek emphasizes the extreme boldness of Tahtawi's ideas and regards him as the apostle of liberalism in the Arab world. Albert Hourani sees him rather as a thinker marking the transition between traditionalism and liberalism; in his opinion

Tahtawi lived and worked during a fortunate interlude in history, when the tension between Islam and Christianity had become relaxed and was not yet replaced by the new political tension between East and West. . . . France and England then represented science and material progress, not political power and expansion. . . . Muhammad Ali and Ismail . . . were benevolent despots of a kind familiar to Islamic thought, who posed no new problems.[13]

[11]Ibid.    [12]Abdel Malek, *Idéologie et Renaissance nationale.*
[13]Albert Hourani, *Arabic Thought in the Liberal Age, 1798–1939* (Cambridge, 1962), 81–
   83. See also his article "The Present State of Islamic and Middle Eastern Historiography,"

During the 1870s Khair al-Din put forward the same ideas, but at a more advanced stage of development. Although most of his working life was spent in Tunisia, Khair al-Din also served the Ottoman central government in Istanbul. He was not only a writer and thinker, but above all a professional statesman, counsellor, and minister. He lived at a time (1810–1889) when the West was being increasingly viewed as a harbinger not of revolution but, rather, of an expansionism which seemed likely to engulf the rest of the world.

Notwithstanding this, the position taken by Khair al-Din was trenchantly clear: Europe remains the advocate of progress and the champion of modernity. The only salvation for the countries lagging behind, if they wish to escape from the impasse in which they find themselves, is to learn from Europe. One of the objectives of his book *Dqwam al-Masalik*[14] is to study the political institutions of Europe, since it is these institutions that he regards as the basis of real power. He argues that European civilization is based on liberty and justice. Liberty is sacred, but there can be no liberty without justice, and it is through recourse to these two values that social peace and individual security are achieved. Peace and security are states that stimulate people toward creative action. Khair al-Din does not dwell at length on these ideas: the most important thing is to apply them in the real world. In his view, the tide of Western civilization has become so strong that no force in the world can hold it back. The only way to avoid being swept to the bottom of the abyss that threatens the Arab world is to climb aboard the ship flying the European flag.

His observations led him to the following conclusion: in the advanced societies of Europe power tends to become divided and dispersed, whereas in oriental societies social and economic backwardness goes hand in hand with a concentration or excess of power. To oppose this excess of power and despotism is the duty of all who are conscious of the fatal dangers that threaten their country. Consequently, the establishment of a constitutional system of government, along European lines, is the necessary and sufficient condition for escaping from poverty, internal anarchy, and vulnerability to external forces.[15]

Everything therefore depends on a judicious organization of power. Having read the works of writers such as Montesquieu, and having lived

---

in Albert Hourani, *Europe and the Middle East* (Berkeley and Los Angeles, 1980), 161–96.

[14] "Réformes necessaires aux Etats musulmans." Essay forming the first part of the political and statistical work entitled "La plus sure direction pour connaître l'état de nations" (Paris, 1868; Tunis, 1972).

[15] *Mémoires de Kheireddine* (Tunis, 1971), 184–85.

in France, Khail al-Din was familiar with different political systems. He discusses absolute monarchy, constitutional monarchy, and republics and finally opts for the second, or what he prefers to call "the State of the notables." As with Tahtawi before him, he made this choice because it was dictated by the period itself and by political circumstances.[16]

With a view both to the adoption of a constitution and the rational organization of his country, Khair al-Din sought to convince and win over to the side of reform the *Alims,* or traditional intellectuals. He called on the *Alims* to join the politicians in their struggle for progress and to combat the hostility of their people to foreign ideas that were wrongly regarded as being contrary to Islam.

It is well known that the first constitution in this part of the world was proclaimed in Tunisia in 1861; and it is equally well known that in Ottoman territory, in Tunisia, as in Egypt and Turkey, the reforms failed. Chastened by these setbacks, Khair al-Din wrote toward the end of his life that "it is impossible to transplant the instituting of one country into another where the temperament of the people, their manners and education, and also the climate are different." In addition,

there has been a reluctance to carry out boldly and resolutely radical reforms adapted to the needs of the country and to the customs of the people. Instead of persevering in the path traced out, introducing the necessary adaptations as the need arose, as is the practice in the governments of the best informed and most civilized nations, we have adopted superficial half-measures and borrowed various isolated institutions from Europe on the grounds that they produce good results in their countries of origin; we have forgotten that it is the general body of laws of a country which guarantees the advantages of each particular law.[17]

Another idea that came directly from the French Revolution was adopted by this first liberal generation: the concept of the *Watan,* or native land, as opposed to the *Umma,* or religious community, to which one belongs. To the question of whether a real distinction can be drawn between these two concepts, Tahtawi replies in the affirmative:

Everything which links one believer with other believers, his fellow-beings, also links him with the members of his native land (*Watan*) as regards their mutual rights, since there exists between them a patriotic fraternity which unites them irrespective of their religious fraternity.

He adds that there is "a moral obligation upon all those united by the same native land to work together in order to make it a better place to live

---

[16]"Réformes nécessaires aux Etats musulmans," 17, 30, 71, and 72.
[17]*Mémoires de Kheireddine,* 137.

in and to improve all aspects of its organization which will contribute to its well-being, greatness, and prosperity."[18]

There is general agreement, and rightly so, that this marks the first appearance in the Arab world of the specific idea of "territorial patriotism" in the modern sense of the term, in which one's native land becomes the focal point of loyalty. It was during this period that the earliest national histories were written, such as the history of Tunisia by Ahmad Ibn Abu Dhiaf (1802–74). In this work the author deals with governmental succession, the creation of a modern army and the introduction of new taxes to cover the costs of reforms and settle foreign debts. In the social context he also studies popular uprisings, such as the tax revolt of 1864, and the debates among intellectuals on the new situation.

Another very significant aspect is that the first volume of this history is preceded by an introduction which examines power and the disastrous effects of "absolute power." This is yet another indication that, following the French Revolution and the awakening of Europe, all political thought in the Islamic world came to adopt the same view, namely, that a nation's progress or backwardness depends on its political organization. The same approach was adopted by all: the liberal was to appeal to law and the Salafi to the *Shari'a*, but the objective was invariably to limit the exercise of power through the use of constitutional devices.

This was in fact the generation that was the best disposed toward France and Europe. Its influence in the Arab world was to last as long as the aspect of the French Revolution that favored progress and emancipation prevailed over the other aspect of expansion and foreign adventures. Even before the end of the century this generation of liberal optimism, which had supported the *Tanzimat* reforms in the hope of bringing about change in the state through constitutional means, had to admit defeat. The Arab States that attempted to introduce reforms on the basis of a liberal ideology disintegrated one after the other, and the European powers, especially France, occupied their territories in the name of a more decisive reform program. However, as Abdallah Laroui has very clearly shown, the concept of reform took on a new meaning: the aim was no longer the modernization of an existing structure but the erection of a totally foreign structure above the Arab society. "By force of circumstances modernization, liberalization, and colonization became synonymous; and the harmful consequences of this historic conjunction have

---

[18]Quoted in Abdel Malek, *Idéologie et Renaissance nationale*, 286.

continued up to the present day to influence politics and behavior in the Arab world."[19]

The nineteenth-century reform movement sought to establish an abstract, secular, and utilitarian idea of the state. Its leaders were capable of positive dealings with the developed world.[20] A historical compromise was theoretically possible. What actually prevailed was the defensive backward-looking attitude of the Muslim intellectuals, who came to regard the new state as a foreign state. In fact, nothing better illustrates the resentment felt by the Salafists at the new reforms than the criticism leveled by Sheikh Muhammad Abduh against the work of Muhammad Ali. Little known despite its significance and premonition of the future, almost all of this criticism merits another look.

It was in an article published in 1902, on the occasion of the centenary of the founding of the Egyptian State by Muhammad Ali, that Abduh expressed his severest criticisms.[21] "What did Muhammad Ali really achieve?" "He could not bring back to life, but he could deal death." Abduh argues that Muhammad Ali used the army to liquidate all resistance, that he disarmed the population and reduced everyone to the same level; he lowered the status of the great families and promoted parvenus who owed everything to him. The state became nothing more than a machine for levying taxes and raising troops. Muhammad Ali thus destroyed all that was worthwhile and genuine in life—the ability to hold an opinion, the desire to act, independence. For him and his children, the Egyptian people were no more than a flock of sheep.

Aiming to become a king who was independent of the Ottoman Sultan, Muhammad Ali sought the assistance of European citizens, according them exorbitant privileges in return for their services in the army, industry, hydraulic engineering, and hospitals. Furthermore, the various government departments were entrusted to "minorities" such as the Cir-

[19]Abdallah Laroui, "L'Etat dans le monde arabe contemporain: éléments d'une problématique," *Cahier* (No. 3, n.d.). Center for Research on the Contemporary Arab World, Catholic University of Louvain.

[20]Khair al-Din wrote: "It is not by reference to man that we learn the truth, but by reference to truth that we understand man." In this connection see Ahmed Abdesslem, *Les Historiens tunisiens des 17e, 18e, et 19e siècles, Essai d'histore culturelle* (Tunis, 1973); and Sadok Lassoued, "Stratégie et tactique chez Kheireddine," *Actes du Premier Congrès d'Histoire et de Civilisation du Maghreb* (Tunis, 1979), 285–305.

[21]Unless otherwise stated, discussion of Abduh's criticism refers to and quotations are from "Le mythe de Mohammed Ali," in Othman Amin, *L'imam Mohammed Abdou, chef de file de la pensée egyptienne* (text in Arabic) (Cairo, 1966), 279–83.

cassians and the Armenians, with the local inhabitants becoming, in effect, "foreigners in their own country."

Admittedly, groups of students were sent to France, but on their return they were not allowed to communicate what they had learned. To be sure, books were translated on several subjects, but they were then stored in warehouses which remained locked up until the end of the reign of Ismail Pasha. Abduh concludes that this proves that the work of translation was in response to the Europeans' desire to spread their ideas (not to a local initiative) and that the enterprise failed for lack of readers and promoters.

Abduh then examines the major achievements of the regime. While Muhammad Ali built workshops and factories, he did not impart to the Egyptians a love of work or any professional feeling so that they would be able to run a business themselves. Though he created a large army and an immense navy, he did not inculcate in the people "a love of military services, a desire to fight and conquer and be proud of it"; all he inculcated was a desire to avoid service at all costs, which explained the ease with which first the French and later the English occupied the country.

Any examination of the work of Muhammad Ali from Abduh's standpoint must inevitably lead to the conclusion that "he was a great merchant, a brave soldier, and a gifted despot, but he oppressed Egypt and destroyed all forms of independent life there. Whatever signs of life (and progress) are to be seen today come, not from him, but from others."

This text provides a perfect illustration of the lack of enthusiasm of the Muslim intellectuals for a reform program that they rightly regarded as authoritarian, westernizing, and of benefit only to a minority. It was an argument that was to be repeated frequently during the twentieth century, since the Salafist reaction was to become an important feature of political culture and of the debate on modernity in the Arab world and the directions and forms it should take. We now have before us two ideals of political culture: a culture centered on the state, public service, and the social contract, and a culture devoted to the worship of the community and of the charismatic leader. Here we confront a polarized discourse in which constitutional and democratic claims alternate with demands for what Al-Afghani and Abduh call "the just despot: a man born of the people who, through justice, will achieve in fifteen years what reason alone could not conceive in fifteen centuries."[22]

---

[22]Abduh, quoted in Selim Nasr, *La Liberté dans la pensée arabe moderne* (in Arabic) (Damascus, 1983), 467.

## THE STRUGGLE FOR SECULARIZATION

As the colonial system began to lose ground between the two world wars
and national movements emerged, reform once more became the order of
the day but in a new context. While it had been relatively easy for the first
intellectual generation to reach agreement on the subject of a constitution, the same cannot be said of the following generations, since the
constitution, although it represents the fundamental law of the nation,
relates in fact not to an abstract entity but to a particular state. For the
Muslim intellectual it was the *Shari'a* that represented ultimate law, and
this law could not be applied exclusively in one country to the detriment
of the Muslim community as a whole. Given this lack of correspondence
between the state, the religious community and the national community,
the traditional elite was to be an anxious and ambivalent elite, since it
supported the constitutional movement in intellectual terms, while remaining emotionally attached to a larger entity than the country in which
it lives. By contrast, the liberal elite, formed by the tradition of the philosophy of the Enlightenment and the conquests of the French Revolution,
was to take up a clear position in favor of the secular state and nationalism. In their view, "belief" was a feature of solidarity and social harmony,
but it could not be used as the basis for political action.

It will be recalled that the abolition of the Caliphate in Turkey in 1924
had given rise to an extremely lively debate in the Arab world, since the
central issue, apart from the dismantling of the empire, was the republic's
effort to establish a secular state without religious influence in public
affairs. This phrase aptly summarizes the attitude of the modernists and
the direction to be taken by the struggle for secularization.

It was with the Egyptian, Taha Hussein, that the argument for a national, modern, secular, and rationally organized state reached its highest
point. Taha Hussein constantly refers to the national interest in order to
justify the greatest possible openness to world culture and does so with a
degree of optimism which is almost equal to that displayed by the first
liberal generation. He maintains that "independence from the West cannot be attained without adopting the style of the West," that is to say,
without adopting political democracy and rationalizing the economy,
cultural life, and education. Clearly, the contrast with the viewpoint that
now prevails, according to which the degree of independence is measured
in terms of the distance from the Western model, could not be more
striking.

Taha Hussein and his group have been blamed for their "liberalism" and criticized for their readiness to adopt an outlook taken from the West and associated with the rise of the bourgeoisie. The implication of this criticism is that what is good for the West is not necessarily appropriate for the Third World, and that growth, development, and social justice make it necessary to go beyond the "formal liberties" of a liberal revolution. The critics overlooked two points; first, that the Arab intelligentsia had gone beyond the problem of the origins of ideas: ideas now represented an established acquisition for mankind as a whole. Second, a man like Taha Hussein had a more developed conception of the world than that of the traditional liberal. To appreciate this, it is only necessary to examine the role which he assigns to the state in the field of education:

The state has responsibility from beginning to end; it is responsible to individuals and groups and, in addition, it is responsible for an intellectual training which will be compatible with the new national needs . . . which may be summed up as the consolidation of democracy and the preservation of independence.[23]

After the Second World War it was the turn of the Maghreb to refer frequently to the ideals of the French Revolution, subject to maintaining a clear divide between the ideal France of 1789 and the real France, the France of colonization and exclusion. The main principles of the Revolution were invoked as a call to arms, but there is no doubt that these principles had had a deep impact on the imagination of the inhabitants of the Maghreb, as is shown by the words of Kateb Yassine: "I went to prison for having believed too much in the principles of 1789. No French schoolboy has felt such heart-stirrings as I at the accounts of the Revolution."[24] What links the Ataturks, the Bourguibas, the Arab secularists, and the minorities of the Near East to the French Left is precisely a conception of politics that descends directly from the French Revolution. To say that is not to deny the rise of Salafism, nor to conceal the readiness to embrace the Marxist paradigm; it is merely to show one's colors, one's guiding ideas. Some people may wish to go beyond them, while others wish, quite simply, to put them into effect.

[23]Fouad Zakariyya, "Le Moment historique de 'l'Avenir de la culture en Egypte,'" *Al Hilal*, February 1988, 24.
[24]Quoted in André Angsthelm, "1789 dans le discours du mouvement national algérien," *Grand Maghreb*, March 1988, 107.

# 8

The French Revolution and the Middle East

NIKKI R. KEDDIE

The question of the impact of the French Revolution on the Middle East will here be considered under three separate headings, namely: the political-military impact of the French Revolutionary and Napoleonic period; the intellectual-political impact of the ideas of the Enlightenment and of liberal French ideas from the revolutionary period and after; and the development of revolutionary and rebellious movements in the Middle East and their relation, if any, to the French Revolution. Before launching on these topics it is important to note that, from at least the eighteenth century until after World War II, French was *the* language of culture and foreign education throughout the Middle East, as in much of the rest of the world. This meant that persons with foreign language knowledge got most of their European-based ideas from French thinkers, whether or not the recipient had any special "natural" affinity for French above other ideas. Hence, even someone who, left to an open choice, might have tended, say, to adopt English rather than French liberal notions was in fact more likely to read and cite French thinkers. The origins of this pattern antedate the French Revolution and had little to do with that revolution, but it may lead some to overstate the influence of the French Revolution on Middle Eastern ideas.

A problem that enters into almost all discussions of intellectual influence is that it is intrinsically impossible to know if, for example, Middle Eastern figures who cite certain French thinkers would have had more or less the same ideas if they had never come in contact with those thinkers. It seems likely that such Middle Eastern thinkers were stimulated by modern Western thought, but they were also stimulated by elements in their own traditions and by new circumstances that required new approaches; as already noted, they might also have found what additional

140

elements they needed from, say, British, Italian, German, or ultimately American and Russian thinkers had the French not been available. This might have brought different elements to their partial or complete modernism, but it might very likely have led to a result quite similar to their French-influenced views. The main point is that a stress on "influences" often leads scholars to understate the local and internal forces that prompt thinkers and political leaders to find what they know they need from abroad.

Also, consideration of the influence of the French Revolution or of various European movements often leads to an overconcentration on a very few intellectuals and elite figures. There is no doubt that for the Middle East by far the biggest influence came not from the Revolution as such but from the revolutionary and Napoleonic wars that soon affected Egypt, the Ottoman Empire, and even Iran, the three areas to be discussed below. Most scholars seem agreed that the immediate intellectual and cultural influence of the French Revolution was almost nil.[1] In the military and political sphere, which soon spilled over into economic and later cultural developments, however, the Revolution's effect was considerable.

## THE MILITARY AND POLITICAL IMPACT OF THE REVOLUTION

The Near East became almost as centrally involved in the post–French Revolution wars as did most of Europe, so that the region of Europe and the Near East could be considered a single one from this point of view. There will be no attempt to go into details here, but the general outlines of French political and military impact should be clear. There was no positive official reaction to the Revolution or Napoleon. The first major written reaction by an Ottoman statesman to the French Revolution was that it threatened public order by overthrowing religion.[2] Traditional Ottoman friendship with France, as against the Old Ottoman enmities to Austria and Russia, could not withstand Napoleonic advances toward

---

[1] See the disagreements with Bernard Lewis of Serif Mardin, *The Genesis of Young Ottoman Thought* (Princeton: Princeton University Press, 1962), 169ff.; Niyazi Berkes, *The Development of Secularism in Turkey* (Montreal: McGill University Press, 1964), 83–85; and Ibrahim Abu Lughod, *Arab Rediscovery of Europe* (Princeton, N.J.: Princeton University Press, 1963), 134, n. 28.
[2] As cited in Bernard Lewis, "The Impact of the French Revolution on Turkey," *Journal of World History* 1 (July 1953): 105–25.

the Near East in Europe or Napoleon's Egyptian campaign of 1798, before he came to power. There was thus Ottoman warfare against France, and the first foundations were laid for Ottoman dependence on Great Britain, which was to last through most of the nineteenth century.

Just as important was growing Ottoman awareness of the need for military modernization. Already in the early eighteenth century there had been a period of Westernization in the military and cultural spheres, and plans for military modernization were revived by Sultan Selim III, who, by coincidence, came to the throne in 1789. Faced with foreign wars, he got his top advisers to suggest a program centering on military modernization, which was to begin in 1792. Although this was too early to reflect any significant influence of the French Revolution, which was not yet encroaching on the Near East, the program, which failed mainly owing to the opposition of the powerful old military force of janissaries, provides part of the background for later reforms that did reflect influences going back to the French Revolution.[3]

The most important precipitator of French Revolutionary influence in the Ottoman Empire, not only on its semiautonomous Egyptian province but ultimately on the area closer to the capital, Istanbul, was Napoleon's invasion of Egypt in 1798. Although its potential for expansion was soon lost when the British took naval control of the area, the impact of the invasion in Egypt itself was significant and lasting. (There is a tendency among those scholars who want to reverse exaggerations of Western influence in the Middle East to play down that of Napoleon in Egypt, but I find their arguments exaggerated in the opposite direction.) The most important break with the past came when the French forces decisively weakened the ruling and military elite, the Mamlukes, who were never able to take power again. This opened the way for new social groups to take power after the French left. The French also introduced a number of modernizing changes in taxation and administration. Their increased use of local Coptic Christians as a governing and tax-collecting class prefigured the West's favoring of religious minorities in the Ottoman Empire and elsewhere. This led ultimately to greater or complete legal equality for such minorities, which may be said to be a French Revolutionary

[3]See Niyazi Berkes, *Secularism*, chapters 3–4; Bernard Lewis, *The Emergence of Modern Turkey* (London: Oxford University Press, 1961), chapters 3–4; Stanford J. Shaw, *Between Old and New: The Ottoman Empire under Sultan Selim III, 1789–1807* (Cambridge, Mass.: Harvard University Press, 1971).

ideal, although in the Ottoman Empire it was adopted largely for practical, not ideological, reasons. It also, however, associated religious minorities with foreigners, which tended to militate against the very equality and assimilation that some wished to favor.

Those who wish to deny great influence to the Napoleonic expedition are probably right to think that French administrative and taxation changes did not go nearly as far in practice as was intended. But it seems impossible that the innovative post-French ruler, Muhammad Ali (1805–49), could have taken power and accomplished all he did without the prior breakup of the old regime by the French. Muhammad Ali, an Ottoman military leader of Albanian origin, was able, through various maneuvers, to establish himself as autonomous ruler of Egypt within a relatively short time after the French departure. The most important way he took advantage of the French legacy was in killing off at one blow the remaining Mamlukes—had he had the whole Mamluke force to face his coup might not have been possible. It was only then that he could launch a series of radical reforms, many of which built on the Napoleonic precedent, while others were aided by France, his only European ally.

Some of these reforms, undertaken after the fall of Napoleon, had a direct relationship to French revolutionary influences. The most important of these was the sending of a group of students to France. Their religious guide, the young shaikh Rifa'a al-Tahtawi, became interested in secular subjects and, among other things, wrote a laudatory book on French realities and ideas some years after returning to Egypt. This attitude toward France was, however, in a sense an accidental outcome of Muhammad Ali's reform program, most of which, as was true of other initial reform programs in Asia and Africa during the nineteenth century, had the main practical aim of military self-strengthening. With the Mamlukes eliminated, Muhammad Ali was free to turn to building a new model army, which enabled him not only to become essentially independent of his Ottoman overlords but to expand his territory and ultimately, to threaten the Ottoman rulers in battle. Auxiliary to this military program were programs of education, translation, and radical economic reform including industrialization. Although Muhammad Ali did far more than carry forward the program of the Napoleonic invasion, without that invasion it seems exceedingly unlikely that he could have succeeded to the degree that he did. His ultimate military defeat, followed by forced acceptance of a reduced army and economic conditions that made industrialization impossible, came only via an alliance between the Ottoman sultan and the main European Powers.[4]

A contrast to the radical Egyptian changes that have their origins in the French revolutionary period is found in the Ottoman Empire where, for example, Selim III was not able to neutralize the janissaries as the French and Muhammad Ali were able to neutralize the Mamlukes. Selim's reforms and then his rule had to be abandoned after a revolt that combined the janissaries and some of the religious leaders, or *ulama*. His reforming successor, Mahmud II, had to put many years of preparation into his own massacre of the janissaries in 1826, which he knew was a necessary prelude to military and other reforms. In this case the French revolutionary period had little to do directly with reform; it was much more an indirect consequence, resulting from the Ottoman leaders' recognition of a threat from Muhammad Ali, compounded by their inability to do anything effective against revolts in Serbia, Saudi Arabia, and Greece. (In the last two cases Muhammad Ali had to be called in to help, and he put stiff conditions on his aid.) Like Muhammad Ali, however, Mahmud encouraged education and translation, and he also opened up permanent embassies in a number of European countries. These contacts with foreign thought and practice, along with the increased numbers of foreign specialists and advisers who came to both the Ottoman Empire and Egypt, gradually led to a situation where political and cultural ideas as well as technical and scientific materials were studied.

The case of Iran, much farther from continental Europe than Egypt and Turkey and having much less pre–French Revolution contact with Europe, is nonetheless interesting for showing how far the military-political impact of the French Revolution spread. Iran fought several wars with the Russians in the eighteenth century, but in the Napoleonic period Iranian involvement with Europe deepened greatly; both France and Great Britain made increased efforts to establish ties with Iran, using military aid and trade incentives, which for the Iranians were mainly desirable for the help they gave against the Russians. A treaty signed with Sir John Malcolm of the East India Company in 1801 had an anti-French element and was undermined when Britain and Russia (Iran's main enemy) came together as enemies of Napoleon. The French took advantage of the Iran-British estrangement to build up relations and in 1807 signed

[4]The vast bibliography on Muhammad Ali and this period may be approached by reference to the most recent Western-language work on him, Afaf Lutfi al-Sayyid Marsot, *Egypt in the Rein of Muhammad Ali* (Cambridge: Cambridge University Press, 1984).

with Iran the Treaty of Finkenstein and other accords, which provided for French military advisers and training. These came with the mission of General Gardane beginning in 1807. The Persian heir-apparent, Abbas Mirza, was a prince who saw the need for a Western-style military and education, and he continued efforts in this direction from his seat in Tabriz, Azerbaijan, for years after the French mission ended. Unfortunately, the constant changes in European alliances in the Napoleonic period worked to Iran's disadvantage. The accords of 1807 with France, which explicitly pushed out the British, were followed in the same year by the reversal of alliances in the Treaty of Tilsit between Napoleon and Alexander I of Russia, which made them allies and reinstituted Great Britain as an opponent of France's Russian ally. This rearrangement brought British efforts to replace French influence in Iran, culminating in a new treaty negotiated by Sir Harford Jones in 1809. All the while Iran was at war with Russia, for which the British now gave some aid. They even strong and successfully advised Iran not to accept a Russian peace offer but to keep on fighting.

The new reversal of alliances that came after Napoleon's invasion of Russia in 1809 made Russia again an ally of the British. The British now reversed their advice and pressure in Iran, encouraging Iran to accept Russian terms for peace that were worse than those the British had advised them to reject in 1812. Without either French or British aid, the Iranians had no choice but to accept the Treaty of Gulistan, the first of its major unequal treaties, with Russia in 1813.

Although Iran was less developed to begin with and less touched by French events of 1789–1815 than were the Ottomans or Egypt, the effect of this period on Iran's government and military was not negligible. The period saw the first significant agreements with European powers— agreements that had military, training, and trade aspects. It also saw the beginning of Western-style military training, dress, and more modern armaments, even though this was not to lead to much, given that before the mid-nineteenth century nobody in the top ranks of government besides Abbas Mirza was dedicated to military or other modernization.[5]

An ironic outcome of the Revolution and the Napoleonic period in all the Middle Eastern areas under discussion was that a more or less brief burst of French influence in the military and foreign policy spheres was

[5]A brief coverage of nineteenth-century developments, along with bibliographical references, is found in Nikki R. Keddie, *Roots of Revolution: An Interpretive History of Modern Iran* (New Haven: Yale University Press, 1981).

followed, after Napoleon's defeat, by a long-term decline in the influence of France, which was replaced generally in turn by that of Great Britain, Russia, Germany, and the United States. In the Ottoman Empire and Iran the nineteenth century was primarily a period of Russo-British rivalry in which other powers played a major role. The French in the Middle East essentially bet on Muhammad Ali, to whom they provided all sorts of advisers, but when all the other powers combined to stop Muhammad Ali's military advance against the Ottomans and to end his economic independence, France was unable to resist. Although the French continued to have some reduced importance in Egypt, it was ultimately the British who won out there. Thus, when looking at French cultural influence one must not exaggerate its political importance: the British appeared content to let the French subsidize schools in the region and students in France, as well as to influence intellectuals, provided the British could export their goods and exercise political influence or control.

## THE INTELLECTUAL AND POLITICAL INFLUENCE OF THE IDEAS OF THE REVOLUTION

In a well-known article, Bernard Lewis suggested that the French Revolution was the first Western movement that could be really influential in the Muslim world, and that this was because as a secular movement it did not arouse the traditional Christian-Muslim religious opposition among Muslims. This thesis has been strongly criticized by other scholars, who tend to find the immediate intellectual influence of the French Revolution in the Middle East almost nonexistent. Insofar as people were aware of the Revolution and its secularism, they seem to have been hostile to it, and Lewis himself gives almost no evidence of Muslims living close to the time of the French Revolution who welcomed it, either for the reasons he cites or for any other reason.[6] Indeed, the generalization about secularism and the French Revolution's influence, presented early in Lewis's article, sits uneasily in an essay that contains much interesting information mainly on points having little relation to this generalization. Lewis discusses the presence in the Ottoman Empire of prerevolutionary French citizens; French efforts to spread the ideas of the Revolution; and hostility to the

[6]Lewis, "Impact." See Serif Mardin, *The Genesis of Young Ottoman Thought,* 169–70n1; Niyazi Berkes, *The Development of Secularism in Turkey,* 83; and Ibrahim Abu Lughod, *Arab Rediscovery of Europe,* chapter 6. All three of these books have useful material on the later influence of the French Revolution.

Revolution by the Ottoman ruling elite. This article is in fact more notable for showing early Ottoman and Middle Eastern elite opposition to the Revolution, primarily on the grounds of its secularism or hostility to religion (which to them meant hostility also to political stability), than it is for demonstrating early Muslim support for the Revolution.

High level Ottoman hostility to the French Revolution was increased by the eastward movement of French armies toward the Ottoman sphere, and by the Napoleonic invasion of Egypt, officially and in tax terms an Ottoman province. In 1798 a high Ottoman official was asked to prepare a memorandum concerning the invitation of the anti-French allies to the Ottomans to join their coalition. Lewis had usefully quoted at length from this memorandum, which seems to have reflected a widespread Ottoman view:

It is one of the things known to all well-informed persons that the conflagration of sedition and wickedness that broke out a few years ago in France, scattering sparks and shooting flames of mischief and tumult in all directions, had been conceived many years previously in the minds of certain accursed heretics . . . , the known and famous atheists Voltaire and Rousseau, and other materialists like them, had printed and published various works, consisting, God preserve us, of insults and vilification against the pure prophets and great kings, of the removal and abolition of all religion, and of allusions to the sweetness of equality and republicanism, all expressed in easily intelligible words and phrases, in the form of mockery, in the language of the common people. Finding the pleasure of novelty in these writings, most of the people, even youths and women, inclined towards them and paid close attention to them, so that heresy and wickedness spread like syphilis to the arteries of their brains and corrupted their beliefs. When the Revolution became more intense, none took offence at the closing of churches, the killing and expulsion of monks, and the abolition of religion and doctrine: they set their hearts on equality and freedom, through which they hoped to attain perfect bliss in this world, in accordance with the lying teachings increasingly disseminated among the common people by this pernicious crew, who stirred up sedition and evil because of selfishness or self-interest. It is well known that the ultimate basis of the order and cohesion of every state is a firm grasp of the roots and branches of holy law, religion and doctrine; that the tranquillity of the land and the control of the subjects cannot be encompassed by political means alone; that the necessity for the fear of God and the regard for retribution in the hearts of God's slaves is one of the unshakably established divine decrees; that in both ancient and modern times every state and people has had its own religion, whether true or false. Nevertheless the leaders of the sedition and evil appearing in France, in a manner without precedent, in order to facilitate the accomplishment of their evil purposes and in utter disregard to the fearsome consequences, have removed the fear of God and the regard for retribution from the common people, made lawful all kinds of abominable deeds, utterly obliterated all shame and decency . . . in order to keep other states busy with the protection of their own regimes and thus forestall an attack on themselves, they had their rebellious declaration which they call "The Rights of Man" translated into all languages and published in all parts, and strove to incite the common people of the nations and religions to rebel against the kinds to whom they were subject.[7]

Notable in this report is the presentation of religious belief, including fear of retribution for transgressions among the common people, as the foundation of social and political order. This view has been a predominant one in Islamic history, found among rationalist philosophers, theologians, and authors of books of advice to kings, as well as among many Islamic reformers like the nineteenth-century Sayyid Jamal al-Din al-Afghani.[8] (Ironically, I heard frequently from Iranian intellectuals in the 1960s the statement that it was important for the masses to have religious belief, or else they might become disorderly or rebellious.) While the word "secularism" may sound relatively innocuous in the modern West, it did not sound innocuous in the nineteenth-century Middle East. To most Middle Eastern Muslims, "secular" implies "antireligious." Although the quotation above is from an official, the lack of favorable contemporary Muslim citations on the French Revolution suggests that the traditional view regarding attacks on religion was probably the prevalent one.

A second point to be noted in this report is its hostility to writing in a simple language accessible to the common people so that ordinary people and even women and youths could understand and enter into politics. The Revolution was rightly seen as a challenge to the traditional modes of Middle Eastern politics and religion.

The first break with these modes in the Ottoman Empire did not come from intellectuals but from men in the government who made up part of the self-strengthening movement that got its serious start with Sultan Mahmud II. Their activities required education and diplomatic missions abroad and translations of a number of European works. It was essentially as a by-product of governmental and military modernization that some educated men in the Ottoman Empire, as elsewhere in the Middle East, came into contact with Europe, especially France, and began to read French works and to learn French history.

It is difficult, however, to separate out the influence of the French Revolution from other French or even European influences. For example,

[7]Ibid., 121–22.
[8]See Nikki R. Keddie, *An Islamic Response to Imperialism: Political and Religious Writings of Sayyid Jamal ad-Din "al-Afghani"* (Berkeley and Los Angeles: University of California Press, 1968), chapter 2.

one of the earliest French works translated and published, first into Turkish and later into Arabic and Persian, was not any contemporary work but the seventeenth-century "mirror for princes" *Télémaque* by Fénelon. This novel advocated a monarch's good conduct and concern for his subjects' welfare; though it might have been seen as political criticism, as in Fénelon's day, it was hardly revolutionary. Of course, a more radical work could not have been published and might have gotten its translator into trouble, but we do not know that any such translations were contemplated. A short-lived Istanbul salon composed of Ottoman officials in the 1820s was the first group to discuss Enlightenment science, philosophy, and literature, but it met with suspicion from the government.

Ottoman officials of the first half of the nineteenth century were less openly influenced by French revolutionary political thought than was the Egyptian shaikh, Rifa'a al-Tahtawi, who was at the same time a functionary of the Egyptian government and a promoter of certain aspects of liberal French thought and practice. The closest Ottoman analogue was Khaireddin Pasha (1825–90). Interestingly, he was a native of Tunisia and not of Istanbul. He promoted reform as a functionary in Egypt and as chief minister of Tunisia and was strongly influenced by French liberal and constitutional thought. French Enlightenment influence on Ottoman thought and practice may, in less liberal form, be discerned in such advocates of legal reform from the top down in the 1830s and 1840s as Sadik Rifat Pasa and Mustafa Reşid Pasa.

The stronger strain of French liberal and Enlightenment influence came later, from a group of Ottomans who opposed the centralizing, and in the eyes of some people tyrannical, trends in the Ottoman government in the time of Mahmud II, and came particularly under the ministers who ruled after his death in 1839 in the period known as the *Tanzimat,* or "reordering." It is usually the reformist side of this period that is stressed, with its introduction of schools and new tax and fiscal measures, and particularly the point most pushed on the Ottomans by the European powers—de jure and increasingly de facto legal equality for minorities, mainly Christian. But it is also possible to stress the negative features of the period, particularly the Anglo-Ottoman commercial convention of 1838, which obviated protection for Ottoman crafts and industries, and the increasingly centralized rule of the state by a few men, with the accompanying decline of local and group autonomy. The first organized, and in part liberal, opposition to these moves came from a group generally called the Young Ottomans, who were active in the 1860s and 1870s.

They were preceded by an Enlightenment-oriented intellectual, Sinasi, who spent most of his life in France. Their most important intellectual leader, Namik Kemal, was a man of many parts and talents. In relation to the influence of the French Revolution, Kemal is notable for trying to reconcile both Montesquieu and parliamentary constitutionalism with Islamic traditions. He, like a number of later Islamic modernists, tried to equate the Islamic legal system (the *Shari'a*) with the natural law advocated by Enlightenment thinkers. He also defended certain parts of Ottoman tradition against the innovations of the *Tanzimat*, saying that the idea of the separation of powers had been seen in older Ottoman days, with the janissaries representing the populace, and Islamic justices the judiciary.[9] As is usual in such cases, it is difficult to tell whether Kemal believed everything he said on such subjects or whether he was trying to present Western constitutionalism and parliamentarism in a guise that would make it more palatable to his countrymen. Perhaps it was some combination of the two that even Kemal himself would not have been able to sort out.

Certainly Kemal seems to have been more tied to fairly orthodox views on Islam than was another nineteenth-century reformer whose ideas in some ways resembled Kemal's—Sayyid Jamal al-Din al-Afghani. Afghani, an Iranian by birth and schooled in the ideas of philosophers like Avicenna, traveled to Istanbul for the first time in 1869–70; there, he had contact with some advanced thinkers, especially in the field of educational reform and modernization. We do not know if he was in contact with Young Ottoman thought, but some of his later ideas resembled theirs, especially Kemal's. Afghani is known as the intellectual advocate and leader of Pan-Islamism, a movement for the unity of Muslim peoples against the West. In fact, intellectual Pan-Islamism was advocated over a decade before Afghani first wrote of it by certain of the Young Ottomans, particularly Namik Kemal. It was a type of nationalist movement for some kind of political unity against outside encroachment. Insofar as modern nationalism started with the French Revolution, Pan-Islamism, though more often related to movements for Italian, German, and Slavic unity, has its ultimate origins (aside from official advocacy by Ottoman rulers) in the French Revolution.

Kemal's nationalism shows up in his popularizing for the Ottomans of the term *watan*, which had meant home area, to mean the French *patrie*,

[9]Serif Mardin, *Genesis*, chapter 10, and the relevant references in Berkes, *Development*.

or fatherland. His French-style liberalism shows up in his popularizing the word *hurriyet,* which had meant nonslave status, to mean *liberté.* Both these shifts of meaning subsequently took hold in all the main Middle Eastern languages. Kemal and other Ottomans had to fudge the meaning of terms like *Watan* and *Umma* ([Islamic] community), since they wanted to retain their vast Christian territories in the Balkans. There was thus an understandable vagueness about just who comprised the *Watan* and *Umma,* and the terms were used differently in different contexts. Only after some decades did a number of Ottoman thinkers begin to make their nationalism either exclusively Muslim or exclusively Turkish, and only after the loss of non-Turkish and Christian territories after World War I were large numbers of Turks ready to accept a nationalism based mainly on language, culture, and economic ties, of a type similar to that expressed in the French Revolution.

To return to the comparison of Kemal and Afghani, it is striking that although Kemal had more contact with Western thought early in his life, it was the Iranian-born Afghani who took more radical positions on a number of matters. In large measure this radicalism was based on Iranian philosophical and religious traditions, notably the Shaikhi religious movement that formed the background of the Babi-Baha'i offshoot from Shi'ism. Afghani was also well schooled in the Islamic and Iranian philosophical traditions that stressed reason, antinomian mysticism, or both. Along with the Islamic philosophers he believed that literalist religion was good to keep the masses orderly but that the intellectual elite could dispense with it for a more rationalist truth based on a Greek-style philosophy founded on natural law. These philosophical notions fit well with the Deism of Enlightenment thinkers. It was, therefore, easy for Afghani to adopt a number of Western-style ideas without breaking radically with his own particular background. Although he did not visit France and England until his early forties and does not seem to have had extensive contacts with Western thought before then, he was able to learn and adapt very quickly and to impress an antireligious rationalist like Ernest Renan as a man of his own stripe.

Renan had given a lecture saying that Islam was intrinsically hostile to science, tying this to the supposed unscientific nature of Semites like the Arabs. Both Afghani and Namik Kemal wrote answers to this printed lecture, but their tones were entirely different. Namik Kemal, writing in Turkish, produced an apologetic defense of Islam and its scientific abilities and achievements. Afghani, on the contrary, wrote that all religions were hostile to science and that Christianity, as an older religion, had a head start in freeing science from religious oppression, but the Muslim world could move in the same direction. He added that most people, except for the intellectual elite, preferred religion to science, so that the struggle between them would not end. Renan then wrote praising Afghani's intelligence and rationality, attributing them largely to the fact that he was not a Semite.[10]

Within the context of this discussion of the influence of French revolutionary thought, an important thing about these exchanges is that it was possible for someone coming out of a particular Iranian unorthodox background to appear more attuned to Westerners and Western ideas than someone with a more "Western" formation. Renan was not the only Westerner or Frenchman to record his high opinion of Afghani. There was, in other words, a living unorthodox tradition in Iran that drew upon both rationalist philosophy and mysticism and prepared some people for at least partial acceptance of modern ideas. Partly because of this, Iran had more rebellions and revolutions in the nineteenth and twentieth centuries than any other Middle Eastern country, even though Iran was less touched by economic and political influence from the West than were Turkey and Egypt. This pattern, manifested as late as the revolution of 1979, owes something to Iranian intellectual and cultural traditions.

There were also nineteenth-century Iranian reformers more influenced by French thought than was Afghani. The most notable was Malkom Khan, the son of an Armenian convert to Islam who, like his son, was in government service. Malkom Khan was educated in France and introduced into Iran a group based on French freemasonry. He also called, with increasing boldness after he lost his ambassadorship to Britain, for the rule of law and even a constitution. The influence of French liberal thought on Malkom Khan also showed up in his organization of a society of humanity, based on a religion of humanity on the model of Auguste Comte's ideas.[11]

Not only for Malkom Khan but also for a number of other Middle Eastern thinkers, postrevolutionary French thought and organization had a considerable influence. Freemasonry was not exclusively French in the

[10]Keddie, *Islamic Response,* chapter 2 and part II.

[11]On Iranian internal traditions see Mangol Bayat, *Mysticism and Dissent: Socio-religious Thought in Qajar Iran* (Syracuse: Syracuse University Press, 1982); a very critical view of Malkom Khan is found in Hamid Algar, *Mirza Malkum Khan: A Study in the History of Iranian Modernism* (Berkeley and Los Angeles: University of California Press, 1973).

Middle East, but many lodges were, and in both the Ottoman Empire and Egypt some Masonic lodges (such as that led by Jamal al-Din al-Afghani in Egypt in the 1870s or the Young Turks' lodges) had an important political role. The Saint-Simonians were active and influential in the Middle East, and Comte and others were known. As the case of Malkom Khan suggests, ideas like that of a "religion of humanity" had a resonance among Middle Eastern thinkers who, like some Frenchmen, wanted to find salvation in a kind of secular religion. Particularly appealing to such men were all-encompassing ideologies that promised a solution to all problems if only the proper path were followed.

A slightly less influential friend of Malkom Khan's, Mirza Yusuf Khan, made an even more systematic appeal to French revolutionary ideas as a partial salvation for Iran. In his main work, *Yek Kalemeh* (One Word), he spoke of law, on the model of the French civil code, as the salvation of Iran. He also freely translated the Declaration of the Rights of Man and Citizen. Like the Young Ottomans before him, he tried to reconcile Western law with Islam and the Quran.

To deal briefly with the Egyptian case, the writings of Tahtawi praising much about French life and politics have been mentioned. It may be a pure historical accident that there was no Tahtawi figure in Istanbul. What is rather similar regarding Egyptian and Ottoman reaction to French ways is that an autocratic type of Westernization came to be practiced by the government in both countries, and that this, along with the growth of Western economic and political control of one's country, brought a reaction in both countries against pure Westernization. Similar reactions came later in Iran.

In the case of Egypt this changeover from high-level Westernism to an anti-Western reaction was especially clear. Tahtawi, a government official for most of his life, was not only a great admirer of French ways and the first almost pure Westernizer but also for a long time the most important Western-influenced thinker who could be considered a major reformer. Although he was careful not to write about sensitive subjects such as the legitimacy of monarchy and may not have favored parliamentarianism, his description of France makes it clear he favored almost pure Westernization in a variety of political, educational, and social spheres. However, he was writing before Westerners took over the economic and eventually the political life of Egypt, beginning in the 1870s. Once this had happened, an ironical yet logical change occurred among intellectuals. The most nationalist and radical of them rejected large elements of Western thought and practice, which henceforth came to be associated with elite-class liberal moderates.

This pattern can be discerned in a number of fields, but here we will limit ourselves to views on the position of women. Radical anti-British Egyptian politicians of the late nineteenth and early twentieth centuries who generally came from a petty-bourgeois background, including most notably the radical nationalist leader Mustafa Kamil (no relation to either Turkish Kemal), defended traditional and "Islamic" practices regarding women and rejected their reform as a Western plot. (This was despite Kamil's close ties to and correspondence with a liberated French woman.) It was moderates like Ahmad Lutfi al-Sayyid who adopted a more "Western" position on reform as on other subjects.[12] (Similar anti-Western radicals, such as Tilak in India, are found in other countries under colonial rule.) This situation suggests that it may be especially problematic to try to assess the influence of the French Revolution by the time a generation or two had passed. Who is the more "influenced"—the conservative to moderate Westernizer or the anti-Western radical? By the time Western-style education became really widespread the French Revolution was so intermixed with other trends in intellectual life, including nationalist anti-Westernism, that it is almost impossible to separate out French Revolutionary influences. In Iran, the recurrent alliances since 1890 between radical intellectuals and clerics hostile to the government and to foreign control often discouraged the open voicing of secular or Enlightenment ideas. Lesser restraints were present elsewhere in the Middle East.

## THE INFLUENCE OF THE FRENCH REVOLUTION ON MIDDLE EASTERN REVOLTS

In rebellious or revolutionary movements in the Middle East, it is again difficult to separate out French Revolutionary influences. It should be noted, however, that ideas stemming ultimately from the influence of the French Revolution, such as constitutionalism, parliamentarianism, liberty, and the fatherland were important in the ideologies of various revolutionary and rebellious movements. They were important in the movement for a constitution in the Ottoman Empire that came to fruition in 1876

[12]Juan Ricardo Cole, "Feminism, Class, and Islam in Turn-of-the-Century Egypt," *International Journal of Middle East Studies* 13 (November 1981): 387–407; Keddie, "Western Rule vs. Western Values: Suggestions of a Comparative Study of Asian Intellectual History," *Diogenes* 26 (1959): 71–96.

with the dethroning of a sultan and the introduction of a constitution. This constitution, however, conceded so much to the executive that, without its violation, it could be used to support the autocratic rule of Sultan Abdulhamid II. In Egypt the various moves by Arab military officers and constitutionalists against Khedive Ismail and against foreigners out to control Egypt culminated in the Urabi Rebellion, which some authors have called a revolution, in 1881–82. Here, it was intervention by the British that put down the revolt and put Egypt under de facto British rule.[13] The revolt's ideology was populist and antiforeign nationalist with strong constitutionalist elements.

In Iran, the most rebellious and revolutionary country of the Middle East down to today, even though it long felt much less European influence than the central Middle East, the French Revolution's influence on revolts was somewhat less but still existed. The heretical Babi Revolts of the 1840s owed nothing to the French Revolution; even the mass movement against a British tobacco monopoly in 1891–92, led ideologically by the *ulama*, owed more to widespread antiforeignism and to the self-interest of the traditional bourgeoisie than it did to any Western ideology. It was only in the Constitutional Revolution of 1905–11 that Western ideology began to play a major role. Constitutionalism—stemming distantly from the French Revolution and more proximately from the Ottomans; from constitutional Japan's victory over the Russians; and from adoption of a constitution in Russia after the revolution of 1905—became the central demand. As a result, a constitution was attained in 1906–7. Some of the rhetoric of the Constitutional Revolution was French-influenced; specifically, that of the radical newspaper that threatened the shah with the fate of Louis XVI if he continued to defy the parliament. (Indeed, there was an assassination attempt against Shah Muhammad Ali, who was ultimately exiled—a French-style execution would in practice have been unthinkable.)

Appeals to the French Revolution were notable both during the Iranian constitutional revolution and especially during the Ottoman Young Turk revolt that reinstated the constitution of 1876 in 1908 and, after a counterrevolutionary interval, overthrew Sultan Abdul Hamid. By this time, both in France itself and in the Middle East and elsewhere, the French Revolution had become a kind of myth in which the revolutionary slogan,

---

[13]The newest work on the period is Juan R. I. Cole, *Colonialism and Social and Cultural Origins of Egypt's 'Urabi Movement* (Princeton, N.J.: Princeton University Press, 1993).

Liberty, Equality, and Fraternity, came to stand for human rights, the rule of law, and parliamentary government, while the darker side of the Revolution was played down or essentially forgotten. In autocratic monarchies like Iran and the Ottoman Empire this myth had a special appeal and relevance, since it meant that such monarchies could be limited or overthrown by revolutionary action by the populace or its representatives and replaced by just representative institutions. One can understand why this view of the meaning of the French Revolution should have a special appeal in autocratic countries, quite apart from the hegemony of French culture in these countries. French Revolutionary slogans, in their original form or combined with local ideas, were widespread in the Ottoman 1908 movement, and may be found in the press, in artwork, and in the coinage.[14]

The stress in these early Middle Eastern revolutions on parliamentary constitutionalism is quite typical of such initial revolutions almost everywhere. The French Revolution was only one of the influences that produced this emphasis; it was even less important in influencing the timing and course of these revolutionary movements, which owed much more to local social, economic, and political circumstances. Nevertheless, the original vision and rhetoric of the French Revolution often finds echoes in these first revolutionary movements in the Middle East. The positive aspects of the French Revolution provided an effective model for the overthrow of autocratic rulers and the institution of representative government and the rule of law. Neither in France nor in the Middle East could postrevolutionary reality equal the model.

In sum, the most direct and important influences of the French Revolution in the Middle East came from the political and military changes felt in that area in the period 1789–1815. In the sphere of ideology, French influence was both considerably later and more diffuse—mixed with a variety of influences and of specific local circumstances. And when we look at Middle Eastern revolutionary movements this diffusion is increased, with the French influence having entered into a stream of ideo-

[14]After this chapter was originally written, I attended a session of the American Historical Association in December 1989, San Francisco, on "The French Revolution in Middle Eastern Revolutionary Consciousness." I thank the three participants for sending me their fine and useful papers: Palmira Brummett, "The French Revolution: Language and Press in Ottoman Istanbul 1908–1911"; Rashid Khalidi, "The French Revolution as Model and Exemplar: The Arabic Press after the 1908 Ottoman Revolution"; and Mohamad Tavakoli-Targhi, "Constitutionalist Imagery in Iran and the Ideals of the French Revolution."

logical views combining a number of foreign and domestic sources, while specific local circumstances became increasingly crucial. Nonetheless, as a specific model or myth of revolution, the influence of the French Revolution in the Middle East was not equaled by any other until the Russian Revolution came to rival it. And in many ways it has continued to be significant throughout the twentieth century.

# 9

━■┅●┅●┅●┅●┅●┅●┅●┅●┅●┅●┅●┅●┅●┅●┅●┅●┅●┅●┅●┅●┅●┅●┅■━

## The revival of political history and
## the French Revolution in Mexico

### CHARLES A. HALE

The significance of the French Revolution in the history of Latin America can hardly be taken for granted after two centuries. In fact, twenty-five years of indifference may be just now beginning to give way to a revival of interest in the French Revolution among historians of Latin America. How significant the French Revolution is perceived to have been in Latin America depends on the weight given by historians to national politics, particularly to the politics of the nineteenth century. It also depends on the weight given to ideas. The history of both politics and ideas experienced a sharp decline in the mid-1960s, as an increasingly professional cadre of historians reacted against traditional political history, against *historia patria*, in pursuit of presumably more fundamental economic patterns, cultural continuities, and social and regional variations.

The French Revolution as a source of influence or as a model for understanding the Latin American experience has had little place in these historiographical departures. Both the economic and the cultural interpretations have emphasized Latin American dependence, and they have construed the nineteenth century (and even in some cases the twentieth century) to be a neocolonial era, when the formal ties to Spain and Portugal were replaced by informal ties to world capitalism or to Western liberal ideas. The implication of these interpretations is that independence is superficial and that dependence is the deeper experience of the region. A further implication is that true autonomy, economic or cultural, can come only through popular anticolonial revolution or through the recovery of autochthonous Iberian cultural mores. The burgeoning social and regional historiography, whether Marxist or non-Marxist, has sought out

the class or ethnic peculiarities of the subcontinent and has often ignored
national politics and traditional political milestones.

Moreover, there is little evidence that the long-dominant social or
class-based interpretations of the French Revolution itself, the accounts
by Jean Juarès, Albert Mathiez, Georges Lefebvre, and Albert Soboul,
among others, have had much impact on the social and economic historiography of modern Latin America. The reason is probably that the
social interpretation necessarily depicted France's bourgeois and then
proto-socialist revolution as an internal European phenomenon, an upheaval directed against a French old regime. France's experience could
hardly provide a model for understanding a dependent neocolonial region bound to the industrialized nations of northern Europe or to a
capitalist world-system. In fact, France itself might be considered a part of
that oppressive system. Nor could French society be profitably compared
to the ethnically diverse and racially mixed society of Latin America.

The significance of the French Revolution for Latin America depends,
therefore, not only on the weight historians give to politics but also upon
a political interpretation of the Revolution itself. The two naturally flow
together when historians of modern Latin America recognize the com-
monplace and traditional fact of political independence as the point of
departure of their studies, a political independence achieved during what
R. R. Palmer called the "Age of the Democratic Revolution." While acknowledging that ties of dependence and social peculiarities permeate the
history of Latin America, we must also emphasize its uniqueness among
other ex-colonial regions of the so-called Third World. Latin America, by
virtue of its early nineteenth-century achievement of political independence, had a liberal century, during which the French Revolution served
as a continual point of reference for political ideas and policies. "Liberal"
and "liberalism" as political terms were first used in Spain in the Cortes
of Cádiz (1810–12), and they signified (as they did in France) an acceptance, albeit critical, of French revolutionary doctrines.[1] From Spain the
terms passed naturally to colonies struggling for their independence.

Strong evidence of the revival of Latin American political history is the
recent magisterial work by François-Xavier Guerra, *Le Mexique: De
l'Ancien Régime á la Révolution*.[2] Guerra's volumes not only revise our

[1] See Juan Marichal, "España y las raíces semánticas del liberalismo," *Cuadernos* 11 (1955):
53–60; also "The French Revolution Background in the Spanish Semantic Change of
'Liberal' (1810)," *American Philosophical Society Yearbook* (1955), 291–93.
[2] François-Xavier Guerra, *Le Mexique: De l'Ancien Régime á la Révolution*, 2 vols. (Paris,

view of Mexican history from the late colonial era to the beginning of the
Revolution of 1910 but they also demonstrate anew the relevance of the
French Revolution for understanding modern Latin America. Let us re-
view the work briefly as an introduction to this chapter.

Guerra's theme is the establishment of modern political culture in
Mexico, the entry of modern ideology and values into a traditional or
"holistic" society. He also construes this process to be the result of a
conflict between two *sociabilités politiques,* two modes of conducting
political activity: (1) the traditional, which is based on concrete personal
and family ties, accepted hierarchies, and community, group, and religious identities, and (2) the modern, which is based on abstract and
impersonal notions of individualism, equality, and legal uniformity, and
on secular values. Guerra argues that modern political culture had its
origin in the Enlightenment, was implemented in the French Revolution,
and passed on to liberal Spain and thus to Mexico. The Mexican liberal
program of the nineteenth century was based on this new ideology and
was epitomized in the democratic provisions of the Constitution of 1857,
whose immediate model was the French republican Constitution of 1848.
The regime of Porfirio Díaz (1877–1911) represented a compromise between the traditional and the modern, and thus, the progress of modern
ideology was arrested until it was given new impetus after 1900 by the
liberal clubs, the radical Partido Liberal Mexicano, and finally by Francisco I. Madero's democratic movement of 1908 to 1911.

In formulating his study of Mexico, Guerra draws explicitly on the
insights of François Furet, the leader in the now ascendant political interpretation of the French Revolution. Furet, in turn, has revived the early
twentieth-century work of Augustin Cochin, which focused on the *sociétés de pensée,* the literary and philosophical societies of eighteenth-
century France that articulated the new conception of politics based on
ideas.[3] For Cochin, these societies were the forerunners of the Jacobin

1985). A two-volume Spanish edition has been recently published (Mexico, 1988). See also
"Lugares, formas y ritmos de la politica moderna," *Boletín de la academia nacional de la
historia* [Caracas] 71 (1988): 2–18. The interest Guerra's work has aroused in France and
in Latin America can be demonstrated by the large number of students pursuing theses
under his direction at the Sorbonne and by the papers presented at a recent symposium in
Paris, "L'Amérique latine face á la Révolution française."

[3]François Furet, *Interpreting the French Revolution* (Cambridge, 1981; French edition,
1978); Augustin Cochin, *Les Sociétés de pensée et la Révolution en Bretagne, 1788–1789,*
2 vols. (Paris, 1925). Guerra also draws on the theories of the anthropologist Louis Dumont, who distinguishes sharply between traditional or "holistic" society, based on hier-
archy as a value, and modern society based on equality and individualism. See Dumont,

clubs that became the vehicle for implanting modern political culture during the Revolution. Guerra finds the Hispanic counterpart of the *sociétés de pensée* to be the free-thinking Masonic organizations of Spain, which were replicated in nineteenth-century Mexico and to which a large number of leading politicians and intellectuals belonged.

However, the core of Guerra's work deals with traditional political culture or *sociabilité*. He presents a massive compilation of biographical information on five thousand individual "political actors" of the late Díaz years, along with some three thousand more groups, communities, and localities, all of which Guerra tabulates by computer to demonstrate the vast and complex network of traditional ties that in his view formed the "reality" of nineteenth-century Mexican politics, ties reminiscent of old-regime Europe. Juxtaposed to this elaborate corpus of data and this analysis of political reality are the harbingers of modernity, the liberal and democratic ideas that seep in after about 1800 (especially through the Masonic lodge) and produce the "fictions" of "the people" and "the nation" that appear in Mexico's constitutions, in short, modern ideology. It is toward Guerra's concept of modern ideology that I would like to direct some brief comments.

One is struck in Guerra's work by the contrast between his treatment of society, which is immensely rich and complex, and his treatment of ideas, which is one-dimensional. As noted above, Guerra begins with the Constitution of 1857, which included a declaration of the rights of man, a pronouncement of popular sovereignty, and provisions for legal equality, separation of powers, federalism, popularly elected judges, a single-chamber legislature, and a limited executive. These are the ideas that seem to make up Guerra's modern ideology—the ideas that were propagated by the Masonic lodges, by the liberal elite, by the Díaz regime (paradoxically) in promoting state-directed public education, and ultimately by the liberal clubs that preceded the Revolution of 1910.

Absent from Guerra's otherwise impressive study is a systematic analysis of political ideas. He scarcely acknowledges the role of conservative thought or the existence of ideological conflict (in the sense of a conflict of ideas). The liberal elite of the nineteenth century, he asserts, "has no theoretical enemies; facing it is only the weight of social reality," that is, the traditional *sociabilité*.[4] Moreover, except during the Díaz period,

*Homo Hierarchicus. The Caste System [of India] and Its Implications*, rev. English ed. (Chicago, 1980) and *From Mandeville to Marx: The Genesis and Triumph of Economic Ideology* (Chicago, 1977).
[4]Guerra, *Le Mexique*, 1:183 (Spanish ed., 1:202).

Guerra does not identify conflicts within the liberal elite; even then, the contention between "positivist liberals" and "historic liberals" dissolves in the pursuit of a common modernizing project. Liberal and democratic ideas become homogenized in Guerra's treatment as the ingredients of an all-embracing modern ideology. Of course, the main reason for this one-dimensional treatment of ideas is that Guerra's concern is not ideas per se, but modern political culture, that is, the new conception of political activity and power relationships based on rational thought, which through civic education became in effect a new political value system.[5]

Instead of viewing ideas as an integral part of politics and policy formation, Guerra tends to regard ideas as an imposition, as "fictions" imposed on an existing "reality." Imposition requires agents, which Guerra identifies in the first instance as the Masonic lodges, the Mexican counterparts of Cochin's and Furet's *sociétés de pensée*. However, we know practically nothing about the Masonic lodges, and Guerra does not advance our knowledge. For instance, Guerra often relies for information on Catholic "Masonic plot" literature, which is even less reliable in Mexico than it is in France.[6] Thus, it requires a leap of faith to accept the Mexican Masonic lodges as direct analogues of the thoroughly investigated French *sociétés de pensée*. Future study of the Masonic lodges may prove Guerra right, but such study will not replace an analysis of the complexities of Mexican thought itself, an essential ingredient of any revival of political history. In particular we must understand the complexities of liberalism, the dominant set of political ideas in the nineteenth century.

Guerra is certainly correct in emphasizing the French and Spanish sources of Mexican thought as well as the importance of the French Revolution as a point of orientation. However, he fails to emphasize the

---

[5]The reader will note that in summarizing Guerra's argument I have used his terms "modern ideology," "modern political culture," and even "sociabilité moderne" interchangeably. A closer analysis of Guerra's use of terms may reveal distinctions that are not readily apparent to me. My notion of "ideology," namely, as constituting the propositions or rhetorical positions of a political program that are directed in defense of or in opposition to an institutional and social order, is clearly narrower and less inclusive than Guerra's. His definition of ideology might be closer to Dumont's, that is, "the totality of ideas and values common to a society or group of people in general": *From Mandeville to Marx*, 7. Guerra's phrase is from *Le Mexique*, 1:166 (Spanish ed., 1:184).
[6]Guerra cites particularly Félix Navarrete, *La Masonería en la historia y en las leyes de Méjico*, 2d ed. (Mexico, 1962). Navarrete was the pseudonym of Jesus García Gutiérrez (1875–1958), a prominent Catholic journalist and author of tracts attacking anticlerical legislation. The book is strongly polemical in tone. Guerra does note the need for a documented history of freemasonry: *Le Mexique*, 1:411, n. 13 (Spanish ed., 1:67, n. 12).

distinctiveness of Mexican political ideas by virtue of their development in a newly independent nation, an American ex-colony of Europe. When he says that Mexican liberalism was "a prolongation of Spanish liberalism and not a reaction against conservative Spain," Guerra oversimplifies Mexico's struggle to establish its identity as a New World republic. Moreover, Guerra's effort to find in the French Revolution of 1789 the model for understanding the Mexican Revolution of 1910 distorts the nineteenth-century experience and opens his work to the criticism that it is Euro- and even Francocentric.[7]

In order to demonstrate the complexity of Mexican thought and also to explore a less-appreciated dimension of the impact of the French Revolution, let us consider how Mexican liberals used the ideas of Benjamin  Constant, Edouard Laboulaye, and Hippolyte Taine in their unsuccessful effort to establish a system of "constitutional balance," a system that would prevent the extremes of "anarchy" and "despotism." The elements of this system were an effective separation of powers, an ambivalence if not hostility toward popular sovereignty, and a tie between individual rights and propertied interests as the guarantee of stability. The system was elitist, antidemocratic, and theoretically antistatist, though it came to include a strong state if properly limited by constitutional means. It drew inspiration from French historical constitutionalism, a current of thought that had its origins in Montesquieu and was developed in the nineteenth century by Tocqueville, as well as by Constant, Laboulaye, and Taine. French constitutionalists idealized English (and in one instance, North American) institutions and made their point of departure a critique of the French Revolution and the egalitarian or "Jacobin" revolutionary tradition. I will examine three episodes in Mexican constitutional liberalism from the 1820s to the 1890s, each of which was guided by French experience and French thought. I will then conclude by suggesting the possible influence of this nineteenth-century critique of the French Revolution on its present-day interpreters, including François-Xavier Guerra.

The first episode came in the aftermath of the Revolution for Indepen-

[7]These epithets are used by Alan Knight in his several critiques of Guerra's work. See review in *Hispanic American Historical Review* 68 (1988): 137–43; "Interpreting the Mexican Revolution," Texas Papers on Mexico, Institute of Latin American Studies, University of Texas, Austin; and his reply to Guerra in *HAHR* 69 (1989): 385–88. I admit to ambivalence on this matter, because it is in part Guerra's continental (that is, Spanish and French) perspective on Mexico that attracts me to his work. It should also be noted that Guerra's current research focuses on the independence era and its aftermath and gives closer attention to political ideas. See "Le peuple souverain: fondements et logiques d'une fiction (pays hispaniques aux xix<sup>e</sup> siècle)," in press.

dence and can be traced in the ideas of José María Luis Mora, Mexico's leading liberal theorist of the postindependence generation. Besides directing two important journals between 1821 and 1830, Mora was the prime mover in drawing up the first constitution for the state of Mexico, by far the new nation's most populous entity within the federal system established by the Constitution of 1824. The constitutionalism of the 1820s was a response to the revolutionary turmoil of the previous decade, which began with Miguel Hidalgo's popular insurgency in 1810 and ended with the creation of a Mexican empire by Agustín de Iturbide in 1822. Mexican constitutionalism was also a continuation of the enthusiasm generated in 1820 by the restoration of the Spanish Constitution of 1812 that remained in effect after independence in 1821 and became the principal model for both the national and the state code.

Though liberal Spain provided much of the specific guidance for Mexican constitution makers of the 1820s, postrevolutionary France provided the theoretical impulse, particularly through the ideas of Benjamin Constant. Constant was the classic continental constitutionalist, whose cardinal principle was the defense of individual liberty against the invasions of arbitrary authority. He upheld that principle in widely differing regimes from 1796 to 1830. Beginning as a moderate republican during the Directory, he was eliminated from his post in the Tribunate by Napoleon in 1802 and remained a bitter opponent of the emperor until 1814. Nonetheless, the following year he accepted a position in the Council of State during Napoleon's Hundred Days and wrote his major work, *Principes de politique,* at this time. While the specific form of government was not his concern, constitutional monarchy was the context in which Constant was most at home; and following in the spirit of Montesquieu, England was his model. With England in mind, he emphasized the need for "a numerous and independent representation" and for "intermediate bodies" to act as positive safeguards between the individual and the state.[8] There was much in Constant that was faintly aristocratic, as there was with all nineteenth-century liberals of his persuasion. Yet he condemned the pre-1789 nobility as a privileged corporation without function and

---

[8]Benjamin Constant, "Principes de politique applicables à tous les gouvernements représentatifs et particulièrement à la constitution actuelle de la France" (1815), *Cours de politique constitutionnelle ou collection de ouvrages publiés sur le gouvernement représentatif,* ed. Edouard Laboulaye, 2d ed., 2 vols. (Paris, 1872), 1:146. The work has been recently reprinted (Geneva, 1982). I have drawn this section of the chapter from my earlier work, *Mexican Liberalism in the Age of Mora, 1821–1853* (New Haven, 1968), chapters 2 and 3.

looked instead to the parliamentary heritage of the early years of the Revolution.

Constant could well have written Mora's first articles of 1821 and 1822. Although Mora quoted Montesquieu more frequently than Constant did and regarded him as the "pathfinder for liberal institutions," Mora also emphasized that Montesquieu lived before the era of "political revolutions" and thus could not "know the spirit of contemporary monarchies and republics."[9] It was Constant's ambivalence toward the French Revolution that made his thought directly relevant to Mora's Mexico. Constant shared Tocqueville's later dictum that "in the French Revolution there were two impulses in opposite directions, which must never be confounded; the one was favorable to liberty, the other to despotism."[10] The problem was how to consolidate the liberty that had been gained, particularly "when twenty-five years of storm have destroyed the ancient institutions of a people." Far from an absence of government, Constant saw in the Revolution the "continuous and universal presence of an atrocious government," guided by Rousseau's doctrine of popular sovereignty.[11]

Like Constant, Mora did not categorically deny popular sovereignty. Neither could have done so and remained a liberal. Yet both began with a critique of Rousseau and the misuse of his ideas by revolutionary governments after 1792. "As the celebrated Constant observes," wrote Mora, "the horrible outrages against individual liberty and civil rights committed in the French Revolution arose in large part from the vogue of this [Rousseau's] doctrine, which is not only illiberal, but the fundamental principle of despotism."[12] Examples from recent French history permeated Mora's political thought of the 1820s. Whenever he turned to the question of civil rights, to the separation of powers, and particularly to judicial independence, he was likely to include a reference to the Reign of Terror or to Napoleon. Mora regarded Iturbide as Mexico's Napoleon, an analogy that became even closer when Iturbide abandoned the pretense of constitutionality.

[9]*Actas del congreso constituyente del estado libre de México,* 10 vols. (Mexico and Toluca, 1824–31), 6:892 (24 February 1826).
[10]Alexis de Tocqueville, *Democracy in America,* 2 vols. (New York, 1954), 1:100.
[11]Constant, "Observations sur le discours prononcé par S. E. le ministre de l'intérieur en faveur du projet de loi sur la liberté de la presse" (1814–18), *Cours,* 1:504; "De l'esprit de conquête et de l'usurpation, dans leurs rapports avec la civilisation européene" (1814), *Cours,* 2:239.
[12]José María Luis Mora, "Discurso. La Suprema Autoridad civil no es ilimitada" (1822), *Obras sueltas,* 2d ed. (Mexico, 1963), 473.

In the debates over federalism versus centralism of the 1820s, Mora took a position that was often judged to be centralist but was, in effect, inspired by Constant's "new type of federalism." Having lived through the Revolution, Constant assumed the continuity of centralized authority and rejected the loose association of powers that heretofore had been called federalism. He called particularly for the revival of municipal autonomy as a part of his system of guarantees. He even romanticized village magistrates and savants who kept local customs alive. In reaction to extreme Napoleonic centralism, he issued his famous dictum, "variety is life; uniformity is death."[13] Mora likewise sought, within the assumptions of a centralized administration, to revive the municipalities of the state of Mexico. As a Mexican Creole, he made no effort to romanticize what he saw as degenerate Indian communities too often controlled by corrupt caciques, but he did favor a measure of autonomy along with a system of control by prefects modeled on that of France. Mora's proposal prevailed in the state constitution of 1827.

At the heart of Mora's constitutional liberalism, like that of Constant, was the idea that individual liberty could be best guaranteed if the political process were entrusted to property holders. The experience of the Revolution confirmed the importance of property for Constant. Without it as a balance, he said, men of all professions took up "chimerical theories" and "inapplicable exaggerations."[14] Mora expressed similar views in the debates over the electoral law for the state of Mexico, and they were only strengthened by the factional and social turmoil of 1827 to 1829. In fact, Mora's hostility to egalitarian political democracy came through most clearly during these years, which culminated in the popular upheaval that brought Vicente Guerrero to the presidency. Constant's attachment to property revealed aristocratic leanings, though as a postrevolutionary liberal he could not use the term. Mora did use the term in 1830, which in Mexico revealed a Creole elitism that became a central feature of Mexican constitutionalism.

The weakness of constitutional liberalism as a political program became apparent to Mora after 1830. As a liberal he could no longer overlook, as he had in the 1820s, the reality of entrenched corporate privilege, epitomized by the juridical privileges of the church and the army and by the vast ecclesiastical property holdings. Mora realized that

[13]Constant, "De l'esprit de conquête," *Cours*, 2:174.
[14]Constant, "Principes de politique," *Cours*, 1:61.

the state, instead of being further restricted, must be strengthened if equality under the law and individualism were to have meaning. Thus, he turned away from constitutionalism. Benjamin Constant and postrevolutionary France became less relevant to him, and he began to refer increasingly to the Spanish philosopher Gaspar Melchor de Jovellanos. He even reprinted several of Jovellanos's writings. Despite differences of detail, Mora shared with Jovellanos the dilemma of Spanish constitutionalism—the dilemma of trying to forge a constitutional system where historic precedents were weaker than in France (non-existent in Mexico), where monarchical attachments were strong, and where the regime of corporate privilege was still intact. As theorist for the first Mexican reform government of 1833, Mora sensed that the "constitution" had to give way to a fiscally strong administrative state that could secularize society, institute legal equality, and yet avoid the democratic extremes of the French Jacobins or of the Cádiz radicals. Thus, it was the Spanish Bourbon tradition that provided the most relevant model for anticorporate reform.[15]

The second constitutionalist episode came in the aftermath of the Reforma, Mexico's mid-century ideological and civil conflict that in many respects had been foreshadowed in 1833. The year 1867 marked the restoration of the liberal republic (and the gaining of Mexico's "second independence") under Benito Juárez, in triumph over the French army of Napoleon III, Emperor Maximilian of Austria, and the native conservatives. A month after the liberal victory, the Juárez government issued the *convocatoria,* a call for elections that marked the official return to constitutional government following the de facto wartime dictatorship of Juárez. However, the *convocatoria* aroused great hostility because it included a proposal to modify the Constitution of 1857 that had been the banner of the liberal cause, even if it had been only briefly put into practice. In defending the changes, Minister Sebastián Lerdo de Tejada argued that to complete the Reforma, Mexico must abandon "convention government" in favor of "good administration" and "constitutional balance." The constitution, we will recall, had proclaimed popular sovereignty and had provided for a parliamentary regime on the French model of 1848. Under the constitution, said Lerdo, the unicameral legislature was everything, the executive nothing. As a vehicle of "social reform" in the trying circumstances of 1857 to 1863, convention government might

---

[15]For further discussion of the shift in Mora's thought in the 1830s, see my *Mexican Liberalism,* chapter 4.

have been justified, but "in normal times, the despotism of a convention can be as bad as the despotism of a dictator, or worse."[16]

The opposition to the *convocatoria* and its call for constitutional reform came from state governors whose power as regional chieftains had grown during the war years. It also came from doctrinaire defenders of the constitution, later labeled "metaphysicians" or "Jacobins," who were spokesmen for the more egalitarian tendencies of the Reforma. The first were opposed to the *convocatoria* because it would strengthen the central government and the executive power, the second because it would undermine the democratic provisions of the constitution. The only reform proposal eventually to succeed called for the re-creation of a senate, provided for in 1824 but abandoned in 1857. Lerdo argued that the Senate was a way "to consolidate our institutions" in the post-Reforma era. It would allow the states more authority to legislate and to curb the rash of local rebellions. The Senate would have the power to declare the "disappearance" of constitutional government in a state and to call for federal intervention. Thus, "consolidation" in effect meant the strengthening of central authority as well as the controlling of excessive democracy. After several years of congressional debate, the Senate was finally adopted in 1874.

In promoting the Senate, the Juárez government published in 1870 a Spanish-language edition of Edouard Laboulaye's *Histoire des Etats-Unis*, translated by Manuel Dublán, a stalwart of the regime. Without making direct reference to a senate, Dublán's introduction did maintain that Laboulaye's work could provide Mexicans with valuable lessons on the "instability of power." Moreover, it can teach us about "liberty without revolution" (a phrase Dublán repeated several times). The congressional committee's recommendation of December 1869 was more explicit. Approximately half of it consisted of sections from Laboulaye's discussion of the Senate in the United States constitution, a discussion the authors deemed particularly relevant to Mexico.[17]

Now largely forgotten except for his role in the creation of the Statue of Liberty, Laboulaye was a supporter of the Orleans monarchy before 1848, a leader of the liberal opposition to Napoleon III, and after 1870 a

---

[16]The "*Convocatoria para la elección de los supremos poderes*" and Lerdo's "*Circular de la ley de convocatoria*" (both dated 14 August) can be found in Manuel Dublán and José María Lozano, *Legislación mexicana*, 34 vols. (Mexico, 1876–1904), 10:44–56.
[17]Edouard Laboulaye, *Historia de los Estados Unidos*, 2 vols. (Mexico, 1870); "*Dictamen de la comisión de puntos constitucionales*" (1869), in Jorge L. Tamayo, ed., *Benito Juárez. Documentos, discursos y correspondencia*, 15 vols. (Mexico, 1967), 14:403–39.

strong adherent of Adolphe Thiers and the conservative republic. Laboulaye's history consisted of three series of lectures delivered at the Collège de France, begun in 1849 in the wake of democratic revolution and continued in 1863 and 1864. In his preface to the first series, Laboulaye said that the United States, where "customs upheld the laws," had been a kind of "revelation" to him "in a moment of crisis and danger." Its experience might demonstrate "what the lasting conditions of liberty were and how a country [like France] that suffers from anarchy can reform its institutions."[18]

Laboulaye saw the French Constitution of 1848 as abstract and unworkable, one that had inevitably led to Caesarism because a single chamber could provide no resistance to tyranny. Its creation, he reiterated in 1866, was the constitution's "capital error."[19] "In France," wrote Laboulaye in a passage cited in the Mexican committee report of 1869, "we have always confused the nation with its representation. Since the nation is sovereign, [we assume] its representatives must be also." The result is "usurpation and anarchy," which can be prevented only by dividing the legislature so that "the spirit of consequence and moderation" may reign. Pointing to the frequent violation of individual guarantees since 1861 in Mexico, the constitutional reform committee maintained that the nation's history fully confirmed the theories of Laboulaye. If a senate is adopted, said the authors, "dictatorship will be less frequent among us."[20]

Laboulaye was a constitutionalist in the tradition of Montesquieu, Constant, and Tocqueville. Besides his two editions of Constant's works in 1861 and 1872, he published an important essay on Tocqueville and a seven-volume edition of Montesquieu in 1875. He noted the variable fortunes of Montesquieu in France. Sometimes praised as "the master of political science," sometimes "denounced as the worshipper of the past and the apostle of privilege," Montesquieu has survived all our revolutions and "reappears whenever France takes up liberty anew."[21]

---

[18]Laboulaye, preface (dated 15 July 1855) to vol. 1 of *Histoire des Etats-Unis*, 6th ed., 3 vols. (Paris, 1877), ii–xiii. Vol. 1 was first published in 1855, vols. 2 and 3 in 1866. Vol. 3 (vol. 2 of the Mexican edition) was a study of the formation of the American Constitution of 1787.

[19]Laboulaye, *Histoire*, 3:27.

[20]Tamayo, *Benito Juárez*, 14:419–20 (quoted from Laboulaye, *Histoire*, 3:375–76); also 426. Presumably the committee did its own translating, since the wording of the passages translated from Laboulaye in the committee report of 1869 differs from that in the Dublán translation.

[21]Laboulaye, *avertissment* to Montesquieu, *Oeuvres complètes*, 7 vols. (Paris, 1875).

Laboulaye's attachment to Constant was even stronger than it was to Montesquieu. Yet Laboulaye was less legalistic than Constant, for he also adhered to the German historical and comparative school of law derived from Friedrich Carl Von Savigny. Therefore Laboulaye was not in principle hostile to the state, which, as representing nationality and justice, "encompasses what is greatest and most sacred within human institutions."[22] He spoke of the reconciliation of power and liberty. Laboulaye's concern was to set limits to state authority, to avoid tyranny through constitutional restraints and through civic education and participation. He equated this tyranny with the revolutionary doctrine of popular sovereignty and its sequel, the Caesarism of the two Napoleons. Thus, like the Mexicans who cited him, Laboulaye distinguished between dictatorship and strong government. The Senate was an important part of his vision, because through it men of merit, moderation, and substance could complement as well as limit administrative authority. In introducing the Constant edition of 1872, Laboulaye wrote that France "wants to found a government which will assure public peace, while providing a solid guarantee for every interest and every right." Such phraseology, joining interests, guarantees, and the authority of the state, struck a responsive chord in the liberal establishment of post-Reforma Mexico.

The third constitutionalist episode, which took place in the early 1890s, marked the culmination of a new departure in politics. Yet it was closely related to the second episode. It reflected the flowing together in Mexican political thought of the historical constitutionalism of Laboulaye and the new doctrine of "scientific politics" that increasingly provided the intellectual basis of policy assumptions in the era of Porfirio Díaz. Scientific politics was enunciated in 1878 by a self-styled new generation of intellectuals under the leadership of Justo Sierra. Their organ was the newspaper *La Libertad* that was subsidized by the fledgling Díaz regime. Scientific politics was drawn from the positivism of Henri de Saint-Simon and Auguste Comte and entailed a critique of liberal and particularly of egalitarian ideas. Politics must not be based on abstractions, but upon science, that is, upon empirical study, history and social reality, and practical economic concerns. The *La Libertad* group contrasted scientific politics with the "metaphysical politics" of "old liber-

---

[22]Edouard Laboulaye, *L état et ses limites* (Paris, 1863), 96. See also Guido de Ruggiero, *History of European Liberalism* (Oxford, 1927), 197–99. On Savigny, see Hermann Kantorowicz, "Savigny and the Historical School of Law," *Law Quarterly Review* 53 (1937): 326–43. Laboulaye published an essay on Savigny in 1842.

als" of the Reforma era, particularly the constitution-makers of 1856–57, whom they compared with the "Men of '93" in France. Sierra and his colleagues insisted they, too, were liberals and constitutionalists, but "new" or "conservative" liberals who sought to strengthen government and to make the constitution conform to social reality. For them revolution, anarchy, and politics as usual must give way to administration. The term "conservative-liberalism" became the correlate of scientific politics.[23]

The program of *La Libertad* was only in part inspired by positivism. It also had contemporary political models, the conservative republics of France and Spain, led by Adolphe Thiers, Jules Simon, and Emilio Castelar. Moreover, in emphasizing administration, the advocates of scientific politics also regarded the *convocatoria* proposals of 1867 as a precedent; they upheld the newly reestablished Senate; and they quoted Edouard Laboulaye with approval. They found relevant the confluence in France of formerly antagonistic elements of political liberalism, the system of constitutional guarantees and the centralized state. In promoting the Third Republic, Laboulaye combined Constant's *garantisme* with Savigny's reverence for the state as a product of natural growth.

This confluence of ideas was epitomized in the Ecole Libre des Sciences Politiques, established in 1872 as a private institution to train an elite cadre to administer the French state in the modern world. Laboulaye was among the Anglophile founders who were thoroughly elitist and hostile to "*la démocratie.*" As a mirror of the Third Republic itself, the Ecole Libre "system" was also guided by the assumptions of a generalized positivism, what Paul Janet later called the "experimental school" of philosophy led by Hippolyte Taine. These assumptions included an antipathy toward theoreticians, toward doctrines of rights, and toward abstraction, and a fondness for practitioners, for "social facts," and particularly for history. The historical method was seen at the Ecole as the scientific way of approaching any subject. Taine was also a founder of the Ecole, a longtime board member, and a close friend of Emile Boutmy, the first director.[24] Though the Ecole Libre had no direct influence

[23]The contemporary concept of scientific politics and its relation to liberalism is the central theme of my *The Transformation of Liberalism in Late Nineteenth-Century Mexico* (Princeton, 1989).
[24]On the Ecole Libre, see Thomas R. Osborne, "The Recruitment of the Administrative Elite in the Third French Republic, 1870–1905: The System of the Ecole Libre des Sciences Politiques," Ph.D. diss., University of Connecticut, 1974. For an example of the ties between founders of the Ecole Libre, see Emile Boutmy, *Taine, Scherer, Laboulaye* (Paris, 1901).

on Mexican education, the cast of mind—indeed, the vocabulary and phraseology—of the Ecole Libre group closely resembled those of the advocates of scientific politics. It was the language of an intellectual and social elite that infused "science" into liberal discourse, producing an amalgam of formerly conflicting concepts.

The third episode itself entailed the founding of the National Liberal Union in 1892 and the subsequent campaign from within the official circle to reform the constitution. The leader of this campaign, as in 1878, was Justo Sierra, who, joined by some old and some new colleagues, used the scientific arguments of *La Libertad* to propose reforms that would limit, not enhance, the power of Porfirio Díaz. By 1893, the advocates of scientific politics were still calling for a strong constitutional government, but their sense of it had changed with the political situation. The weak executive of 1878 had now become too strong. The key reform proposal was to make judges irremovable, that is, appointed for life rather than being popularly elected (and thus subject to political manipulation) as provided for in the Constitution of 1857. The proposal sparked a major debate in congress and in the press. In the course of debate the reformers were labeled "*científicos*," and the opponents of reform, defenders of the pure constitution, "Jacobins."[25] Thus, 1893 marked the entry of these two epithets into the vocabulary of Mexican politics, to be used constantly thereafter.

The *Científicos* presented the elements of historical constitutionalism in the language of the new sociology. Justo Sierra argued that the effective separation of powers was no more than the creation of a healthy autonomy among the interdependent vital organs of a vigorous social body. *El Universal*, the chief journalistic advocate of irremovable magistrates, called the doctrinaire defenders of the constitution "new reactionaries," trying to stop evolution as if they were zoological organisms trying to retain their rudimentary members. Liberty can never come from declarations, continued *El Universal*, but only from the needs experienced by society after a long and painful struggle to surmount obstacles. In short, liberty is the product of "positive facts," not of "metaphysics."[26] The reformers also used the terms of traditional constitutionalism. Justo Sier-

[25] I have omitted reference here to the split in November 1893 among the former advocates of scientific politics and the emergence of a third position in the debate, opposing irremovable judges and advocating a kind of democratic Caesarism. Its main spokesmen were Carlos Olaguíbel y Arista and Francisco Cosmes. For details see my *Transformation of Liberalism*, chapter 4.
[26] *El Universal*, 22 November 1893.

ra recounted the epic struggle for a free judiciary through history, emphasizing that in France it had taken a century to surmount the ravages of Jacobin and Napoleonic tyranny that had laid waste to an independent judiciary.

Sierra's reference to the French Jacobins reminds us that the case for irremovability included an assault on popular sovereignty and a suspicion of democracy, as well as a resistance to dictatorship. Yet as members of the official circle, the *Científicos* made no direct attack on Porfirio Díaz. Constant had emphasized the need for irremovable judges instead of the popularly elected judges of the Revolution, a guarantee of liberty repeated by Laboulaye in his critique of the Constitution of 1848.[27] In his eloquent remarks to the Mexican congress, the *Científico* Francisco Bulnes warned against committing the error of the opponents, "the same one committed by the Jacobins of 1793, that is, believing that liberty and democracy are the same thing, or that liberty necessarily emanates from democracy."[28] As the advocates of scientific politics had done in 1878, Bulnes was linking his opponents' adherence to popular sovereignty to their defense of the Constitution of 1857. Now, however, the former label "metaphysician" was giving way to the new label "Jacobin."

It was Hippolyte Taine who was responsible for the use of "Jacobin" in Mexico as a political epithet. His passionate attack on France's revolutionary tradition, written in reaction to the republic of 1848 and particularly to the Commune of 1871, had appeared between 1876 and 1891, paralleling the rise of scientific politics in Mexico. The first two volumes of *Les Origines de la France contemporaine* attracted some attention from the *La Libertad* group in the late 1870s; but it was clearly Taine's trenchant indictment of the Jacobin mentality, first published in 1881, that influenced the debate of 1893. For Taine Jacobin "psychology" was the bane of French politics. Its indestructible roots, he wrote, are "exaggerated pride" and "dogmatic reasoning" that exist beneath the surface of society. When social bonds dissolve (as in France in 1790), Jacobins spring up "like mushrooms in rotting compost." Their principles are the simplistic axioms of "political geometry" espoused by the young and the unsuccessful and then imposed on a complex society by "the philosopher

[27]Constant, "Principes de politique," *Cours*, 1:154–55; Laboulaye, introduction (1861) to ibid.; Laboulaye, *Histoire*, 3:490–98, passages from which Sierra probably drew his historical argument in the debate of 1893.
[28]Francisco Bulnes, speech of 12 December 1893, *Diario de los debates*, 16th Congress, 4 vols. (Mexico, 1892–1905), 3:495.

legislator." But, added Taine decisively, they are imposed in vain, because society "is not the product of logic, but of history."[29]

Taine was frequently cited in the Mexican press and in the chamber in 1893. Oblique and disparaging comments about "our Jacobins" could be counted on to bring applause. These were men who followed "absolute principles," who had no respect for the past, who looked for immediate transformation instead of introducing reforms by careful, scientific study in accord with evolving customs and social relations. Manuel Flores ridiculed the doctrinaire stance of *El Monitor republicano* as a "Jacobin symphony."[30]

Although Taine was not a constitutional theorist like Constant and Laboulaye, his political position and his sociological critique of the revolutionary tradition, presented with great literary flair, gave strong reinforcement to Mexican historical constitutionalism in the age of positivism. Despite the failure of the *Científicos* to limit Porfirio Díaz, the 1893 episode left a legacy in Mexican politics. It appeared in the second convention of the National Liberal Union in 1903, the denouement of 1893, which was highlighted by the speech of Francisco Bulnes advocating "institutions" versus "personal government." The rhetorical centerpiece of Bulnes's speech, a prelude to his notorious works attacking the Juárez myth, was a Tainean diatribe against mid-century Jacobinism, which Bulnes identified as attitudes and polities emanating from unicameral parliamentary government.[31] The less-polemical and highly influential *La Constitución y la dictadura* of 1912, by the jurist and politician Emilio Rabasa, followed squarely in this tradition, with frequent references to Jacobins and Jacobinism. Scientific politics as constitutionalism, guided by the French critique of Rousseau and of 1793, 1848, and 1871, may have been present in the ideology of the revolutionary decade of 1910 to 1920, particularly in the programs of Francisco I. Madero and

[29]Hippolyte Taine, "Psychologie du jacobin," *Revue des deux mondes* (1 April 1881): 536–59, reprinted the same year in *Les Origines de la France contemporaine*, 6 vols. (Paris, 1876–94), 3 (*La Révolution*, 2 ["La Conquête jacobine"]):3–39. The *Revue* was much read in late nineteenth-century Mexico, and it may have helped to popularize "Jacobin" as an epithet.

[30]See particularly Justo Sierra, speech of 11 December 1893 in *Diario de los debates*, 16th Congress, 3:175; Emilio Pardo, ibid., 456; *El Universal*, 29 November 1893; Manuel Flores in ibid., 23 November.

[31]Bulnes, *Discurso pronunciado por el Sr. ingeniero D. Francisco Bulnes delegado del estado de Morelos, en la sesion del 21 de junio de 1903, presentando y fundando la candidatura del señor general Porfirio Díaz* (Mexico, 1903); idem, *El verdadero Juárez y la verdad sobre la intervención y el imperio* (Mexico, 1904); idem, *Juárez y la revoluciones de Ayutla y de reforma* (Mexico, 1905).

Venustiano Carranza. Thus, it may have modified or at least survived the implantation of *l'idéologie moderne*. Perhaps the constitutionalist legacy of 1893 even persists today as one element guiding the attempt to reform the Mexican political system.

The constitutionalist tradition just identified, with its positivist infusions of the late nineteenth century, is not only of importance substantively as demonstrating the complexity of Mexican liberalism. It also appears to have influenced the assumptions of the new political historiography itself. Suggestive bits of evidence emerge. The most obvious is the widespread acknowledgement of inspiration from Tocqueville. Furet speaks of Tocqueville as the first to treat the Revolution as a problem instead of merely commemorating it.[32] There is a Tocquevillean current in Mexican historiography as well, evident in the work of Jean Meyer as well as in that of Guerra, focusing on the continuity of state authority.[33] More pertinent here is the apparent attraction of Constant's critique of arbitrary power in France for several of the authors of the recent impressive volumes, *The French Revolution and the Creation of Modern Political Culture*.[34] Although Laboulaye does not seem to have enjoyed this revival, it should be noted that his edition of 1872 of Constant's writings, with his extensive commentaries, has been recently reprinted.

More elusive, yet perhaps more significant, is the possible influence of Taine on the new historiography. Although Taine seems to be rejected by the revisionist school because of his faulty research and his "counter-revolutionary bias," Furet does find his work to be of "considerable interest."[35] Alfred Cobban, perhaps a precursor of the French revisionist school, devoted his final article to Taine, calling him "the most influential and stimulating, the most dazzling, in a word perhaps the greatest of bad historians."[36] Augustin Cochin, whom Furet has revived and to whom Guerra refers frequently, was one of those influenced directly by Taine. In

---

[32] Furet, *Interpreting the French Revolution*, 14–18, 132–63.

[33] See Jean Meyer, *La Révolution mexicaine* (Paris, 1973); also Meyer's review of Guerra's *Le Mexique* in *Vuelta* (Mexico), no. 116 (July 1986), 38–42.

[34] For examples, see Mona Ozouf's conclusion to "L'opinion publique," and Lucien Jaume, "Citoyenneté et souveraineté: le poids de l'absolutisme," in Keith M. Baker, ed., *The French Revolution and the Creation of Modern Political Culture*, vol. 1 (Oxford, 1987); also Bronislav Baczko, "L'Expérience thermidorienne," in Colin Lucas, ed., *The French Revolution and the Creation of Modern Political Culture*, vol. 2 (Oxford, 1988). Also relevant is Furet, "Une Polémique thermidorienne sur le terreur; autour de Benjamin Constant," *Passé présent* 2 (1983): 44–55.

[35] Furet, *Interpreting the French Revolution*, 83–84.

[36] Alfred Cobban, "Hippolyte Taine, Historian of the French Revolution," *History* 53 (1968): 331.

fact, Cochin defended Taine at length in 1909 against Alphonse Aulard's devastating attack on Taine's research methods.[37] More significant for us is the reliance by François-Xavier Guerra on the Mexican positivists and advocates of scientific politics, all admirers of Taine, to support his conception of the liberal and democratic "fictions" in contrast to the sociological reality of politics. As Knight has pointed out, Guerra cites Francisco Bulnes frequently as an authority, as an acute analyst of Mexican society and politics. He also uses Emilio Rabasa, Andrés Molina Enríquez, and Jorge Vera Estañol in the same way. In doing so, Guerra may indirectly reveal his attraction to the judgments as well as to the insights of Taine, particularly Taine's condemnation of Jacobinism and the Jacobin tradition. Knight accuses Guerra of nostalgia for the *sociabilité traditionnelle* of old-regime Mexico and of a hostility toward the modernizers— Bourbons, liberals, and Jacobin revolutionaries. Knight's criticism is too harsh, but it does suggest the problems that can arise when a historian uses as an authority a notorious polemicist like Bulnes, who, according to Francisco Cosmes, imagined himself the Mexican Taine.[38]

One antidote for the distortions that use of such sources can impose on an interpretation of Mexican political history is a critical, albeit sympathetic, appreciation of the ideas of the late nineteenth-century liberal establishment. By analyzing these ideas in comparative historical context we can avoid falling prey unwittingly to the assumptions of the era. The ideas themselves in all of their complexity are an essential ingredient of Mexican political culture, then and now.

[37] Augustin Cochin, "La Crise de l'histoire révolutionnaire: Taine et Aulard" (1909); *Les Sociétés de pensée et la démocratie* (Paris, 1921), 43–140; Alphonse Aulard, *Taine. Historien de la Révolution française* (Paris, 1908). It should be noted that despite his general admiration for Taine, Cochin was critical of his emphasis on Jacobin "psychology."

[38] Francisco Cosmes, *El verdadero Bulnes y su falso Juárez* (Mexico, 1904), 3–12. Cosmes highly approved of Taine as a model but accused Bulnes of imitating him badly. Federico Gamboa, writing in 1920, was more positive toward Bulnes and went as far as to say that his several polemical volumes constituted a Tainean "Los orígenes del México contemporaneo": "prólogo" to Bulnes, *Los grandes problemas de México* (Mexico, 1926), vii–xi.

# 10

## The French Revolution and Chinese socialism

### MAURICE J. MEISNER

When in their imminent flight across Asia our European reactionaries will ultimately arrive at the wall of China, at the gates that lead to the very stronghold of
arch-reaction and arch-conservatism, who knows if they will not find there in the
inscription:

> République Chinoise,
> Liberté, Égalité, Fraternité.

So wrote Karl Marx in 1850,[1] paradoxically speculating on the possibility that backward China—a land he was inclined to characterize as a
"living fossil" and a society "vegetating in the teeth of time"—might
become the repository of the radical battle cries of the French Revolution that conservative mid-nineteenth-century Europe seemed to have forgotten.

It was a time when Marx anticipated a radical upsurge against the
conservative regimes that held sway in Europe after the failures of the
revolution of 1848, when he was inclined to look to the more economically backward countries (such as Germany) for the starting points of
revolutionary revival; when he had raised the slogan "the revolution in
permanence"; and when he was passing through what some of his later,
more conservative, interpreters have called a brief "Jacobin-Blanquist aberration."[2] It was also a time when Marx was filled with moral outrage
over the atrocities that the British government carried out against China
during and after the Opium War—an outrage that was to find written
expression in the famous articles Marx wrote for the *New York Tribune*

[1] Karl Marx, "Revue," in Karl Marx and Frederick Engels, *Werke* (Berlin, 1964), 7:
222.
[2] George Lichtheim, *Marxism: An Historical and Critical Study* (New York, 1961),
125.

in the 1850s.[3] It was in one of those articles that Marx suggested that the Taiping Rebellion in China would "throw the spark into the overloaded mine of the present industrial system [of the Western capitalist countries] and cause the explosion of the long-prepared general crisis, which, spreading abroad, will be closely followed by political revolutions on the continent." Invoking Hegel's "law of the contact of extremes," Marx wrote that "a striking illustration of it [Hegel's law] may be seen in the effect the Chinese revolution seems likely to exercise upon the civilized world. It may seem strange, and a very paradoxical assertion that the next uprising of the people of Europe, and their next movement for republican freedom and economy of government, may depend more on what is now passing in the Celestial Empire—the very opposite of Europe—than on any other political cause that now exists. . . . Now, England having brought about the revolution in China, the question is how that revolution will in time react on England, and through England on Europe."[4]

This "paradoxical assertion" of 1853 proved a passing fancy. Marx, of course, was far more interested in the impact of Western imperialism on "the Celestial Empire" than in the fanciful notion that any nineteenth-century revolution in China would stimulate revolutionary movements in Europe. The main thrust of Marx's views on the matter was that the dynamic forces of Western capitalism, via the agency of imperialistic expansion, would destroy traditional China's stagnant socioeconomic formation, which he assumed was incapable of moving into modern history on its own accord;[5] that the forces of capitalist-imperialism would "batter down all Chinese walls" (as he put it in the Manifesto);[6] that this

[3]Most of Marx's articles dealing with China are collected in [Dona Torr, (comp.),] Marx on China (London, 1951). For a brief review of some of the themes in these articles, see Maurice Meisner, "The Despotism of Concepts: Wittfogel and Marx on China," The China Quarterly, no. 16 (October–December 1963): 99–111.

[4]Karl Marx, "Revolution in China and Europe," New York Tribune, 14 June 1853.

[5]For the purposes of the present discussion, there is no need to take up the controversial question of whether Marx viewed imperial China as an example of the Asiatic mode of production. It is sufficient to note that he saw the traditional Chinese economic system as both precapitalist and unchanging.

[6]As Marx wrote: "The bourgeoisie, by the rapid improvement of all instruments of production, by the immensely facilitated means of communication, draws all, even the most barbarian, nations into civilization. The cheap prices of its commodities are the heavy artillery with which it batters down all Chinese walls, with which it forces the barbarians' intensely obstinate hatred of foreigners to capitulate. It compels all nations, on pain of extinction, to adopt the bourgeois mode of production; it compels them to introduce what it calls civilization into their midst, i.e., to become bourgeois themselves. In one word, it creates a world after its own image" (Karl Marx and Frederick Engels, Selected Works [London, 1950], 36–37).

would result in the introduction of the capitalist mode of production in China and, thereby, in turn prepare the conditions for a bourgeois-type revolution.

From these perspectives Marx's speculations about a "République Chinoise" proclaiming the French Revolutionary ideals of liberty, equality, and fraternity was historically logical and not mere political fancy. For the French Revolution, in Marx's view, was the principal historical model of a bourgeois revolution. The historic tasks and functions of such a revolution, according to Marxist theory, was to break down feudal (or precapitalist) restraints on capitalist economic development, facilitate the flourishing of bourgeois property, and eventually result in the political triumph of the bourgeoisie as a class—ideally in the institutional form of a democratic republic. With what Marx assumed to be the inexorable development of capitalism in China, albeit a capitalism introduced from without, it could further be assumed that a bourgeois-democratic revolution would soon head the Chinese historical agenda. "The laws of social development," Marx wrote, "are now pushing their way with iron necessity, and the underdeveloped countries have to pass through the same phases of economic development which the developed ones have already completed; the country that is more developed industrially only shows, to the less developed, the image of its own future."[7] China would not prove an exception to this universal process of capitalist development, either economically or politically.

Yet if Karl Marx in the middle of the nineteenth century could muse over the possible future influence of the French Revolution on China and the forthcoming appearance of a "République Chinoise," the Chinese themselves at the time did not. While there was a considerable and growing interest in Western technology in mid-nineteenth-century China, Confucian Chinese remained as indifferent to European political history as was the Qianlong emperor in 1793, who at the radical height of the French Revolution informed the British envoy Lord Macartney that "we possess all things" and "set no value on objects strange and ingenious." It was not until nearly a century after the event that Chinese intellectuals began to find political relevance in the French Revolution.

The initial lessons drawn from the history of the Great Revolution were hardly revolutionary. For the reformers who rose to prominence (but not to power) during the waning years of the Qing dynasty, the French Revo-

[7]Karl Marx, "Preface to the First German Edition of *Kapital*," in Marx and Engels, *Werke*.

lution was a negative model which revealed the unhappy consequences for old regimes that failed to undertake timely reforms. Wang Tao (1828–97) was perhaps the first Chinese intellectual to write on the French Revolution. In his *General History of France*, written following visits to France in the 1860s and after, and published in full in 1890. Wang Tao denounced "the calamitous violence" engendered by the French and English Revolutions and the "cruel fury" of the "rebel parties" who had "brazenly dared to commit regicide." "In all of history," he wrote, "surely there have been no rebellions worse than these. . . ." But the cause of the French disaster, he concluded, was the irresponsible behavior of the French king and his failure "to conciliate the masses and win the hearts of the people."[8] The lesson for the Chinese monarchy was clear.

Kang Youwei, the leader of the abortive Hundred Days Reform of 1898, and his disciple Liang Qichao attempted to impart a similar message in their commentaries on the French Revolution. Kang actually wrote *An Account of the French Revolution,* a short booklet he presented to the Guangxu Emperor in 1898. Condemning "the bloody revolution," he commented that "there has never been anything more disastrous than the cruelties committed by modern revolution." But Louis XVI, he went on to argue, brought the disasters onto himself and the French nation by failing to undertake needed reforms in due time:

His [Louis XVI's] promise to grant a constitution was not of his own will but was given under pressure. His hesitation and oscillation, his initial recourse to arms and later disbandment of his guards, and finally his appeal for foreign intervention and flight to Varennes, ended in stirring up the indignation of the people against him so much so that he was sent to the guillotine and became the laughing stock of the world.[9]

This, to be sure, was a rather blatant attempt to play upon the fears of the Guangxu Emperor and others at the court, but it did nonetheless reflect Kang's abiding belief that the establishment of a constitutional monarchy under an enlightened emperor who would initiate reforms from above was far preferable to mass revolution from below.

The political thought of Liang Qichao, Kang's one-time disciple, was more complex—or at least more eclectic—but he also presented the

---

[8]Wang Tao, *Fa-kuo chin-lueh* (1890), translated and cited in Paul A. Cohen, *Between Tradition and Modernity: Wang T'ao and Reform in Late Ch'ing China* (Cambridge, Mass., 1974), 126–27.

[9]Kang Youwei, "Preface" to *An Account of the French Revolution.* Cited in Zhang Zhilian, "The Repercussions of the French Revolution in China." Paper presented at conference, China and the French Revolution, Shanghai, March 1989, 4.

French Revolution as essentially a negative model, as a warning of the perils that might befall a nation that did not undertake reformist changes in due time. Liang on this, as on other matters, was not entirely consistent. While denouncing the bloodshed and anarchy of the French Revolution, he also introduced and promoted the ideas that had gone into the making of the French upheaval, not excluding the works of Jean-Jacques Rousseau. "Bloodless destruction" was his vague political prescription.[10]

It was not until the first decade of the twentieth century that the French Revolution was harnessed to the cause of revolution in China, as opposed to its earlier image of an unnecessary "bloody revolt" that ought to have been avoided through the institution of timely reforms. The failures of reform movements under the old imperial regime, especially the dramatic failure of the Hundred Days Reform of 1898, bred revolutionaries, and China's modern revolutionaries eagerly took up the French Revolution as the greatest of all historical models to emulate. In the early years of the century, standard and radical Japanese histories of the French Revolution were translated and published in Chinese, primarily by anti-Manchu students and political exiles living in Tokyo.[11] The imagery and ideals of the French Revolution filled the pages of *Minbao* and other revolutionary periodicals, exerting an enormous influence on the consciousness of China's early revolutionaries. "Liberty, Equality, and Fraternity" became one of the more prominent slogans and one of the proclaimed goals of Sun Yat-sen's Tongmenghui (Alliance Society), the predecessor of the Guomindang.

Most early revolutionaries were vaguely socialists of one sort or another, and most held the hope that China might avoid a capitalist phase of development in achieving the goal of a "strong and wealthy nation." Thus, Chinese revolutionaries in the first decade of the century largely ignored social interpretations that presented the French Revolution as a "bourgeois revolution" opening the way for the unfettered development of modern capitalism and the triumph of the bourgeoisie and bourgeois society. They were attracted, rather, to the political and ideological as-

---

[10]On Liang's sometimes contradictory views on the French Revolution and French revolutionary thought, see Joseph R. Levenson, *Liang Ch'i-ch'ao and the Mind of Modern China* (Cambridge, Mass., 1959), especially 104–7, 156–58. As Levenson paraphrases Liang's general view: "The French Revolution stained the nation's history with blood," says Liang, "and for more than a thousand years, people who hear of it will tremble and grieve" (156–57).

[11]Chinese publications on the French Revolution are discussed by Zhang Zhilian in "A Century of Chinese Historiography of the French Revolution, 1889–1989." Paper presented at conference, China and the French Revolution, Shanghai, March 1989.

pects of the French Revolution—to heroic examples of revolutionary self-sacrifice; to the radical ideas of the Enlightenment and the principles of the Declaration of the Rights of Man; to the necessity of revolutionary violence; and to the need for firm and united revolutionary leaders, for which the Jacobin Club was taken as the prototype. Above all, the lesson derived from the French Revolution was that all attempts to carry out gradual reforms under the Old Regime were futile endeavors. The total destruction of the existing monarchy through revolutionary action, they insisted, was the essential precondition for national regeneration and modern development.[12]

The Revolution of 1911, of course, accomplished little and disappointed many. The Qing dynasty was removed from the historical scene but the plight and problems of China remained and indeed deepened. China's republican revolutionaries had been fond of drawing parallels between Manchu China and Bourbon France, but as revolution 1911 barely qualified as even a caricature of 1789.

Nonetheless, the French revolutionary tradition, if not necessarily the French Revolution itself, continued to exert a powerful influence among the modern Chinese intelligentsia during the second decade of the century. This was particularly the case with many of the intellectuals associated with the *New Youth* magazine, most notably, Chen Duxiu, the founder of that extraordinarily influential periodical and the acknowledged leader of the "Westernized" intelligentsia during the period of the New Culture Movement (1915–19). For Chen, France, more than any other Western country, embodied the values of modern Western civilization that China needed to adopt—not only for national survival but also because he believed Western values and ideas to be morally and socially superior as well. In his highly influential article "The French and Modern Civilization," published in the September 1915 inaugural issue of *New Youth* (then simply entitled *Youth*), Chen credited the French revolutionary and intellectual tradition as the main carrier of the three theories he regarded as the most important components of modern Western civilization—democracy, evolution, and socialism.[13]

---

[12]These are among the themes which appear in such articles as Wang Jingwei, "Refuting the View That Revolutions Breed Internal Strife," *Minbao* 9 (1907).

[13]Chen Duxiu, "Falanxi ren yu jinshi wenming," *Qingnian* 1 (September 1915). Chen frequently used French sources in his writings, and although he never actually visited France, as hitherto widely believed, he did dispatch his two sons to study in France. For a recent biography that questions the depth and extent of Chen's Francophilism, see Lee Feigon, *Chen Duxiu: Founder of the Chinese Communist Party* (Princeton, N.J., 1983).

Unlike some of the revolutionaries of the pre-1911 Tongmenghui (Alliance Society) era, the New Culture Movement intellectuals were not attracted to the French Revolution as a political model. Indeed, the *New Youth* intelligentsia had rejected all active political participation, at least in principle. Convinced that the problems and plight of China were mainly to be attributed to grave deficiencies in traditional Chinese culture, they believed that their first and essential task was to rid China of its pernicious and persisting cultural-historical heritage. They assumed that the total destruction of the evil values and culture of the Chinese past, and their replacement by the modern scientific and democratic values of the West was the necessary precondition for effective political action and social change.[14] Thus, insofar as the *New Youth* intellectuals looked to France for inspiration, as many of them did, they were attracted not so much to the French Revolution as a political event as to the radical and antitraditionalist intellectual currents that preceded 1789 and followed from it. They were drawn to the Enlightenment though: to the rationalist faith in science as a force corrosive of old traditions and as a guide to the construction of a new society; to the strain in Rousseau (and the Rousseauian tradition) that condemned all social conventions and that called for the creation of a new type of man with a new mentality and new values; to those aspects of French revolutionary thought that demanded a break with old traditions and the destruction of all forms of superstition; and to the anticlerical strands in the French Revolution and its intellectual legacy. Such were some of the aspects of the French Revolution—or, more precisely, the ideologies associated with the French Revolution—that New Culture Movement intellectuals enlisted in their iconoclastic crusade against the Chinese cultural tradition.

With the politicization of the *New Youth* intelligentsia under the twin influences of the Russian Revolution and the May Fourth movement, foreign revolutionary models again came to the fore, but now it was of course the Bolshevik example rather than the French one that assumed

[14]This assumption and the iconoclastic assault on traditional culture and ideas in general was reflected in the intelligentsia's call for "cultural revolution" (*wenhua geming*). For a discussion of the origins and meaning of "cultural revolution" in early twentieth-century Chinese thought (and in latter Maoist ideology), see Maurice Meisner, "Iconoclasm and Cultural Revolution in China and Russia," in Abbott Gleason, Peter Kenez, and Richard Stites, eds., *Bolshevik Culture* (Bloomington, Ind., 1985), 279–93. For insightful treatments of the iconoclasm of the modern Chinese intelligentsia, see Lin Yu-sheng, *The Crisis of Chinese Consciousness: Radical Antitraditionalism in the May Fourth Era* (Madison, Wis., 1979); and Joseph Levenson, *Confucian China and Its Modern Fate: A Trilogy* (Berkeley and Los Angeles, 1968).

immediate political relevance. Yet the French Revolution remained very much a part of the historical consciousness of radical Chinese intellectuals drawn to the October Revolution in Russia. They frequently drew parallels between the two great upheavals, and indeed, the French Revolution served for a time as the standard by which to measure the significance of revolutionary events in Russia. Li Dazhao, for example, the first of the *New Youth* intellectuals to proclaim his adherence to Bolshevism and Marxism (and who, along with Chen Duxiu, was to be a cofounder of the Chinese Communist party), initially announced his acceptance of the messianic message of the Russian Revolution in an article entitled "A Comparison of the French and Russian Revolutions." In that treatise, written in the summer of 1918, Li predicted that the Russian Revolution would mold world history in the twentieth century much as the French Revolution had molded the history of the nineteenth century. But now China could become part of world history. For, whereas the French Revolution, according to Li, was a nationalistic revolution with a "social revolutionary flavor," the Russian Revolution was a socialist revolution with "a world revolutionary color." And while China had remained immune to the influence of the French Revolution, it could now, in accordance with the internationalist message of the October Revolution, fully participate in a universal process of revolutionary transformation.[15]

At the same time that Li Dazhao was celebrating the worldwide "psychological transformation of twentieth-century humanity" heralded by the Bolshevik triumph and relegating the French Revolution to a matter of mere historical significance (and merely Western historical significance at that), the influence of the French revolutionary tradition was finding a concrete Chinese expression in the communal work-study movements that soon would send thousands of young Chinese students to France, the country still viewed by most members of the radical intelligentsia as the homeland of modern revolution. It was in Paris that many of these students would become converts to Russian Bolshevism, eventually returning to their homeland to make up a large part of the early leadership and

---

[15]Li Dazhao, "Fa geming shi bijiaoguan," in Shi Cun, ed., *Zhongguo jindai sixiang shi cankao ziliao jianbian* (Source Materials for the Study of Modern Chinese Thought) (Beijing, 1957), 1201–4. Li's attraction to the Russian Revolution preceded his acceptance of, or even knowledge of, Marxist theory. In 1918 he still spoke of the Bolshevik Revolution in terms of bringing about the "psychological" and "spiritual" transformation of humanity and saw Russia as uniquely situated to "harmonize Eastern and Western civilizations." "The creation of a new civilization in the world that simultaneously retains the special features of Eastern and Western civilizations, and the talents of the European and Asian peoples, cannot be undertaken except by the Russians," he wrote (Ibid., 1203–4).

membership of the Chinese Communist party. Among their numbers were such future Communist luminaries as Zhou Enlai and Deng Xiaoping.

The work-study movement, so thoroughly anti-Confucian in content and purpose, owed its origins to Chinese anarchists who absorbed the French revolutionary tradition in Paris in the early years of the century. Returning to China after the Revolution of 1911, two leaders of the Parisian anarchist group, Wu Zhihui and Li Shizeng, established the Society for Frugal Study in France, in 1912, and the Society for Diligent Work and Frugal Study, in 1914. The communitarian ideals and activities of the anarchists merged with and reinforced the Francophilism and radical iconoclasm of the New Culture Movement intellectuals, and no doubt anarchism contributed much to the radical temper of China's new intelligentsia.[16]

Perhaps the most tangible contribution was "the diligent work and frugal study" movement, which aimed to send Chinese students to France, and which captured the imagination of so many leading intellectuals and student leaders, not excluding Mao Zedong and his New People's Study Society. Although Mao was not among the two thousand or so students who departed for France between 1918 and 1920 (or among the others who followed later), Mao's closest friend and comrade, Cai Hesen, did journey to Paris, where he proceeded to organize the French branch of the Chinese Communist party, a group probably larger than the Party organization in China itself in the early 1920s. During the May Fourth era, the image of a "revolutionary France" still loomed large in the consciousness of radical Chinese intellectuals. And a good many young Chinese did indeed become radicalized in the French intellectual and political environment. Zhou Enlai embarked on the journey to what he called "the homeland of Liberty" in 1920—and returned to China four years later as a committed Communist.

Yet the French Revolution as a political model faded into insignificance as the Chinese Communist movement developed in the 1920s and after. In the early 1920s the leaders of the new party looked to the Bolshevik Revolution as the socialist example for China to emulate, and then under Soviet pressure, allied themselves with the Guomindang in what was called "the national revolution," a narrowly restricted version of the

---

[16]Argued in convincing and detailed fashion in Arif Dirlik, *Anarchism in the Chinese Revolution* (Berkeley and Los Angeles, 1991), chapter 6.

concept of a bourgeois-democratic revolution. While the radical slogans and battle cries of the French Revolution may have echoed briefly in the Shanghai insurrection of March 1927 and during the short-lived Canton Commune at the end of that year, the success of the Guomindang counterrevolution confined the revolution to China's rural hinterlands, thereby severing the links between an increasingly insular Chinese Communism and the Western revolutionary tradition. In a Maoist revolutionary strategy based on harnessing the forces of peasant revolt to "surround and overwhelm" the conservative cities, little of political relevance or inspiration could have been derived from memories of the French Revolution.

To be sure, Mao Zedong formally insisted that a bourgeois-democratic revolutionary stage would precede the arrival of the socialist stage in the revolutionary process. But he also made clear that China's bourgeois-democratic revolution would not take the form of the "old, now obsolete" Western type but rather would be a new type of democratic revolution suited to the particular needs of semicolonial China—a "New Democratic" revolution that would be led by the Communist Party rather than the bourgeoisie and one that would be part and parcel of "the proletarian-socialist world revolution."[17] Mao attributed the difference, in part, to the weakness and peculiar character of the Chinese bourgeoisie, a class molded under the conditions of a colonial and semicolonial country oppressed by imperialism. "The bourgeoisie in China," he emphasized, "differs from the earlier bourgeoisie of the European and American countries, *and especially of France*. When the bourgeoisie of those countries, *and especially in France,* was still in its revolutionary era, the bourgeois revolution was comparatively thorough, whereas the bourgeoisie in China lacks even this degree of thoroughness"[18] (emphasis added). The clear implication was that the French Revolution, the Marxian model par excellence of a bourgeois-democratic revolution, offered no historical precedent for even the bourgeois phase of the Chinese revolutionary process.

Ironically, it was not until well after the Chinese Communist victory in 1949 that aspects of the French Revolution and the revolutionary traditions that the great upheaval bequeathed to later generations were re-

---

[17]Mao's views on China's "new-type" of bourgeois-democratic revolution are formulated principally in his essays "The Chinese Revolution and the Chinese Communist Party" (1939) and "On New Democracy" (1940). See *Selected Works of Mao Tse-tung* (Peking, 1967), 305–34 and 339–84.

[18]Mao Zedong, "On New Democracy," 349.

vived. The French revolutionary legacy assumed a new political significance in the dramatically changed historical circumstances. To fully appreciate this rather curious phenomenon, it would be necessary to discuss the peculiar nature of the French Revolution and the extraordinarily diverse political currents that went into the making of its history. It would further be necessary to examine the role of the French Revolution in the birth of modern socialism and the special place that this model of "bourgeois revolution" (and of the revolutionary process in general) occupies in the Marxist tradition.

This is obviously not the place (and certainly there is not sufficient space) to discuss these complex and controversial topics. For the purposes of the present inquiry, it is perhaps sufficient to note that all revolutions generate radical aspirations and movements that go well beyond the historical limitations of their times. Just as the seventeenth-century Puritan Revolution produced (and soon dispensed with) the egalitarianism of the Levellers and the agrarian communism of the Diggers, the French Revolution yielded the sansculottes, Jacobinism, and Hebertists, the *Enragés*, and Babouvism. These socially radical tendencies could not be contained within the limits of what was in fact a bourgeois revolution, certainly in its ultimate outcome, even if that outcome took nearly a century of French history to fully reveal itself.[19] But if the radical political sects and communistic social movements of the early and mid 1790s did not long survive the course of the Revolution, memories of them remained in the historical consciousness of succeeding generations of radicals, inspiring new political and ideological movements that borrowed the forms and slogans of their French revolutionary models. Just as one cannot seriously discuss the history of democracy and republicanism in modern history without reference to the French Revolution,[20] neither can one seek the sources of modern socialism without reference to the French Revolution. As George Lichtheim has observed "a history of socialism must begin with the French Revolution, for the simple reason that France was the cradle of

---

[19]If one takes as the essential feature of bourgeois revolution a socio-political upheaval that creates conditions in which bourgeois property can flourish (e.g., Isaac Deutscher, *The Unfinished Revolution* [New York, 1967], 22), then the bourgeois character of the French Revolution was quite apparent in the 1790s. Yet it may well be argued that the eminently bourgeois social outcome of 1789 was not fully consolidated and apparent until the establishment of the Third Republic in 1871.

[20]For an insightful analysis of the French Revolution as the source for democratic republicanism (and indeed for most essential aspects of modern politics) in the nineteenth and twentieth centuries, see Lynn Hunt, *Politics, Culture and Class in the French Revolution* (Berkeley and Los Angeles, 1984).

'utopian socialism' and 'utopian communism' alike . . . ; both currents stemmed from the great upheaval of 1789–1799."[21] And both currents later fed into Marxism. Even if the proposition is much too simplistic and more than a bit historically misleading, there nevertheless is an essential truth in the old formula that the Marxist theory was a synthesis of French socialism, English political economy, and German philosophy.

Beyond the general incorporation of the French Revolution (or, at least, its radical symbols and terminology) into the global Marxist tradition, it is the term and concept "commune" that most significantly links post-1949 Chinese history with the great French upheaval of 1789. The link, to be sure, is indirect. And save for Chinese historians specializing in the study of the French Revolution, it is also a mostly unconscious tie. The direct tie between Chinese communism and the French revolutionary tradition is, of course, the Paris Commune of 1871, or, more precisely, Marx's description of the Commune of 1871 in *The Civil War in France*. But the historical line, in fact, extends back to the era of the French Revolution, for the Communards of 1871 consciously modeled their extraordinary revolutionary government on the famous Commune of Paris of 1792–94, an event that lived on into the nineteenth century in historical memory, conveyed mainly by the utopian socialist ideologies that grew out of the French Revolution.

The Commune of Paris was the most notable institutional expression of popular democracy during the most radical phase of the French Revolution. While perhaps harking back nostalgically to the more or less independent and autonomous communes of the Middle Ages, the Commune of Paris was a modern administrative unit, one of a multitude of communes in municipalities and rural towns throughout France that the Constitution of 1791 recognized as the basic-level subdivision of the departments, which in turn had replaced the chaotic administrative system of the Old Regime. Over the years 1790–92, the communes were generally the most democratic of administrative organs yielded (or reorganized) by the Revolution. Half their members were elected annually, and they were, as Mathiez has written, "in constant touch with the people, whose sentiments they faithfully reflected."[22] The Revolutionary Commune of Paris was founded on the basis of the insurrection of 10

---

[21]George Lichtheim, *Origins of Socialism* (London, 1969).
[22]Albert Mathiez, *The French Revolution* (New York, 1962), 90. The brief discussion of the Commune of Paris that follows is drawn from Mathiez's classic work.

August 1792, when the commissaries of the various Parisian sections convened at the Hôtel de Ville.

What above all distinguished the Commune was its democratic character, the fact that its representatives, as Mathiez has put it, "derived their power from the direct choice of the people."[23] In contrast to the Assembly, whose members were selected by indirect franchise by men of property, the Commune "represented a new type of legality." Implicit in this new legality, though not necessarily consciously recognized at the time, was the emergence of a proto–class struggle within the ranks of the revolutionaries. For the Commune—composed of artisans, laborers, and other Parisian commoners—was locked in constant battle with the Gironde, the representative of the property-owning classes.

The Commune of Paris was far more than simply a municipal governing organ. Its leaders conceived of the Commune as the incarnation of the popular revolutionary will, they attempted to establish links with communes in other cities and in the rural towns, and they spoke in the name of the revolutionary French nation as a whole. Patriotic as well as revolutionary, the Commune took the lead in defending France against foreign invasion; it was instrumental, for example, in mobilizing battalions to lift the siege of Verdun in September 1792. Iconoclastic, as revolutionaries tend to be, the Commune expressed its antitraditional proclivities primarily in the form of anticlericalism, forbidding priests to wear clerical garb save in the performance of their strictly religious ceremonies, for example, and abolishing public religious processions in accordance with the decree that religion was to be a strictly private matter.

A particular intriguing aspect of the Commune of Paris—and a prophetic pointer to the future of radical politics—was the attempt to combine "democracy" and "dictatorship." Although an eminently democratic organ in form and substance, the Commune, at the urging of Robespierre (the link between the Commune and the Convention), asserted its right to exercise dictatorial authority over the enemies of the Revolution.

The Commune of Paris was of course short-lived. Its demise was signaled on 11 Thermidor (29 July 1794) when seventy members of the Commune were guillotined in summary fashion following the fall of Robespierre. But the idea and ideals of the Commune survived and were to be re-created nearly a century later by the Parisian Communards.

---

[23]Ibid., 165.

The year 1871 saw two re-creations: the re-creation of the Commune of Paris and Karl Marx's re-creation of the events of 18 March to 28 May in *The Civil War in France*. I shall not pause here to inquire into the relationship between the two, save to note that the latter was perhaps the more significant of the two, serving to convey to future generations an example of heroic popular revolution that arouses our passions and imaginations to this very day—even in this not-too-revolutionary age. Marx's description and analysis of the Commune has traveled over vast reaches of historical time and space, partly inspiring such diverse historical events as Lenin's Bolshevik Revolution and Mao's Cultural Revolution—and today stands ironically as a critique (indeed, as the antithesis) of the bureaucratic Communist states that twentieth-century, Marxian-led revolutions have yielded. It is this latter role, at this moment in history, that lends Marx's *Civil War in France* its continuing political and historical relevance.

The main themes in Karl Marx's treatise on the Commune of 1871 are well known and need not be repeated here. It is perhaps sufficient to observe that many of the ideals and measures adopted by the Communards of 1871 that Marx found so praiseworthy had been foreshadowed by the Commune of 1792–94, especially the forms of direct and popular democracy that Marx called "the self-government of the producers."[24] Indeed, the enduring fascination of the Commune (and Marx's account of it) largely derives from the image of the centralized state (and what Marx termed "its ubiquitous organs of standing army, police, bureaucracy, clergy, and judicature") being replaced by a simple administration made up of ordinary working people who were directly elected and subject to immediate popular recall, who performed public service at ordinary wages, and who enjoyed no special status or privileges. Other features of

[24]As Marx glowingly wrote: "The Commune was formed of the municipal councillors, chosen by universal suffrage in the various wards of the town, responsible and revocable at short terms. The majority of its members were naturally working men, or acknowledged representatives of the working class. The Commune was to be a working, not a parliamentary body, executive and legislative at the same time. Instead of continuing to be the agent of the Central Government, the police was at once stripped of its political attributes, and turned into the responsible and at all times revocable agent of the Commune. So were the officials of all other branches of the Administration. From the members of the Commune downwards, the public service had to be done at workmen's wages. The vested interests and the representation allowances of the high dignitaries of State disappeared along with the high dignitaries themselves. Public functions ceased to be the private property of the tools of the Central Government. Not only municipal administration, but the whole initiative hitherto exercised by the State was laid into the hands of the Commune" (Marx and Engels, *Selected Works*, 1:471).

the nineteenth-century Parisian Commune harked back to its eighteenth-century prototype: an armed populace who combined a patriotic defense of the nation with a struggle against internal class enemies; a federalist scheme that would link the Commune of the capital with semiautonomous communes in the provinces and rural hamlets; and an iconoclastic anticlericalism that promised a radical break with the repressive traditions of the past.

As has often been noted, Marx's views on the Commune were ambiguous from the outset and conflicting over the years. In 1871 he celebrated the Commune as an "essentially working-class government, the product of the struggle of the producing against the appropriating class, the political form at last discovered under which to work out the economic emancipation of labour."[25] But ten years later he wrote: "The Commune was merely the rising of a town under exceptional conditions, the majority of the Commune was in no sense socialist, nor could it be."[26] It was left to Engels, in his 1891 preface to Marx's *Civil War in France,* to canonize the Commune as the model of the Marxian concept of the dictatorship of the proletariat,[27] thereby providing a uniquely important place for the Paris Commune in radical Marxist thought—although not in the thought of the dominant social-democratic Marxists during the period of the Second International. It was, of course, the radical legacy of Marx and Engels that Lenin seized upon, reproducing the major themes and revolutionary imagery of *The Civil War in France* in *State and Revolution* on the eve of the Bolshevik Revolution, however incongruous the original Marxian model of proletarian dictatorship was with actual Communist political practice. And it was largely through Lenin's influential treatise that Marx's description of the Paris Commune was initially conveyed to Chinese Marxists.

Having inherited the Marxian model of the Commune along with orthodox Marxism-Leninism, Chinese Communists duly celebrated the event over the revolutionary and postrevolutionary periods, largely in accordance with Marx's interpretation as presented in *The Civil War in France* and in Lenin's *State and Revolution.* Among the first to do so was

[25] Karl Marx, "The Civil War in France," in Marx and Engels, *Selected Works,* 1:473.
[26] Karl Marx and Frederick Engels, *Selected Correspondence* (New York, 1935), 386–87.
[27] The oft-quoted last paragraph of Engels's preface reads: "Of late, the Social-Democratic philistine has once more been filled with wholesome terror at the words: Dictatorship of the Proletariat. Well and good, gentlemen, do you want to know what this dictatorship looks like? Look at the Paris Commune. That was the Dictatorship of the Proletariat" (Marx and Engels, *Selected Works,* 1:440).

China's first Marxist, Li Dazhao, who in 1923 published an article praising the Paris Commune, summarizing Marx's original analysis, and emphasizing the compatibility between social revolution and nationalism.
"The people of Paris," he emphasized, "rose up to resist a traitorous
government."[28] Other writings on the Commune followed over the years,
rarely departing from standard Marxist-Leninist views. With the Chinese
Communist victory and the proclamation of the People's Republic, the
constitution of the new regime decreed that the anniversary of the Paris
Commune was to be celebrated annually as one of eight official holi-
days—a bow to a fading Marxian internationalism by the eminently
nationalistic leaders of a profoundly nationalist revolution.

While many Chinese Communists were no doubt genuinely attracted
to the Commune as a symbol of a heroic revolutionary tradition to which
they now had contributed and continued, the Marxian model of the
Commune (as earlier suggested) had no real political relevance in the
modern Chinese historical situation and in the making of the Chinese
Communist Revolution. Nor did it assume any new relevance in the early
years of the People's Republic. Celebrations of the Paris Commune by
China's Communists were purely ritualistic observances, no more than a
matter that was merely *historically* significant (to borrow Joseph Levenson's suggestive phrase). They were simply an aspect of a general ideological legacy handed down from one generation of Marxists to another,
seemingly devoid of any real political message for the present or the
future.

Yet the image of the Paris Commune did come to convey messages of
real historical and political significance in the history of postrevolutionary China, a curious phenomenon closely bound up with the increasingly
utopian character that Maoism came to acquire after the mid-1950s.
There are three periods in the history of the People's Republic when the
canonized Paris Commune was removed from the museum of Marxist
historical exhibits and pressed into the political service of the present:
first, in promoting the social radicalism of the Great Leap Forward campaign; second, in contributing to political radicalism of the Cultural
Revolution; and third, in support of various democratic movements in the
post-Mao era. The three episodes can be only very quickly sketched here.

The "people's communes" that were organized during the Great Leap
derived their name from the hallowed place that the term "commune"

[28] *Li Dazhao Zuanji* (Beijing, 1959), 447–56.

occupies in the Marxist tradition. If the movement as such was not necessarily inspired by the Marxian model of the Paris Commune, that model was prominently invoked to ideologically sanctify communication and no doubt contributed greatly to the utopianism and social radicalism of the time.[29] Undoubtedly, the most radical utopian feature of the Great Leap in 1958, when the people's communes briefly approached the Marxian ideal of the Paris Commune, was the role initially assigned to the communes in the reorganization and exercise of political power. In the radical Maoist literature of the time, the communes were hailed as organs of "proletarian dictatorship," albeit sans urban proletariat. The commune's assumption of the administrative functions of the *xiang* (the administrative village, the basic unit of the formal state apparatus) was interpreted by Maoist theoreticians as making the commune a political organ "performing the functions of state power" and "the most desirable organization form" to carry out all the radical social transformations Marxist theory envisions in the period of the transition from socialism to communism. The communes were celebrated not simply as productive units but, of equal importance, as organizations that "combined economic, cultural, political and military affairs," and that merged "workers, peasants, merchants, students and militiamen into a single entity." In support of these utopian visions, references to Marxist writings on the Paris Commune were frequently invoked. As one radical Maoist ideologist typically observed, "the integration of the *xiang* with the commune will make the commune not very different from the Paris Commune, integrating economic organization with the organization of state power," a step hailed as the beginning of the disappearance of the internal functions of the state.[30]

This vision of the "withering away" of the state was the most utopian of all the utopian goals proclaimed in the early Great Leap period—and it probably struck responsive chords among the peasantry, for it promised fulfillment of traditional peasant anarchist dreams of freedom from the tyranny of officials and bureaucrats. As it was, the movement soon degenerated into organizational and political chaos, and it ended in an enormous economic and human disaster.

The Marxist model of the Paris Commune was once again revived at the beginning of the Cultural Revolution. The "Sixteen Articles," the

---

[29]Portions of this paragraph are adapted from my book *Mao's China and After* (New York, 1986), 240–41.

[30]For example, Guan Feng, "A Brief Discussion of the Great Historical Significance of People's Communes," *Zhexue yanjiu* (Philosophic Research) no. 5, 1958.

charter of the upheaval promulgated in August 1966, proclaimed that "it is necessary to institute a system of general elections like that of the Paris Commune" a month after Mao Zedong had hailed one widely celebrated "big-character poster" as "the manifesto of the Chinese Paris Commune," whose significance, he pronounced, would surpass that of the Paris Commune itself. Yet when an attempt was made (however flawed in conception and practice) to actually reorganize political power on the basis of the Marxian model—in the form of the Shanghai Commune of February 1967—Mao rejected the results as premature and un-Leninist, beginning a long and agonizing Maoist retreat from the original principles of the Cultural Revolution. Yet the ideal of the Paris Commune remained in the chaotic political realm of the time, lingering on mainly among revolutionary organizations that the Maoist regime branded (and suppressed) as "ultra-leftist." A January 1968 manifesto of one such group declared:

The commune of the "Ultra-left faction" will not conceal its viewpoints and intentions. We publicly declare that our object of establishing the "People's Commune of China" can be attained only by overthrowing the bourgeois dictatorship and the Revisionist system of the revolutionary committee with brute force. Let the new bureaucratic bourgeoisie tremble before the true socialist revolution. . . . The China of tomorrow will be the world of the "Commune."[31]

Finally, in the post-Mao era, the Paris Commune model appears prominently in the writings associated with the ill-fated Democracy Movement of 1979–81, especially among such disillusioned Maoists as Wang Xizhe and Chen Erjin, who sought to preserve the original radicalism of the Cultural Revolution and combine it with some form of representative democracy.[32] And following the suppression of the Democracy Movement, more moderate Party reformers who advocate the gradual democraticization of the state—through such measures as direct elections of officials, the right of popular recall, and limitations on bureaucratic privileges—sometimes invoke Marx's analysis of the Paris Commune in support of political reform. After two centuries, echoes of the French Revolution, however faint and indirect, are still to be heard in China.

[31]Shengwulian (Hunan Provincial Proletarian Great Alliance Committee), "Whither China," appendix in Klaus Mehnert, *Peking and the New Left, At Home and Abroad* (Berkeley and Los Angeles, 1969).
[32]See, for example, *Wang Xizhe Lunwen Ji* (Hong Kong, 1981), and Chen Erjin, *China: Crossroads Socialism* (London, 1984).

# About the authors

JERZY W. BOREJSZA is Professor of History at the Historical Institute of the Polish Academy of Sciences in Warsaw. Professor Borejsza's publications include *The Wondrous Nineteenth Century* (1990; 1984) and many scholarly articles.

JACK CENSER is Professor of History at George Mason University. Professor Censer's publications include *The French Revolution and Intellectual History* (1989), *The Press and Politics in Pre-Revolutionary France* (1987), and *Prelude to Power: The Parisian Radical Press, 1789–1791* (1976).

ROBERT FORSTER is Professor of History at the Johns Hopkins University. He is the author of *Merchants, Landlords, Magistrates: The DePont Family in Eighteenth-Century France* (1980), *The Nobility of Toulouse in the Eighteenth Century* (1960), and *The House of Saulx-Tavanes: Versailles and Burgundy, 1700–1830* (1971).

CHARLES A. HALE is Professor of History at the University of Iowa. Professor Hale's publications include *The Transformation of Liberalism in Late Nineteenth-Century Mexico* (1989), *Political and Social Ideas in Latin America, 1870–1930* (1986) and *Mexican Liberalism in the Age of Mora, 1821–1853* (1968).

MICHAEL H. HALTZEL is Chief of the European Division at the Library of Congress and former Director of the West European Studies program at the Woodrow Wilson Center. He is the author of *Der Abbau der deutschen ständischen Selbstverwaltung in den Ostseeprovinzen Russlands 1855–1905* (1977), coeditor with Joseph Klaits of *Liberty/Liberté: The American and French Experiences* (1991), and the author of many articles.

195

ELBAKI HERMASSI is Professor of Literature and Languages at the University of Tunis. His published work includes *The Third World Reassessed* (1980), *Leadership and National Development in North Africa* (1977), and *Society and State in the Arab Maghrib* (1975).

NIKKI R. KEDDIE is Professor of History at the University of California at Los Angeles. A former Woodrow Wilson Center Guest Scholar, she is the author of *Women in Middle Eastern History* (1991), *Roots of Revolution: An Interpretive History of Modern Iran* (1981), and *Iran: Religion, Politics, and Society* (1980).

JOSEPH KLAITS is Program Officer of the Jennings Randolph Program for International Peace at the U.S. Institute for Peace. His publications include *Servants of Satan: The Age of the Witch Hunts* (1985), *Printed Propaganda under Louis XIV: Absolute Monarchy and Public Opinion* (1976), and *Animals and Man in Historical Perspective* (1974).

LLOYD S. KRAMER is Associate Professor of History at the University of North Carolina, Chapel Hill. Professor Kramer's publications include *Threshold of a New World: Intellectuals and the Exile Experience in Paris, 1830–1848* (1988) and *Paine and Jefferson on Liberty* (1988).

MAURICE J. MEISNER is Harvey Goldberg Professor of History at the University of Wisconsin–Madison. Professor Meisner is the author of *Post-Mao China: An Inquiry into the Fate of Chinese Socialism* (forthcoming), *Mao's China and After* (1986), and *Marxism, Maoism, and Utopianism* (1982).

CHRISTOPHER L. MILLER is Professor of French and Professor of African and Afro-American studies at Yale University. He is the author of *Theories of Africans: Francophone Literature and Anthropology in Africa* (1990), *Blank Darkness: Africanist Discourse in French* (1985), and many scholarly articles.

DMITRY SHLAPENTOKH is Assistant Professor of History at Indiana University at South Bend. He is the author of *Soviet Ideologies in the Period of Glasnost: Responses to Brezhnev's Stagnation* (1988) and several articles on the French Revolution and Russian life.

# Index

# 200 Index

206

*Index*

Politics, Culture, and Class in the French
    Revolution (Hunt), 14–16
polygamy, 109–11
popular sovereignty, 5, 165, 170, 173
*Porcupine's Gazette*, 34
Portugal, Latin America and, 158
positivism, 170–71, 174–76
Potocki, Ignacy, 58
power: absolute, 135; constitutional gov-
    ernment and, 133–35; modernization of
    state and, 129–30; of Paris Commune,
    189; political institutions and, 133; rev-
    olutionary discourse and, 12–13; ro-
    mance of, 16–17; of Russian autocracy,
    75
*Pravda*, 86
press: African, 125; American, 30–31,
    34–35, 39, 45; Chinese, 182; French
    Revolution and, 34–35, 84, 86; Mexi-
    can, 174; political culture and, 39, 174;
    Russian, 84, 86
Price, Richard, 100
*Principes de politique* (Constant), 164
privilege: abolition of, 8, 14, 20; corpo-
    rate, 166–67; French monarchy and,
    12–13; French revolutionaries' view of,
    11; Mexican liberalism and, 166–67
proletariat: Chinese communes and, 193;
    European, 83; Marxist theory and, 191;
    Russian, 83; see also working class
*Proofs of a Conspiracy against All the
    Governments and Religions of Europe*
    (Robison), 48
property rights, 91, 96–97
Protestantism, French Revolution and
    American, 46–50
Prussia, 58, 60
psychology: Jacobin, 176n37; revolution-
    ary politics and, 16–17
public opinion, U.S. politics and, 28–29,
    32–33, 38–39
public sphere, politics and, 32–34, 38–39,
    45, 54
Pulszky, Ferenc, quoted, 70

Qing dynasty, 179, 182

Rabasa, Emilio, 176; *Constitución y la
    dictadura* by, 174
race relations on Saint-Domingue, 4, 89–
    104
racism: assimilation and, 116–17; Euro-
    centric culture and, 104; U.S. politics
    and, 29n3
radicalism: American fear of, 28–39, 44;
    Egyptian, 143–44, 153–54; French, 23,

25, 28–39, 80–81, 187–88; see also
    Jacobins; revolutionaries
Raimond, Julien, 92–93, 95–96, 98, 100,
    103, 104
rebellions: in China, 177–78, 182, 185–
    86; in Egypt, 155; in Middle East, 129,
    140, 143–44, 149–50, 152, 154–57; in
    Poland, 58–61, 66, 74; in Russia, 74–
    75, 79; slave, 44n39, 100–4
*Rech'*, 84–85
*Reflections on a Civil War in the Vendée*
    (Jasienica), 68–69
Reforma, Mexican political culture and,
    167
reformers: Chinese, 179–84; Iranian, 152;
    Islamic, 148–54; see also names of indi-
    vidual reformers
reforms, political: of Alexander II, 75;
    Arab intellectuals and, 136–37; in
    Egypt, 143–44; French monarchy and,
    80–81, 180; and Mexican Constitution,
    172; Ottoman Empire and, 128–30,
    142, 144, 149–50
Reign of Terror: French, 8, 13–14, 19–23,
    73, 77; Russian, 84–87
religion: African, 101–2, 104; Catholic,
    189; French colonialism and, 104, 111;
    French revolutionary ideology and,
    146–47, 189; Islamic, 134–35, 138,
    147–48, 151–52; national identity and,
    134–35; Protestant, 27, 46–50; science
    and, 151–52; social order and, 147–
    48; in United States, 27, 46–50
religious community, Islamic, 134–35,
    138
religious movements in Middle East, 151–
    52
Renan, Ernest, 151–52
republicans, 15; American, 29–40, 42, 45,
    47–48; Chinese, 182; democratic, 14–
    15, 36–39, 42; Polish, 62
Resnick, Daniel, 99
revisionism, 9–10, 17–18, 22, 24, 40,
    175
revolution: bourgeois, 179, 181, 186–87;
    cultural, 183n14; democratic, 186; of
    1830 (France), 132; for Independence
    (Mexico), 163–64; of 1911 (China),
    182, 185; of 1905 (Russia), 75, 79; Pol-
    ish concept of, 55–56, 69; see also
    names of individual revolutions
revolutionaries: Chinese, 181–82; French,
    4, 11, 15–17; Hungarian, 69–70; Pol-
    ish, 65–66; on Saint-Domingue, 94–95,
    98–99; see also names of individual rev-
    olutionaries

CPSIA information can be obtained at www.ICGtesting.com
Printed in the USA
BVOW031646080812

297327BV00001B/2/A